"With this latest work, Myerson brings a reader-friendly simplicity to teaching and effectively communicating the vast web of interconnected processes within demand and supply chain planning, along with finely illustrating the dynamics and intricacies involved for their successful execution in a global economy increasingly more volatile and uncertain. To that end, through an array of case studies, Myerson provides practical tips and insights demonstrating real-world application of best practices in particular scenarios as well as 'hard to see' pitfalls to avoid."

– **William J. Bajor, Ph.D.**, Senior Director for Administration and Special Projects, Academic and Student Affairs, Office of the Chancellor, Pennsylvania's State System of Higher Education

"The ability to plan effectively is perhaps the most important determinant of supply chain success. This book does a solid job of presenting the need for effective planning as well as covering the relevant topics that are part of the demand and supply chain planning process. It explains in a clearly written manner what supply chain professionals must understand to be successful."

– **Robert J. Trent, Ph.D.**, Supply Chain Management Professor Emeritus, Lehigh University

"Connecting the dots between demand, supply, and transportation to make, move and sell goods around the world has never been more important – or challenging. Meyerson demystifies what's required for a connected supply chain, why it's a game changer and how to get there."

– **Ron Kubera**, President, Distribution Sector, e2open

"Paul Myerson's latest book a great how-to text for a class on demand and supply chain planning for students as well as a guide for supply chain professionals looking to meet the challenges of today's volatile global environment."

– **Dr. Mikhail M. Sher**, Leon Hess Business School, Monmouth University

The Art and Science of Demand and Supply Chain Planning in Today's Complex Global Economy

The demand and supply chain planning process for manufacturers, distributors, and retailers has evolved over the years. It has gone from a disjointed, unconnected, slow, inaccurate, fairly manual set of processes to an integrated, timely process enabled by the use and coordination of highly trained people, lean, agile processes, and cutting-edge technology.

To make this set of processes work effectively, one has to fully understand and appreciate that there is an "art and science" aspect to the process which can take years of education and experience to fully understand.

Essentially, this book will offer the reader a chance to fully understand the interconnected set of processes in a "best-practice" application. Furthermore, examples and cases will be used to illustrate its practical application in today's complex global supply chain.

In addition, readers will understand and be able to apply and articulate the concepts, tools, and techniques used in the efficient supply of goods and services in today's changing global economy. It will help them to learn how businesses, through their supply chain, work both internally and with their trading partners – both upstream and downstream – to build strong relationships and integrate demand and supply planning activities across the supply chain to deliver customer value efficiently and effectively. They will learn about the tools and technologies enabling integration, and the critical drivers and key metrics of supply chain performance.

The Art and Science of Demand and Supply Chain Planning in Today's Complex Global Economy

Paul Myerson

Routledge
Taylor & Francis Group

A PRODUCTIVITY PRESS BOOK

First published 2023
by Routledge
605 Third Avenue, New York, NY 10158

and by Routledge
4 Park Square, Milton Park, Abingdon, Oxon, OX14 4RN

Routledge is an imprint of the Taylor & Francis Group, an informa business

© 2023 Paul Myerson

ISBN: 978-1-032-43420-9 (hbk)
ISBN: 978-1-032-24991-9 (pbk)
ISBN: 978-1-003-28107-8 (ebk)

DOI: 10.4324/9781003281078

Typeset in Minion
by Deanta Global Publishing Services, Chennai, India

Contents

SECTION I   Supply Chain Strategy

SECTION II   Demand-Side Planning

SECTION IV   The Road Ahead

Preface

In 2014, when I was preparing to teach a demand and supply chain planning course for the first time at Lehigh University, the department chair and I were unable to find a suitable text for the course.

In the end, we had to cobble together a text using sections from a number of books (with permission), along with articles and cases from other sources.

Fast-forward to 2020, when, after publishing my sixth book on supply chain and logistics management and personally observing and analyzing demand and supply issues during the COVID-19 pandemic (as well as other seemingly continuous challenges such as tsunamis, hurricanes, tariffs, etc.), I realized the time had come to create a unified book on the subject that could act as a sort of handbook to help educate students and professionals on how to build and manage a harmonious, integrated demand and supply chain planning process that can withstand this type of volatile environment.

The "best-practice" planning process should, at the same time, also be built to support the lean, agile supply chain operation that is required today to make sure supply adequately meets demand while maintaining desired cost and profit goals.

This book, then, is the result, where I have tried to put into clear, common-sense terms not only the basics of an integrated, harmonious demand and supply chain planning process but also the strategies needed to implement and manage it.

I've also included a variety of cases as examples for the reader, as well as lecture slides and chapter questions and answers for educational purposes (available for download, free, at Routledge.com).

I hope this book helps both students and professionals (and their employers) to better navigate and indeed thrive during these turbulent times, as change is always inevitable and needs to be embraced, not avoided.

About the Author

Paul Myerson is currently an adjunct professor of Supply Chain Management at Kean University. He holds a BS in Business Logistics from Pennsylvania State University and an MBA in Physical Distribution from Temple University.

Myerson has an extensive background as a supply chain and logistics professional, consultant, and teacher (both full-time at Monmouth and Lehigh Universities and at various times as an adjunct at Kean University and New Jersey City University).

As an industry professional, trainer, and consultant, Myerson has been a successful change catalyst for a variety of clients and organizations of all sizes. His 40 plus years of experience in supply chain management, logistics strategies, and operations systems have resulted in bottom-line improvements for companies such as General Electric (GE), Unilever, and Church and Dwight (Arm & Hammer).

Myerson created and marketed a supply chain planning software tool for Windows from 1998-2013 and, more recently, with a technology partner, is creating a multi-platform supply chain planning app for small businesses (www.forecisely.com).

He is also the author of seven books on supply chain and logistics management and has written a column on lean supply chains for *Inbound Logistics Magazine*, both since 2012.

Section I

Supply Chain Strategy

1

Introduction to Demand and Supply Chain Planning in Today's Complex and Increasingly Uncertain Global Economy

The demand and supply chain planning (D&SCP) processes for many larger manufacturers, distributors, and retailers have evolved over the years. They have gone from a disjointed, unconnected, slow, inaccurate, fairly manual set of processes to an integrated, timely process enabled by the use and coordination of highly trained people, lean, agile processes, and cutting-edge technology.

At the same time, while the improvements in global supply chain management have been substantial over the past 30+ years (which, at least in part, has helped to keep prices down), the recent pandemic has shown us that perhaps we were not in as good a shape as we thought we were (which has been exacerbated by an acceleration toward e-commerce and ultimately omni channel retail driven in part by the pandemic), as there have been shortages everywhere ranging from microchips to uncertainty whether there would be enough Xboxes as gifts for the holidays.

At least partially a result of these shortages and delays, inflation is at its highest rate since at least 2008, and core inflation, which strips out volatile items such as food and energy, leaped to the highest level since 1992. What was initially a supply crunch is instead morphing into a full-blown crisis featuring a shortage of energy, labor, and transportation.

So, we can conclude that there are still many lessons to be learned here since continuous improvement is a necessity for survival in today's volatile environment.

DOI: 10.4324/9781003281078-2

HOW THIS BOOK CAN HELP

In order to enable our demand and supply processes to work effectively and harmoniously, one has to fully understand and appreciate that there is an "art and science" aspect to each step in the D&SCP process (Figure 1.1).

While it's required to work in this field, it is not enough to just understand how a supply chain works; one must also understand and be able to articulate and apply the concepts, tools, and techniques used in the efficient supply of goods and services in today's changing global economy.

This book will help with that by offering you a chance to fully understand the interconnected set of processes in a "best-practice" sense from strategic, tactical, and operational views. Furthermore, examples and cases will be used to illustrate its practical application in today's complex, uncertain global supply chain.

In this book, we will discuss how businesses, through their supply chains, work internally and with their trading partners – both upstream and downstream – to integrate demand and supply planning activities across the supply chain and build strong, collaborative relationships to efficiently and effectively deliver customer value. Readers will learn about tools (and the "art & science" involved in applying them) and technologies enabling integration, and the critical drivers and key metrics of supply chain performance.

Ultimately, both students and business professionals want (and *need*) to know how to allow the people, processes, and technology of demand

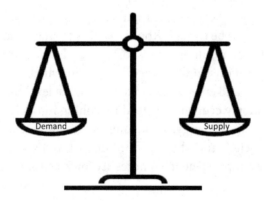

FIGURE 1.1
Supply and demand balance and harmonization.

and supply planning to all work together in unison for a lean, agile supply chain.

WHERE WE ARE TODAY AND CHANGING STRATEGIES

We are now in a "whitewater rapids" period in terms of the global economy, where organizations exist in an environment that lacks stability and predictability, requiring flexibility from the processes, technology, and people in the supply chain to navigate these rough waters.

Making the transition to a truly flexible and lean supply chain, especially during these turbulent times, involves changing the three elements necessary for successful business transformation: processes, technology, and people.

The transition involves using a structured approach to make sure that changes – which can range from a simple process tweak to major policy or strategy revisions – are implemented successfully if the organization is to achieve its potential.

Revising Processes

Companies can utilize many tools to manage process change in a supply chain in order to gain flexibility and continuously improve. These tools include:

- Benchmarking to clearly identify performance gaps and thus focus supply chain management efforts on the areas most in need of improvement.
- Six sigma to reduce variation and defect rates in production (and, in more recent years, other) processes through statistical analysis.
- Lean strategies to examine and streamline processes by eliminating non-value-added activities or waste within the entire enterprise, including the supply chain.

Transforming Technology

Many companies are using digital technology to transform key business areas, but technology can't be applied haphazardly. When applied properly, however, it can enable good processes.

Technological advancements have made it extremely easy to gather and analyze vast amounts of data. Focusing on key pieces of data used in decision-making saves time and money.

Many leading companies have gone further and have begun to create a true digital organization that automates repeatable tasks to increase efficiency and drive down costs.

Managing People and Change

Few people like change within their organization, but, if management leads the change initiative properly, the process can be successfully implemented with minimal resistance.

To effectively manage change in your organization, you must first educate leaders and gain their commitment and support for the effort. Leaders must communicate why the change is needed and what benefits they expect.

Leaders need to know when change is needed, work on getting the change accepted organizationally, implement change in the best way possible, and relate the need for change directly to the business value proposition.

For example, leadership needs to be able to clearly describe how improved demand planning helps sustain and increase revenues through improved customer satisfaction and reduced production, distribution, and inventory costs.

At this point, it is also important to identify risks and have a mitigation plan in place if issues arise. For example, consider piloting change in one geography or business unit before rolling it out across the entire organization.

Furthermore, clearly defining roles and responsibilities within the organization will help earn employee buy-in and minimize confusion.

Finally, organizations must implement and continuously measure metrics – and design rewards – that reinforce and eventually maintain the desired future state.

In the end, creating a lean, flexible supply chain requires changes in your organization. It's up to you whether to cling to the past, with the inherent risks, or embrace change and look to the future [Myerson, 2019].

WHERE TO LOOK FOR IMPROVEMENT: ON THE DEMAND SIDE

During the pandemic, a lot of the focus on supply chains tended to be on the supply side, and rightly so, owing to the highly publicized sourcing, production, distribution, and transportation issues. As a result, organizations continue to look to increase productivity, flexibility, and agility through programs such as lean, increased automation, robotics, artificial intelligence, etc.

However, the supply side shouldn't be the only area of focus. To one degree or another, human behavior has tended to exacerbate the issue, resulting in volatility on the demand side.

The impact of panic buying, hoarding, and last-mile delivery option changes has created a clear example of the bullwhip effect, where variations at the consumer demand end of the supply chain result in a ripple effect that highlights and exaggerates weaknesses in upstream supply chain, operations, and manufacturing processes.

Improving Timing and Accuracy

This brings us back to visibility, collaboration, and communication as the keys to improve demand timing and accuracy. These strategies can help minimize the impact of a global pandemic or other local and global events that seem to be regularly occurring.

Companies that still primarily rely on using historical demand data to create forecasts are, in effect, driving while looking in the rear-view mirror. We know the result of that.

Not only do we need to collaborate with our key customers, it is also critical to drill down further toward the customer. Using data such as retail and e-commerce point of sale (POS) and customer warehouse withdrawals helps determine what is really going on.

It also helps to monitor events such as weather, environmental issues, and changing tastes and preferences (sometimes triggered by and found on social media), which can cause fluctuations in demand, and assess their possible impacts.

Luckily, we are in a time when we finally have a better set of technological tools to deal with the ever-increasing amount – and speed – of new events and changing tastes and preferences that can increase demand volatility.

Flattening Volatility

Today, organizations need to develop highly robust demand sensing and shaping processes with the aid of technology to flatten out and better predict this volatility, at least to some degree. Organizations also then need to share the resulting, more accurate forecasts up and down the extended supply chain to gain maximum benefit or "surplus" for all participants.

Enabling Accurate Forecasts

As the volume of data coming at us is exponentially increasing, now is the time to finally start embracing the following concepts to enable more accurate forecasts through better, more informed decision-making:

- Supply chain data analytics. This consists of:
  - Descriptive analytics (what happened).
  - Diagnostic analytics (why it happened).
  - Predictive analytics (what is likely to happen).
  - Prescriptive analytics (what action to take).
- Machine learning (ML), which is based on the idea that machines should be able to learn and adapt through experience.
- Artificial intelligence (AI). AI is a broad idea that machines can execute tasks "smartly". AI applies machine learning, deep learning, and other techniques to solve actual problems.

Improving demand processes not only requires using new and better technologies, but it also requires employees who are trained, willing, and ready to use them [Myerson, 2021a].

WHERE TO LOOK FOR IMPROVEMENT: ON THE SUPPLY SIDE

While improved demand accuracy in your supply chain is critical, it is equally important to have supply-side accuracy and timeliness, especially now. The disruption the pandemic caused for global supply chains is getting worse, creating shortages of consumer products and making it more expensive for companies to ship goods where they're needed.

Supply-Side Accuracy and Timeliness

Today's long and complex supply chains – with their increased uncertainty due to the pandemic and environmental and other disruptions – have increased the importance of knowing exactly what inventory you have and where it is, in real time (or as close to it as you can get).

Supply-side accuracy and timeliness refer to the what, where, and when of materials and documents:

- What – inventory control, orders, transfers.
- Where – physical location: plant, warehouse, in transit, or with customer.
- When – timeliness of information.

People, Process, Technology

Where should you look to measure and improve supply-side accuracy?

On a strategic level, when searching for potential business improvements it is often helpful to think in terms of "people, process, and technology" (as we mentioned before). In this case, let us use this to consider how it would be applied on the supply side:

People: Besides identifying, screening, and hiring the best talent, this goes largely to the topic of training once people are onboarded; this pertains to supply chain partners as well. Proper training – and retraining, as well as cross-training – helps to ensure that staff are correctly taught and understand the company's inventory control practices and procedures. Training should be a continuous process in your business operations. Providing ongoing professional development opportunities allows staff to refresh their skills, to retrain, or to update their competencies and experience. As the saying goes, "We're only as good as our people".

Process: Supply chain management, with all its various activities, is the basis of a well-functioning business and requires error-resistant processes. For example, if you do not use best practices such as cycle counting to know how much inventory you have in facilities throughout your extended supply chain (including what inventory your carriers, suppliers, and customers have), as well as accurate and timely paper and electronic order and other transactional documents, then you could be in real trouble.

Technology: Inventory and transportation management systems track the life cycle and movement of stock as it comes and goes out of your business. Today's inventory and transportation management systems make it easier for you to track your inventory throughout the extended supply chain. This gives the right people access to that inventory and enables you to have an accurate record of inventory movement throughout your supply chain and get insight from inventory activity and history. Technology such as electronic data interchange (EDI), barcode scanning, and radio-frequency identification (RFID) helps to minimize errors and improve accuracy. Having real-time inventory visibility up and down the supply chain gives you the additional benefit of anticipating issues before they become a crisis. A number of good cloud-based logistics execution platforms are designed just for this. By focusing on supply-side accuracy and timeliness, you can cut down on unnecessary excess inventory and outages and meet demand more precisely in this volatile environment [Myerson, 2021b].

I think we have made the case in this chapter that we are in for a "white-water rapids" ride for the foreseeable future, and we have discussed some general thoughts on the potential impact and areas of focus needed to survive and thrive.

As the saying goes, "to be forewarned is to be forearmed". So, the question is, how do you plan and react to this turbulent environment?

To do this, we first need to understand our supply chain from both the demand and supply perspective and then create a strategy to deal with constant change. This is the topic of our next chapter.

2

Understanding the Importance of Supply Chain to an Organization and Developing a Strategy for a Sustained Competitive Advantage

HISTORICAL PERSPECTIVE

Up until World War II, logistics was fragmented within business organizations, primarily focusing on transportation and purchasing. In educational institutions, there were no integrated programs. Instead, individual courses were offered in transportation and purchasing.

During World War II, logistics was thought of in military terms for the most part, as the link that supplied troops with rations, weapons, and equipment.

After the World War II, as businesses began to understand the relationships and trade-offs involved, such as inventory costs vs. transportation costs, and with the growth of suburban America with its shopping centers, national highway system, and migration of manufacturing from the cities, logistics gained an important place in the business world as well.

In the 1960s, physical distribution, a more integrated concept that included activities such as transportation, inventory control, warehousing, and facility location had become an area of study and practice in education and industry. Physical distribution involved the coordination of more

DOI: 10.4324/9781003281078-3

than one activity associated with supplying product to the marketplace (i.e. it was more focused on the "outbound" side of manufacturing).

By the mid-1960s, the scope of physical distribution was expanded to include the supply side, including inbound transportation and warehousing, and was referred to as business logistics. In many cases, purchasing was not included and went under the heading of "materials management" or "procurement".

In the early 1980s, as American manufacturing had been hammered by overseas competitors for over a decade and began actively outsourcing materials, labor, and manufacturing overseas, the term "supply chain management" entered the common business lexicon. It defined both the new, complex global world we now live and do business in, and an understanding of the integration and importance of all activities involved in sourcing and procurement, conversion, and logistics management. This includes coordination and collaboration with channel partners, who can be suppliers, intermediaries, third-party service providers, and customers.

As opposed to the past, where physical distribution, logistics, purchasing, etc. were all fragmented, many of today's organizations feature an integrated supply chain organization, in most cases led by a senior level executive (Figure 2.1).

Technology has helped to drive the concept of an integrated supply chain, starting with the development of electronic data interchange (EDI) systems as a standardized format for the electronic transfer of data between business enterprises (which really took off in the 1980s), as well as the introduction of "off the shelf" enterprise resource planning (ERP)

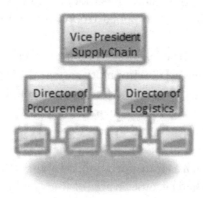

FIGURE 2.1
Supply chain organizational chart.

software systems which featured integrated core business processes in a common database. Furthering this into the 21st century has been the expansion of internet-based collaborative systems.

This supply chain evolution has resulted in both increasing value added and cost reductions through integration and collaboration.

VALUE AS A UTILITY

Utility refers to the value or benefit a customer receives from a purchase. There are four basic types of utility: form, place, time, and possession. More recently, the utilities of information and service have been added. Supply chain management contributes to all of these utilities, as it is all about having the "right product, at the right place and price, at the right time".

Below are descriptions and benefits of each type of utility:

- Form utility – performed by the manufacturers (as well as third-party logistics companies, or "3PLs", that perform value added activities such as kitting and display assembly) making the products useful.
- Time utility – having products available when needed.
- Place utility – having items available where people want them.
- Possession utility – transfer ownership to the customer as easily as possible, including the extension of credit.
- Information utility – opening two-way flows between parties (i.e. customer and manufacturer).
- Service utility – providing fast, friendly service during and after the sale and teaching customers how to best use products. This is becoming one of the most important utilities offered by retailers, which in many ways are part of the supply chain [Myerson, 2015].

CORPORATE, BUSINESS, AND SUPPLY CHAIN STRATEGY

If an organization can identify what adds value to their customers and deliver it successfully, they will have established a competitive advantage, which in essence is the purpose of a strategic plan.

Mission and Vision Statements

In order to do so, you must first establish a broad mission statement, supported by specific objectives for your business. A mission statement is a company's purpose or "reason for being" and should guide the actions of the organization and lay out its overall goal, providing a path and guiding decision-making.

A good mission statement is useful tool for well-run business. It is the "why" of business strategy.

A mission statement defines a company's goals in four important ways:

1. It defines what the company does for its customers.
2. It defines what the company does for its employees.
3. It defines what the company does for its owners.
4. It defines what the company does for its community and for the world.

On the other hand, the vision statement focuses on the future; it is a source of inspiration and motivation. Often it describes not just the future of the organization, but the future of the industry or society in which the organization hopes to effect change.

Strategy Defined

Vision is your forward-looking starting point as it establishes where you want your company to be in the future and why it matters. Mission, on the other hand, captures at a high level what you will do to realize your vision.

The resulting strategy lays out the goals, big themes of work, and marketing approach that will help you achieve both the vision and mission.

Typically, organizations will create corporate and business strategies such as product or service differentiation, low-cost leadership, or quick, consistent, or flexible response (there are a variety of other possible strategies such as "blue ocean", which is a combination of low cost and differentiation for example).

Whatever the selected strategy is, it is extremely important that the functions in the organization are aligned with these strategies. As an example, a supply chain built around a low-cost strategy will not be very effective at supporting a differentiation strategy.

Determining Your Corporate and Business Strategy

In order to determine the appropriate corporate and business strategy, an external scan and internal analysis must be performed.

During external analysis, it must be determined what effects forces in the external environment have on the firm's potential to gain and sustain a competitive advantage, and how the firm should deal with them.

Internal analysis requires finding out what effects internal resources, capabilities, and core competencies have on the firm's potential to gain and sustain a competitive advantage, and how the firm should leverage them for competitive advantage.

This analysis typically culminates with a "strengths, weaknesses, opportunity and threads (SWOT)" analysis, where the information gathered from the external and internal analysis above identifies the organization's internal strengths and weaknesses, as well as its external opportunities and threats. As a result, it can formulate a plan to leverage internal strengths to exploit external opportunities and to mitigate internal weaknesses and external threats.

After gathering and analyzing the competitive data, the organization will formulate the following types of strategies:

- Business strategy: describes how the firm should compete, selecting (or switching) from the cost leadership, differentiation, or response strategies.
- Corporate strategy: determines where the firm should compete (industry, markets, and geography).
- Global strategy: identifies how and where the firm should compete: local, regional, national, or international.

Finally, and probably the area where most companies fall short, there is the *implementation* of a selected corporate, business, or global strategy.

This will include organizational design/redesign, which can involve significant change management and determines how the firm should organize to turn the formulated strategy into action.

Corporate governance and business ethics should be developed at this point to help implement the type of corporate governance that is most effective for a given strategy, as well as how the firm anchors strategic decisions with good business ethics.

Strategic Choices

Strategic choices will be made based upon the results of the SWOT analysis and implementation of one of the competitive priority categories mentioned above – differentiation, low-cost leadership, or response.

The supply chain must then be managed and aligned to support these strategies.

SUPPLY CHAIN OBJECTIVE AND STRATEGIC IMPORTANCE

The typical objective of supply chain and logistics management is to coordinate activities within the supply chain to maximize the supply chain's competitive advantage and benefits to the ultimate consumer.

One goal of a successful supply chain is to maximize what is known as "supply chain surplus".

Supply chain surplus, also known as supply chain profitability, is a common term that represents value added by the supply chain function of an organization. Its operational concept is sharing the profit that remains after subtracting costs incurred in the production and delivery of products or services. Ideally, profit is distributed to supply chain partners via transfer prices. Supply chain surplus is the total profit shared by all the stages and intermediaries; the greater the supply chain surplus, the more successful the supply chain. The success of a supply chain is calculated by its overall surplus, not by the profit at each stage. Supply chain surplus can be calculated by either of the following formulas (one is based upon hard dollars, the other uses the concept of "customer value"):

Supply chain surplus = Revenue generated from a customer – Total cost incurred to produce and deliver the product

Supply chain surplus = Customer value – Supply chain cost

"Outside-In" vs. "Inside-Out" Thinking

The idea of supply chain surplus is aligned with the relatively new concept of "outside-in" vs. "inside-out" thinking. For years, organizations have strived for consistent cost savings through process efficiency in their supply chains, but what we have seen in recent years is that, while these efforts sound good (especially owing to the "leveraging effect" of the supply chain, since it can be 50–70 percent of revenue for a business), organizations are actually seeing limited value from the initiatives. In fact, an Accenture study found that organizations that look to reduce costs by 3–4 percent year over year often do not see a tangible benefit to the bottom line from these efforts.

This is because companies have historically taken an "inside-out" approach, focusing on how they operate in their supply chains to create efficiency. This was built in another business environment that moved slower and evolved less readily. Efficiency is a tremendous strategy in this type of market, as you can consistently improve your process through evaluation of known quantities.

But the world has changed, as the pandemic, environmental disasters, the growing complexity of a global economy, increased security due to acts of terrorism, etc. have shown us. There are few known quantities anymore, and the ones that are known do not always stay the same very long. Change is constant, and process efficiency is being replaced with agility as our business plans and strategies evolve with our markets. Agility is the new driver of business success, because successful companies have learned that adaptation is key to their existence. (Note that some organizations have been able to successfully use lean *and* agile in combination in what is known as a "hybrid" supply chain strategy, which will be discussed in Chapter 6.)

For supply chains, this means being as agile as the other areas of the business, as well as your customers, suppliers, and other partners, and collaborating with them to provide the best experience for the customer. This takes an "outside in" approach to supply chain strategy; one that is customer focused and agile in response to changing customer expectations [Verwijmeren, 2021].

SUPPLY CHAIN STRATEGY "TRANSFORMATION" METHODOLOGY

So how might you go about actually establishing a departmental or functional supply chain strategy for your organization? Paul Dittman, in his book *Supply Chain Transformation* [Dittman, 2012], suggests using nine steps when developing a supply chain strategy, which I have modified slightly for purposes of clarity and results:

1. **Start with customers' current and future needs** – customer value is the customer-perceived benefits gained from a product/service compared with the cost of purchase. Delivering customer value is critical to a business, as mentioned earlier.

However, delivering financial value to your shareholders is also important and is reflected in various business performance measures such as profit and market growth.

A supply chain strategy should aim to deliver customer value, *while at the same time* meeting shareholder needs by enabling reliable supply and logistics service, low inventory cost, and short cash-to-cash cycle times.

The supply chain operations reference (SCOR) model is a management tool used to address, improve, and communicate supply chain management decisions within a company and with suppliers and customers of a company.

Using the SCOR model processes of plan, source, make, deliver, return, and enable can be a great way to make sure that customer and shareholder values are in alignment.

Steps 2–6 that follow involve using a kind of SWOT analysis for your supply chain organization.

2. **Assess current supply chain capabilities relative to best in class** – this can be accomplished through observation, interviews, data gathering, and benchmarking your organization against industry "best in class" performance.

Based upon your organization's overall strategy, some metrics and measurements may be more important than others. For example, if you have a time-based strategy, speed of delivery may be important, while cost of delivery (relatively speaking) may not be as important in terms of achieving "best in class" status.

Developing a "gap analysis" of your current vs. ideal future state based upon this analysis can contribute to a clear and easy to follow road map.

3. **Evaluate supply chain "game changers"** – it is important to scan the environment on a regular basis to see what trends may impact customers and the supply chain. Examples include supply chain collaboration, visibility, sustainability, lean six sigma, etc.

4. **Analyze the competition** – as the saying goes, "keep your friends close but your enemies closer". Competitive analysis is probably not done often enough in terms of an organization's supply chain. If you plan on using your supply chain to achieve a competitive advantage, this is a "must do".

You might evaluate how integrated and responsive the competition's supply chain is when compared with yours and if they offer value added services such as:

- Product customization and testing.
- Kitting.
- Bundling/unbundling.
- Light assembly.
- Packaging, repackaging, and re-boxing.
- Labeling.
- Sorting and recycling.
- Reverse logistics and returns management.
- Environmental impact reporting and management.

5. **Survey technology** – identify not just what is new or being developed, but what is a good fit (functionally and financially) for your company. Sometimes, it's better not to be on the "bleeding edge" when it comes to technology.

6. **Deal with supply chain risk** – risk management needs to be part of the strategy document. External risks which are out of your control can be driven by events either upstream or downstream in the supply chain. Below are the main types of external risks:

- Demand risks – can be caused by unpredictable customer or end-customer demand.
- Supply risks – these types of risks are caused by interruptions to the flow of product for raw material or components within your supply chain. For example, if you are utilizing a just in time (JIT) strategy for a critical part or component, you need to think long and hard as to what risks are involved, as you do not want to risk shutting down a production line owing to a critical part that you have sole sourced becoming suddenly unavailable.
- Environmental risks – come from outside the supply chain. These risks are usually related to economic, social, governmental, or climate factors and include the threat of terrorism.

- Business risks – can include a supplier's financial or management stability or the purchase or sale of supplier companies.
- Physical plant risks – these risks can be caused by the condition of a supplier's physical facility and regulatory compliance.

Now that you have identified what adds value to your customers while making sure it is aligned with shareholder needs, as well as possible current and future performance gaps in your supply chain, a road map for future success can be developed.

7. **Develop new supply chain capability requirements and create a plan to get there** – one way to determine these requirements was formulated by Hau Lee, who concluded that supply chains that offer best value to the customer differ from typical supply chains in how they approach three issues that are closely tied to strategic supply chain management:

- Agility – the supply chain's relative capacity to act rapidly in response to dramatic changes in supply and demand.
- Adaptability – refers to a willingness and capacity to reshape supply chains when necessary.
- Alignment – refers to creating consistency in the interests of all participants in a supply chain [Lee, 2004; Table 2.1].

In Lee's model, these three "As" can be used to service an organization's competitive priorities, as discussed earlier.

8. **Evaluate current supply chain organizational structure, people, and metrics** – there is no one-size-fits-all approach for creating an organization. Traditional supply chain organizations are functionally oriented. In the 1980s and 1990s, companies started to transition to structures that grouped some core supply chain functions within one department. From around 2000 onward, the philosophy of the supply chain as an end-to-end process took hold, more often than not with a director or vice president of supply chain overseeing the operation. This also requires giving that manager a set of cross-functional performance objectives (and metrics) and the resources they require to meet these objectives.

This type of organization requires an evaluation of existing capabilities and identification of any gaps between currently available skills and those needed to support this "end-to-end" strategy.

9. **Develop a business case and get buy-in** – of course, any type of change typically has to be approved by management. To do this, you need

TABLE 2.1

Typical to Best Value Supply Chains

Issue	Typical Supply Chain	Best Value Supply Chain	Example Company
Agility	Moderate capacity to react to changes	Good capacity to anticipate and react to changes	Raytheon Technical Services Company locates an executive office nearby key customers
Adaptability	Focus on efficiency through the use of discrete supply chains	Maintain overlapping supply chains to ensure customer service	Computer Sciences Corporation positions some inventory close to customer locations while other items are warehoused centrally
Alignment	Supply chain members sometimes forced to choose between their own interest and the chain's interest	A rising tide lifts all boats – the interests of supply chain members are consistent with each other	When a supplier's suggestion saves R.R. Donnelly money, the firm splits the savings with the customer.

to develop a business case as, whenever resources such as money or effort are utilized, they should be in support of a specific business need. An example of a business case for a new supply chain strategy might state that

> improvement initiatives outlined in the plan will have a broad impact throughout the entire company, increasing efficiency and aligning business activities across all lines of business. Different aspects of the enterprise can now coordinate their procurement efforts and material flows to increase operating efficiency and take advantage of their combined buying power to negotiate better prices and contract terms.

BUSINESS MODEL CANVAS AND SUPPLY CHAIN MODEL CANVAS

Another creative way to develop your supply chain strategy is by utilizing the output from a business model canvas (BMC), which is a strategic management template used for developing new business models and documenting existing ones; it is a framework to evaluate the key building blocks that make up a company from a competitive advantage standpoint.

Business Model Canvas

The BMC utilizes a visual chart with elements describing a firm's or a product's value proposition, infrastructure, customers, and finances, assisting businesses to align their activities by illustrating potential trade-offs (see Table 2.2).

The nine building blocks of the business model design template that came to be called the business model canvas were initially proposed in 2005 by Alexander Osterwalder. Since the release of Osterwalder's work around 2008, new canvases for specific niches have appeared (including a supply chain canvas that we will look at shortly).

When developing the BMC, we need to gather some information on the nine building blocks:

1. Customer segments – list the top three segments. Look for the segments that provide the most revenue.
2. Value proposition – what are your products and services? What is the job you get done for your customer?
3. Revenue streams – list your top three revenue streams. If you do things for free, add them here too.
4. Channels – how do you communicate with your customer? How do you deliver the value proposition?
5. Customer relationships – how do these show up, and how do you maintain relationships?
6. Key activities – what do you do every day to run your business model?
7. Key resources – the people, knowledge, means, and money you need to run your business.

TABLE 2.2

Business Model Canvas Template

Key Partners	Key Activities	Value Proposition	Customer Relationships	Customer Segments
	Key Resources		Channels	
Cost Structure			Revenue Streams	

8. Key partners – list the partners that you cannot do business without (not suppliers).
9. Cost structure – list your top costs by looking at activities and resources.

Supply Chain Model Canvas

The business model canvas helps to reduce the complexity of designing successful business models. Implementing a supply chain model canvas (SCMC) can contribute to simplifying the process to build supply chain models that create a competitive advantage for our companies.

We need the input of the business model canvas before building a supply chain model canvas, as it must be driven by the company strategy and business model.

Before starting on the SCMC, it's a good idea to create a version of the BMC that focuses on the supply chain. For example, we should develop it using key supply chain partners rather than company partners, or key supply chain activities rather than company activities, or the supply chain value proposition rather than the company one, etc.

The SCMC is a tool that helps a company to build a supply chain that is tailored to its particular value propositions by:

- Defining key activities, key resources, and key partners.
- Visualizing the synchronization of the activities of the network.

Synchronizing network activities is about all the processes created to manage a supply chain such as: demand management, supply planning, matching assets with demand, analytics, available to promise (ATP), and inventory modeling and policy.

To visualize this, Montané [2018] suggests building the SCMC with 15 boxes (see Table 2.3).

The supply chain model canvas focuses on synchronizing a company's supply chain by splitting it into four sections:

1. Delivering value to the customers.
2. Looking for efficiency inside operations.
3. Minimizing costs while maximizing service level.
4. Minimizing fixed assets, inventory, and account payable.

TABLE 2.3

Supply Chain Model Canvas

	Design	Plan	Source & Make	Deliver	Customer	
	Supply Chain Design	Supply Chain Packing	Procurement and Sourcing	Warehousing	Supply Chain Segmentation	Value (Create or Raise)
Efficiency (Eliminate or Reduce)	Supply Chain Analytics	ERP/IT	Manufacturing	Transportation	Quality and Returns
	Fixed Assets	Inventory	Accounts Payable	Cost Improvements	Service Level Improvements
	Balance Sheet			Profit & Loss Account		

The operations of the model are placed on the top ten building blocks, which follow the sequence of the value chain (design, plan, source and make, deliver, and customer). The bottom five building blocks are focused on the supply chain financial impact on the balance sheet and the profit and loss account. Individual blocks can either be more focused on efficiencies or on customer value creation, depending on your particular business strategy (using a continuous improvement tool such as lean, as described in Chapter 6).

To compile the SCMC, it is useful to use a process based on the steps and answers to the following questions:

1. **Supply chain segmentation:** Focus the supply chain to deliver value to customer segments.
   - What are the company's products and services?
   - What are the customer segments? What are the segmentation attributes?
   - What do customer segments value – efficiency or responsiveness?
2. **Quality and returns:** How does the company create value for customer segments by delivering quality products and by managing after-sales issues that may occur?
   - What is the company's differentiated quality process?
   - How is the company managing complaints?
   - How is the company managing supply chain risks?
   - How does the company minimize returns impact?
3. **Warehousing:** How does the company stock and handle items?
   - What storage systems are used?
   - What material is handled?

- What putaway strategy is used?
- Which order types are managed?
- What is the removal strategy?
- How is inventory controlled?

4. **Transportation:** How do we move the items?
   - What is the modal mix?
   - What is the packaging used? Is it the right one?
   - Does the company have its own fleet? What are the right fleet size, equipment mix, and location?
   - What is the number of carriers used? What is the right number?
   - How many routes are there? How many should the company have?

5. **Procurement/sourcing:** How does the company manage purchase, and what are its costs?
   - How does the company optimize the purchasing price?
   - How does the company optimize the operational costs?
   - How does the company optimize the transaction costs?
   - What is the classification of the company's purchasing materials requirements?
   - What are the strategic positioning and the action plan?

6. **Manufacturing:** How does the company manage production?
   - What is the production environment for products (i.e. make to stock, make to order, or assemble to order)?
   - What is the company's production strategy?

7. **Supply chain planning:** How does the company manage planning activities?
   - What is the demand plan (market plan, products/brands plan, sales plan, sales forecast, promotions plan)?
   - What is the production plan (master production scheduling plan, capacity plan, resource plan, production plan, purchasing plan)?
   - What is the distribution plan (inventory plan, distribution plan, warehouse plan, transportation plan)?

8. **IT/ERP:** How are systems used to manage planning activities?
   - Is there a material requirements plan?
   - Is there a warehouse management system?
   - Is there a labor management system?
   - Is there a transportation management system?
   - Is there supply chain optimization software?

- Is there supply chain analytics software?
9. **Supply chain design:** What is the structure of the supply chain?
   - How many warehouses and factories should the company have?
   - Where should they be located?
   - What size should they have?
10. **Supply chain analytics:** What are the key performance indicators (KPIs) and the performance of the supply chain?
    - What are the required KPIs? What is their availability?
    - How is the company performing?
    - What does the company want to happen?
    - How can the company make it happen?
11. **Cost improvements:** What costs can be reduced while giving the same service to the customer?
    - Are there some possible savings (in terms of procurement, inventory carrying costs, total fulfillment costs, total supply chain costs, lean waste costs, reverse logistics costs, cost of poor quality)?
    - What is the cost to serve?
    - What are the supply chain carbon footprint and emissions?
12. **Service-level improvements:** What ways are there to give better service to the customer?
    - How responsive is the supply chain?
    - How flexible is the supply chain?
    - How adaptable is the supply chain?
13. **Fixed assets:**
    - What is the assets turnover?
    - What are the bottleneck operations?
    - What is the outsourcing strategy?
    - What is the capital budget?
    - Should the company make a facility expansion?
14. **Inventory:**
    - What items have to be stocked? Where?
    - What is the optimal size of the inventory?
    - Is the supply chain reliable and responsive?
    - How are the fill rates doing?
    - How is the service level doing?
    - Can the company exploit some risk pooling out of the stock strategy?

15. **Account payable:**
   - What money is owed? What percentage is past due?
   - How quickly is the organization paying?
   - What percentage of accounts are not meeting terms? What is the value of overdue accounts?
   - Which vendors are problematic?
   - What is the average/weighted average days past due?

This framework can help supply chain departments to identify and deliver higher operational and financial performance and help the company figure out how to deliver on its value propositions to its customer segments in order to gain a competitive advantage by making informed decisions.

The SCMC should be revisited as often as need be, with the subsequent output of ideas/changes to be tested and implemented for a continuous improvement in the way a company delivers its value propositions.

However, the success of the implementation of the strategies will likely depend on the expertise of the supply chain strategist as well as the tools used.

SUPPLY CHAIN STRATEGY IMPLEMENTATION METHODOLOGY

Formulating a supply chain strategy is only the first step. As the saying goes, the "best-laid plans of mice and men often go astray". Meaning that a successful implementation is as important in many ways as the plan itself.

One way in which I like to think of any type of business improvement or change is in terms of people, process, and technology. As plans can be strategic, tactical, and operational, I thought it a good idea to overlay the two views creating a general template for it (see generic example in Table 2.4).

The thinking here is that all businesses are made up of the three components of people, process, and technology, and, within each, there are strategic, tactical, and operational goals that need to be established and tracked for successful implementation and alignment with a business strategy.

Within each category and planning horizon, the plans should be set and measured such that they are in congruence with the corporate and business strategy.

TABLE 2.4

Supply Chain Functional Implementation Strategy Example

	Functional – Strategy	Functional – Tactical	Functional – Operational
People	Recruit, train, and retain a supply chain "people" pipeline that fits your strategy and culture	Establish rotational positions, retrain, cross-train, select training partners	Survey results and employee input and satisfaction
Process	Analyze structure annually for strategic fit (supply chain network, CPFR process and scope, S&OP process)	Value stream map (VSM) of selected families of products	Implement process improvements from VSM and measure results
Technology	Evaluate and modify or select technologies that support corporate and business strategies	Implement changes to current or new technologies	Measure results of new/ improved technology performance with employee input/ feedback

So, for example, if our company employs a "cost leadership" business strategy, it will be critical for alignment purposes that our people, process, and technology strategies focus on making this happen.

The "process" *strategy* should, for example, employ a low-cost supply chain network. *Tactically*, we should employ mostly low-cost carriers such as rail and truck, and, *operationally*, we would measure the actual transportation costs against the plan to ensure it is being followed.

What follows are some thoughts on how important these choices are from a people, process, and technology standpoint when employing this type of analysis and implementation of a supply chain strategy (or any strategy, for that matter).

People

The success or failure of a business depends on its employees. If they are not part of an improvement program, it is doomed to failure. Whether you are a manufacturer, wholesaler, or retailer, there has to be both top-down support and bottom-up involvement.

Besides the "what's in it for me" question, employees want to feel that they are listened to and part of the solution, not just viewed by management as part of the problem.

It is useful to think of a kind of change or improvement in terms of Maslow's hierarchy of needs, which states that our actions are motivated in order to achieve certain needs. If we are successful in meeting many of these needs, our employees will tend to be more productive and participate in general and in terms of any kind of participatory program or plan.

Specifically, Maslow's hierarchy of needs points out that people have basic physical requirements, including the need for food, water, sleep, and warmth, which can be viewed in "pyramid" form (Figure 2.2). Once these lower-level needs have been met, they can move on to the next level of needs, which are for safety and security. As people progress up the pyramid, needs become increasingly psychological and social. Then, the need for love, friendship, and intimacy become important. Further up the pyramid, the need for personal esteem and feelings of accomplishment take priority.

The more we can help our employees to progress up this pyramid of needs, the more motivated they will be, and the more successful the organization as a whole will be.

In terms of the success of the implementation of a strategy or program, we need to support (financially, emotionally, and educationally) and empower our employees to fully motivate them.

Something that is known as the "job design continuum" (Figure 2.3) illustrates how we can progress in this task of self-actualization in the workplace (i.e. the top of Maslow's hierarchy of needs).

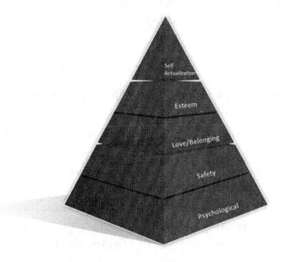

FIGURE 2.2
Maslow's hierarchy of needs.

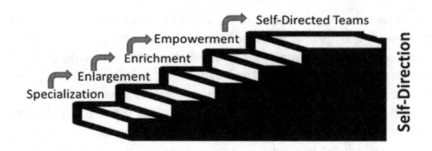

Job Expansion

FIGURE 2.3
The job design continuum.

As we move up the job continuum by enlarging and enriching jobs, we reach a point at which we can empower employees, which is sometimes a very difficult task for some managers to deal with, as they may have to give up some control. Empowerment is the process of enabling an employee to think, behave, act, react, and control their work in more independent ways.

To be truly successful in any type of program or project, we need to establish teams (in some cases self-directed, but not necessarily). This ultimately leads to benefits such as an improved quality of work life for employees, improved job satisfaction, increased motivation, improved productivity and quality, and reduced turnover and absenteeism.

Process

The number of stock keeping units (SKUs) offered in retail has exploded over the past 40 years or so. The average supermarket today carries anywhere from 15,000 to 60,000 items, vs. 5,900 in 1960 (and 7,800 in 1970) [McTaggart, 2012].

As a result, it has become harder and harder for manufacturers, wholesalers, and retailers to manage operations. That is perhaps why collaborative programs such as efficient consumer response (ECR) and collaborative planning, forecasting, and replenishment (CPFR) were created to help manage inventory in the supply chain better.

Additionally, in these volatile economic times, businesses are looking for any edge they can find to improve on thin margins and increase productivity and sales. That is why, throughout this text, I have advocated the need to look beyond the supply chain (which is a great place to start) and include all of the internal processes not just in operations, but also in sales and marketing and finance, as well as including key partners in your extended supply chain as much as possible.

Technology

Technology can enable a good process. The past 30 years have seen exponential gains in technology, including the growth of the internet (for e-commerce, m-commerce, omni channel retail, collaboration, and visibility), enterprise resource planning, supply chain planning, execution systems, and warehouse and store technologies (e.g. radio frequency identification (RFID) and self-checkout).

It is important to stay up to date in terms of technological advances as they are coming at us at such a rapid pace, while at the same time making sure the technology is a good fit for your company's needs.

Now that we have a good idea of the importance of organizational and supply chain strategy, we will next look in more detail at supply chain elements and drivers, and how you can determine fit and scope to ensure alignment with the corporate and business strategies.

3

Supply Chain Performance: Achieving Strategic Fit and Scope

SUPPLY CHAIN STRATEGY ELEMENTS AND DRIVERS

Supply chain strategy defines the connection and combination of activities and functions throughout the value chain to fulfill the business value to customers.

As a result, a good supply chain strategy tends to be driven by the interrelations between four main elements (see Figure 3.1):

1. Industry framework (i.e. the marketplace).
2. Company's value proposition to the customer via its competitive positioning.
3. Managerial focus (relationship between supply chain processes and business strategy).
4. Internal (supply chain) processes.

Industry Framework

Developing an industry framework involves identifying the interaction of suppliers, customers, technological developments, and economic factors that may impact competition.

There are four drivers that can impact supply chain design. They are:

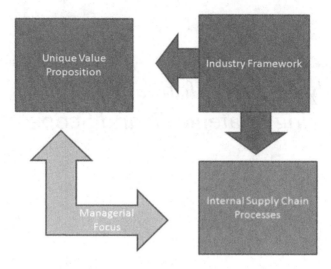

FIGURE 3.1
Four main elements of supply chain strategy.

1. Demand variation – this can affect a wide array of manufacturing and supply chain costs and is therefore a major driver of efficiency and, ultimately, cost.
2. Market mediation costs – these are costs incurred when supply doesn't match demand, often resulting in either lost sales or higher than needed supply chain costs and excess inventory.
3. Product life cycle – advances in technology as well as consumer trends have reduced the time to bring an item to market as well as its useful life. This affects demand variability as well as marketing and supply chain costs.
4. Relevance of the cost of assets to total cost – this largely affects businesses requiring a high utilization rate to remain profitable (e.g. the chemical industry). This encourages a "push" mentality to gain high utilization of assets but can result in higher inventory costs and lower service levels. Industries that have lower cost assets can focus on being more responsive

Unique Value Proposal

The value proposition offered to a company's customer is best understood after the establishment of the competitive priority strategy that the organization has selected in terms of its supply chain. As part of the organization's strategy, it needs to determine what it takes to win business and incorporate that into its value proposition, thereby understanding and incorporating the required key drivers into its supply chain to that, ultimately, the required value is delivered to the customer.

Managerial Focus

In order to be successful, an organization must make sure that its supply chain is linked to and aligned with its competitive priorities. This can only be accomplished via its decision-making process and management focus.

It can be very easy for management to only focus on efficiency-oriented performance measurements at the expense of the competitive priorities set by the company. A misalignment can result in the supply chain being "suboptimized" by attaining local cost efficiencies at the expense of the value proposition offered to the customer.

Internal Processes

Internal processes must be connected and aligned properly. Thinking in terms of the SCOR model processes of source, make, and deliver can help to make sure this occurs. It is of critical importance to determine the appropriate "decoupling point" (i.e. where a product takes on unique characteristics or specifications). This contributes to determining which parts of your internal processes are "push" (i.e. high asset utilization rate; just before the decoupling point) vs. "pull" (i.e. workload driven by customer demand) [Perez, 2013].

SUPPLY CHAIN DRIVERS AND THEIR IMPACT ON ITS CAPABILITIES

Now, let's look a bit more closely at how supply chain capabilities are guided by the decisions you make regarding a slightly different set of drivers than those mentioned above.

The supply chain drivers of production, inventory, location, transportation, and information can be managed for responsiveness or efficiency (or in between, known as a "hybrid" approach and discussed later in this chapter as well as in Chapter 6) depending on changing business requirements (Figure 3.2). When you research how your supply chain works, you can determine the demands it faces and the capabilities it needs to be successful. The supply chain drivers can then be adjusted as needed to acquire those capabilities.

Analyzing the five drivers is a great way to think about supply chain capabilities. The decisions you make about how each driver operates will determine the blend of responsiveness and efficiency a supply chain is capable of achieving.

Let's look at each of the five drivers and their impact on the supply chain's capabilities, which can range from being very efficient vs. very responsive (shown in Table 3.1):

1. Production – this driver can be made very responsive by building manufacturing capabilities that have excess capacity and use flexible manufacturing techniques to produce a wide range of items. Added responsiveness can be achieved by companies producing in smaller plants that are close to demand geographies for shorter delivery times.

   For efficiency, you would typically build factories with very little excess capacity that are focused on producing a smaller range of

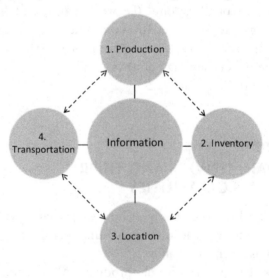

FIGURE 3.2
Five supply chain drivers.

TABLE 3.1

Summary of Supply Chain Drivers and Their Impact on Responsiveness vs. Efficiency

Supply Chain Drivers	Responsiveness	Efficiency
1. Production	Excess capacity, flexible manufacturing, many smaller plants	Little excess capacity, narrow focus, few central plants
2. Inventory	High inventory levels, wide range of items	Low inventory levels, fewer items
3. Location	Many locations close to customer	Few, central locations serve wide areas
4. Transportation	Frequent shipments, fast and flexible modes	Few, large shipments, slower and cheaper modes
5. Information	Collect and share timely and accurate data	Cost of information drops while other costs rise

items. Centralizing production to get better economies of scale can gain even more efficiency, although delivery times might be longer.

2. Inventory – responsiveness can be achieved by stocking high levels of inventory for the full range of your products. More stock keeping locations will also add to your responsiveness by keeping the inventory close to customers.

   Efficiency in inventory management would call for inventory levels of all items to be reduced, especially of slow-moving items. Also, economies of scale and cost savings can be achieved by stocking inventory in fewer, central locations.

3. Location – the closer your locations are to your customers, the more responsive your supply chain can be.

   On the other hand, efficiency can be achieved by operating from fewer locations and centralizing activities.

   The location decision for plants, distribution/fulfillment centers (DCs), and retail facilities is a critical strategic decision for a business and needs to be carefully analyzed (and re-analyzed every few years or so), as we will discuss later, in Chapter 5 (Supply Chain Network Design).

4. Transportation – responsiveness can be achieved by selecting transportation modes that are fast and flexible, such as trucks and airplanes. Many companies that sell products through catalogs or on the internet can provide high levels of responsiveness by using transportation to deliver their products, often within 48 hours, using

small package carriers such as FedEx and UPS. Other companies – especially in e-commerce, such as Amazon – are building and operating their own transportation services in high-volume markets to be more responsive to customer needs.

Efficiency can be maximized by transporting products in larger batches and doing it less often. The use of transportation modes such as railroad and container lines can be very efficient.

5. Information – the data that provide information are expanding every year, almost exponentially, as the technology for collecting data, analyzing them to turn them into useful information, and sharing them throughout the supply chain becomes more widespread, easier to use, and less expensive. Information can directly enhance the performance of the other four supply chain drivers when used properly, hence the "hot topic" of data (or supply chain) analytics lately.

Responsiveness can be achieved as companies increasingly collect and share accurate, timely data generated by the operations of the other four drivers, internally and externally, with customers, suppliers, and other partners.

The best practice in many industries today, such as electronics and consumer package goods (CPG), is for the manufacturers, distributors, and big retailers to collect and share data about customer demand, production schedules, and inventory levels, which will be discussed in Chapter 8 ("Integration, Coordination, and Collaboration in a Supply Chain"). This enables companies in these industries to respond more quickly in today's volatile environment (and hopefully other industries will start to adopt these concepts more rapidly).

In the long run, the cost of information continues to drop while the cost of the other four drivers continues to rise (especially lately with the rapid increase in inflation). Companies that make the best use of information to increase their internal efficiency and their responsiveness to external supply chain partners will gain the most customers and be the most profitable. As the old saying goes, you should always try to "replace inventory with information" where possible.

Efficiency vs. Responsiveness

Until the turn of the 21st century, as a priority, efficiency increased productivity and lowered the prices of products, making them available to a wide segment of the population. However, when striving for efficiency it helps to have predictability and stability.

To plan and manage production and distribution of products efficiently, it helps to have a good idea of what demand will be for those products, as well as the cost of raw materials and the selling prices. That information goes a long way toward maximizing profits.

Efficiency also requires at least a fair degree of stability so that you can plan for future facilities capacity and transportation infrastructure to enable your operating model. Efficiency is most attainable when producing a smaller variety of relatively simple products and services that sell in more predictable and stable markets.

In the 21st century, responsiveness is driving the economy. Responsiveness is what drives continuous innovation in products and technology and continuous change in the ways we organize businesses and serve customers. Twenty-first-century companies still need to be efficient, but their success is based more on their ability to sense and respond quickly to changing markets and evolving customer desires. The "holy grail" is a mass customization process that maintains reasonable (but not the lowest) costs. The lowest price is not always the deciding factor in purchasing decisions as, today, they're more about relationships. People want products and services that respond quickly and meet their changing needs and desires.

While consumers value the quality and innovation offered by companies such as Apple and Tesla, etc., they will pay more for their products. Home "last-mile" delivery of everything from clothes to groceries may cost a bit more, but people value and pay for the responsiveness and convenience of those services. Responsiveness is at its best when providing complex or unique products (i.e. mass customization) and services that sell in constantly changing markets driven by changing technology and new customer needs and desires.

The Right Mix of Efficiency and Responsiveness

Even when supply chains emphasize responsiveness, there are sections or nodes of those supply chains that should focus on efficiency (in lean terms, which will be discussed in Chapter 6, this is referred to as using a "hybrid" approach resulting in a lean *and* agile supply chain).

Efficiency is important when there are high volumes of stable products moving between facilities. For example, the links and nodes of supply chains that connect factories with warehouses or distribution centers should be as efficient as possible. They should use efficient transportation modes and delivery schedules, and the facilities should automate their operations as much as possible.

However, the links and nodes of supply chains that connect distribution centers to end use customers, known as "last-mile" deliveries, usually focus on responsiveness. They use transportation modes and delivery schedules that emphasize responsiveness because customers often require fast delivery of products.

In most supply chains, there are some operations that will need to focus on efficiency, and others that will need to focus on responsiveness. The mix may shift over time, as customer preferences, market conditions, and technologies often change.

There are plenty of new technologies, such as robots, drones, artificial intelligence (AI), and 3D printing, that can impact how supply chains operate to increase efficiency and/or responsiveness.

Zara, for example, is a clothing designer, manufacturer, and retailer of unique clothing products and operates in a constantly changing market shaped by popular fashion and customer desires. It uses a lean hybrid methodology enabled by information and technology to manage its supply chain [Hugos, 2020].

Segmentation Strategy for Supply Chains

It should also be considered that, in some cases, a "segmentation" strategy may be called for. For example, Dell Computers started by offering highly customized, high-end, "make to order" desktop computers, laptops, and tablets at premium prices (and continues to do so). More recently, it began producing standardized "make to stock" desktops, laptops, and tablets that are sold through mass merchandisers, such as Walmart, at lower prices.

Effectively, it has separate, "segmented" supply chains for each of those product lines. If it didn't, it would be hard to manage a single supply chain for customized products – that is, based upon speed and responsiveness – while at the same time also running the standardized, value-priced product lines requiring efficiency and low costs through the same supply chain.

Technology Is a Foundation for an Efficient and Responsive Supply Chain

Companies need access to data (which then must be converted into usable information) to make better decisions about how they manage production, inventory, locations, and transportation.

Thanks to technology today, there is an abundance of data. However, the data is coming from all directions and in granular detail.

In fact, IDC predicts that the collective sum of the world's data will grow from 33 zettabytes (ZB) in 2020 to 175 ZB by 2025, for a compounded annual growth rate of 61 percent.

It also predicts that

- The storage industry will ship 42 ZB of capacity over the next seven years.
- Some 90 ZB of data will be created on Internet of Things (IoT) devices by 2025.
- By 2025, 49 percent of data will be stored in public cloud environments.
- Nearly 30 percent of the data generated will be consumed in real-time by 2025 [Seagate Technology Report, 2020].

So, the high demand for people with data analytics skills isn't that surprising as they are needed to convert large volumes of these data, with the aid of technology, into useful information to support decision-making.

On top of that, this exponentially expanding amount of data is often dispersed across multiple systems that sit in siloed business units. Without transparency and systems integration, leaders have a difficult time establishing and enforcing efficient or responsive processes, much less an efficient or responsive supply chain.

For example, many organizations rely on outdated transportation data and manual efforts to plan and schedule shipments. Any delay in transportation not only prevents the shipper from operating efficiently or responsively, but also impacts how well the rest of the supply chain can do the same, as a (supply) chain is only as good as its weakest link, as the saying goes.

To be efficient and profitable, as well as responsive to customer demands, companies need to utilize technology. There is a lot of valuable data out there, from many different sources, that must be gathered and analyzed.

As a result, we can no longer rely on manual methods, spreadsheets, or disconnected systems to perform the analysis [Bonner, 2020].

ACHIEVING STRATEGIC FIT

The next step in this process is to achieve strategic fit between your supply chain's capabilities and your product or service characteristics.

The idea of achieving a strategic fit of your supply chain with its industry is a competitive strategy where all functional strategies must fit together to form a coordinated overall strategy.

The different functions in a company must appropriately structure their processes and resources to be able to execute these strategies successfully. Ultimately, the design of the overall supply chain and the role of each stage must be aligned to support the supply chain strategy.

Achieving strategic fit should include the following steps:

1. Understanding the customer and supply chain uncertainty – both the supply and demand of your supply chain for an individual product or service (or family of products or services) can range from fairly predictable to highly volatile (Figure 3.3).

   For example, demand and supply for a commodity such as baking soda are very predictable and consistent. On the other hand, a high-tech product such as a new version of a smart TV may be very volatile, such as during the pandemic when microchips were in short supply, or 3D, 4K, or 8K TVs, where demand is very unpredictable. By examining this, you can get a good idea as far as the current and future demand and supply uncertainty for your products or services is concerned.

FIGURE 3.3
Levels of demand and supply uncertainty.

2. Understanding the supply chain – this step involves determining how your company best meets demand.

   As discussed earlier, supply chain responsiveness is the ability to respond to wide ranges of quantities demanded, meet short lead times, handle a large variety of products, build highly innovative products, and meet a very high service level. Of course, responsiveness comes at a cost (e.g. use of faster, premium transportation modes, more automated equipment, etc.).

   Supply chain efficiency, on the other hand, is the inverse of the cost of making and delivering the product to the customer. So, to some degree, you typically will have to give up some responsiveness to achieve lower costs (Figure 3.4).

   For example, a refinery would tend to be very efficient, with production being scheduled weeks or months in advance and with a relatively small variety of items/grades or flexibility. On the other hand, a business such as a convenience store chain with a small store footprint will have to be very responsive to what is being sold each day, continuously changing the merchandising mix by location and time of day.

3. Achieving strategic fit – this step ensures that the degree of supply chain responsiveness is consistent with the implied uncertainty (Figure 3.5). Roles are assigned to different stages of the supply chain, ensuring the appropriate level of responsiveness and that all functions maintain consistent strategies that support the competitive strategy.

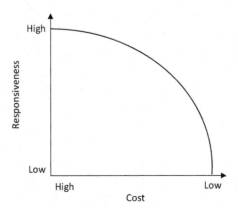

FIGURE 3.4
Supply chain cost–responsiveness relationship.

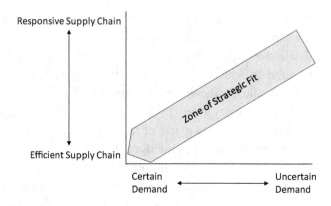

FIGURE 3.5
Zone of strategic fit.

Ideally, your supply chain should end up being in a so-called "zone of strategic fit" to maximize service and minimize cost [Chopra and Meindl, 2016].

The reader should now have a solid understanding of supply chain drivers and the importance of achieving strategic fit and scope. This raises the questions of how good the fit is and whether it is being maintained. This can be determined through setting proper metrics, setting appropriate targets, and ensuring their ongoing measurement.

4

Supply Chain Metrics and Measurements

As the saying goes, "if you don't measure something, you can't manage (or improve) it". This was never truer than in the supply chain and logistics management field. There is an assortment of trade-offs that exist in a supply chain (e.g. cost vs. service) which must be counterbalanced against each other to be successful for the long term.

It is important to match your supply chain performance measures with your company's mission and strategy, keeping in mind that performance measures can affect the behavior of managers and employees.

It is also vital to target and measure supply chain performance to meet customer expectations, improve supply chain capability, improve asset performance, motivate the workforce, and provide stakeholders with a satisfactory return on their investment.

While technology today makes it much easier to gather and analyze data, there is a lot more data available, making it all the more important to measure only the right things and to avoid wasted effort; otherwise, you may fall into the dreaded phenomenon of "paralysis by analysis". The results of analysis should be used effectively.

MEASUREMENT AND CONTROL METHODS

Having an efficient and effective supply chain requires a set of standards to compare with actual performance. These standards are referred to as metrics.

DOI: 10.4324/9781003281078-5

While there are a variety of established metrics for the supply chain, such as those defined by the supply chain operations reference (SCOR) model mentioned in Chapter 2, determining the appropriate metrics for your organization can be a complex problem.

Selecting and measuring the wrong set of metrics can lead your company to follow the wrong goals, as metrics tend to drive behavior.

In supply chain and logistics management, cost metrics need to focus on the entire, extended supply chain (internal and external), not on just one function or one link.

The Evolution of Metrics

Historically, businesses would focus on manufacturing costs as a measure of efficiency. That was eventually extended to include transportation costs in the 1970s. In the 1980s and 1990s, this view was expanded to look at the broader performance of distribution and logistics costs, which were supplemented with more meaningful performance indicators such as the delivery rate and percentage of order fulfillment as a greater focus on customers emerged.

The advent of the global supply chain, the internet, enterprise resource planning (ERP) systems, automated data gathering devices such as barcode scanners, and the IoT allowed organizations both to take an even broader view of their extended supply chains and to gather, measure, and analyze cost and service information more easily.

Today, relying on traditional supply chain execution systems is becoming increasingly difficult, with a mix of global operating systems, pricing pressures, and ever-increasing customer expectations. There are also recent economic impacts such as the pandemic, rising costs, global recessions, supplier bases that have shrunk or moved offshore, as well as increased competition from low-cost outsourcers. All of these challenges potentially create waste in your supply chain. That's where data analytics comes in.

Data Analytics

Data analytics is the science of examining raw data to help draw conclusions about information. When applied to the supply chain, it is often described as "supply chain analytics". It is used in many industries to allow companies and organizations to drive insight, make better business decisions, and implement better actions, as well as in the sciences to verify (or disprove) existing models or theories.

One way to look at data analytics is to break it into four categories:

1. Descriptive analytics – uses historical data to describe a business; is also described as business intelligence (BI) systems. In the supply chain, descriptive analytics help to better understand historical demand patterns, how product flows through your supply chain, and when a shipment might be late.
2. Diagnostic analytics – once problems occur in the supply chain, the source of the problem needs to be analyzed. Often, this can involve analysis of the data in the systems to see why the company was missing certain components or what went wrong that caused the problem.
3. Predictive analytics – uses data to predict trends and patterns; often associated with statistics. In the supply chain, predictive analytics could be used to forecast future demand or to forecast the price of a product.
4. Prescriptive analytics – using data to select an optimal solution. In the supply chain, you might use prescriptive analytics to determine the optimal number and location of distribution centers, set your inventory levels, or schedule production.

Traditional measures tend to be based upon historical data and not focused on the future; don't relate to strategic, non-financial performance goals such as customer service and product quality; and don't directly tie to operational effectiveness and efficiency.

The ever-increasing amount and sources of raw data have compounded the need for the use of data analytics assisted by great technology. This is not just to gather data but to help with the analysis using AI, optimization models, and so forth to translate the data into usable information to support better, faster decision-making.

Measurement Methods

A number of measurement methods have been developed or enhanced in recent times, including:

- The balanced scorecard – a strategic planning and management system that aligns business activities with the vision and strategy of the organization, improves internal and external communications, and monitors organization performance against strategic goals. It adds strategic non-financial performance measures to traditional financial metrics to give managers and executives a more "balanced" view of organizational performance.

- The supply chain council's SCOR model – metrics in this model provide a foundation for measuring performance and identifying priorities in supply chain operations.
- Activity-based costing (ABC) – a costing and monitoring methodology that identifies activities in an organization and assigns the cost of each activity with resources to all products and services according to actual consumption by each product and service.
- Economic value analysis (EVA) – the value created by an enterprise, based on operating profits in excess of capital utilized (through debt and equity financing). These types of metrics can be used to measure an enterprise's value-added contributions within a supply chain (not as useful for detailed supply chain measurements).

No matter which method you use, it is a good idea that the metrics are consistent with overall corporate strategy, focused on customer needs with prioritized expectations, and focused on processes and not functions.

Furthermore, metrics should be implemented consistently throughout the supply chain, with actions and rationale communicated to everyone.

It's also a good idea to use some kind of balanced approach when selecting and developing metrics, using precise costs to measure improvement (in detail and in the aggregate), which can be greatly aided by the use of technology.

MEASUREMENT CATEGORIES

While each method has its own specifics, it is important at least to include the measurement categories of time, quality, and cost in one form or another.

- **Time** – includes on-time delivery and receipt, order cycle time and variability, and response time.
- **Quality** – measures customer satisfaction; processing and fulfillment accuracy, including on-time, complete, and damage-free order

delivery; and accurate invoicing. Also includes planning (including forecasting) and scheduling accuracy.

- **Cost** – this category includes financial measurements such as inventory turns; order-to-cash cycle time; and total delivered costs broken up by cost of goods, transportation, carrying, and material handling costs.

Another way of looking at supply chain measurement categories is in terms of where they will be applied.

- **Strategic level** – measures include lead time against industry norm (i.e. benchmarking, which will be discussed later in this chapter), quality level, cost-saving initiatives, and supplier pricing against market.
- **Tactical level** – measures include the efficiency of purchase order cycle time, booking-in procedures, cash flow, quality assurance methodology, and capacity flexibility.
- **Operational level** – measures include ability in day-to-day technical representation, adherence to developed schedule, ability to avoid complaints, and achievement of defect-free deliveries.

Now, let's look at two of the major models for measuring the supply chain, the balanced scorecard approach and the SCOR model.

BALANCED SCORECARD APPROACH

When using the balanced scorecard approach to the supply chain, one needs to consider it from four different perspectives:

1. Customer perspective – how do customers see us?
2. Internal business perspective – what must we excel at?
3. Financial perspective – how do we look to shareholders?
4. Innovation and learning perspective – can we continue to improve and create value?

Next, we must put it in a framework that integrates the organization's overall goals and strategies with selected supply chain metrics in the categories of customer service, operations, and finance (Figure 4.1).

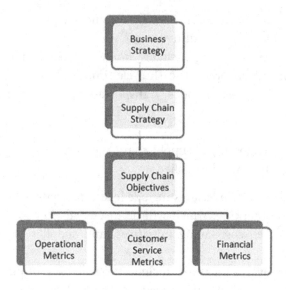

FIGURE 4.1
Supply chain metrics framework.

It is always critical that supply chain and logistics metrics connect to the overall business strategy. For example, if a company uses a cost leadership strategy, a financial metric such as inventory turnover would be critical, demanding top quartile leadership. If they employ a response strategy, then inventory turns might not be as critical as, say, delivery time.

Customer Service Metrics

Customer service metrics indicate a company's ability to satisfy customers' needs by meeting them on a timely basis and creating exceptional value for the customers (Table 4.1).

TABLE 4.1

Customer Service Supply Chain Metrics

Goals	Measures
Flexible response	Number of choices and average response time
Product/service innovation	Customer contact points and product finalization points
Customer satisfaction	Order fulfillment rate
Customer value	Customer profitability
Delivery performance	Delivery speed and reliability

Operational Metrics

Operational metrics come from internal processes, decisions, and actions needed to meet or exceed customer expectations. They are drivers of future financial performance (Table 4.2).

Financial Metrics

Financial metrics indicate whether the company's strategy, implementation, and execution create value for the shareholders by contributing to improvements in profitability (Table 4.3).

Innovation and Learning Metrics

Other metrics to consider (although not included in Figure 4.1) are innovation and learning. These metrics encourage the identification of measures that answer the question "How can we continue to improve, create value, and innovate?". This is analyzed through the investigation of training and knowledge resources.

TABLE 4.2

Operational Supply Chain Metrics

Goals	Measures
Waste reduction	Supply chain cost of ownership
Time compression	Supply chain cycle efficiency
Unit cost reduction	Percent of supply chain target cost achieved
Product/process innovation	Product finalization point
Inventory management	Inventory turns and days of inventory
Supplier performance	Supplier evaluations

TABLE 4.3

Financial Supply Chain Metrics

Goals	Measures
Profit margins	Profit margin by supply chain partners
Cash flows	Cash-to-cash cycle on receivables and payables
Revenue growth	Customer growth and profitability
Return on assets	Return on supply chain asset
Return on equity	Return on supply chain equity

One example would be measuring the time it takes to develop a new generation of products, life cycle to product maturity, and time to market vs. competition. This helps to determine how well information is captured and how effectively employees use that information to convert it to a competitive advantage within the industry.

SUPPLY CHAIN OPERATIONS REFERENCE MODEL

Another, relatively newer approach to measuring the supply chain is the SCOR model that was discussed in Chapter 2. To recap, the SCOR model was designed to help companies to communicate, compare, and learn from competitors and companies both within and outside their industry. It measures an organization's supply chain performance as well as the effectiveness of supply chain improvements and can also help to test and plan future process improvements.

The SCOR model contains over 200 process elements, 550 metrics, and 500 best practices, including risk and environmental management, and is organized around the five primary management processes of plan, source, make, deliver, return, and enable (Figure 4.2).

The model is based on three major "pillars":

1. Process modeling – to describe supply chains that are very simple or very complex using a common set of definitions. SCOR provides three-levels of process detail. Each level of detail assists a company

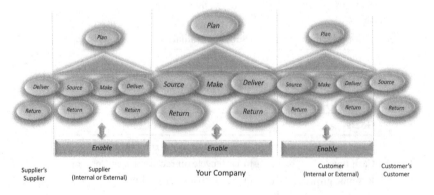

FIGURE 4.2
The SCOR model.

in defining scope (level 1), configuration or type of supply chain (level 2), and process element details, including performance attributes (level 3). Below level 3, companies decompose process elements and start implementing specific supply chain management practices. It is at this stage that companies define practices to achieve a competitive advantage and adapt to changing business conditions.

2. Performance measurements – SCOR metrics are organized in a hierarchical structure. Level 1 metrics are at the most aggregated level and are typically used by top decision makers to measure the performance of the company's overall supply chain. Level 2 metrics are primary, high-level measures that may cross multiple SCOR processes.

3. Best practices – once the performance of the supply chain operations has been measured and performance gaps have been identified, it becomes important to identify what activities should be performed to close those gaps. Over 430 executable practices derived from the experience of supply chain council (SCC) members are available.

Also, as mentioned in pillar 1 above, SCOR "levels" range from broadest to narrowest and are defined as:

- **Level 1**: scope – defines business lines, business strategy, and complete supply chains.
- **Level 2**: configuration – defines specific planning models such as "make to order" (MTO) or "make to stock" (MTS), which are basically process strategies.
- **Level 3**: activity – specifies tasks within the supply chain, describing what people actually do.
- **Level 4**: workflow – includes best practices, job details, or workflow of an activity.
- **Level 5**: transaction – specific transaction details to perform a job step.

Furthermore, all SCOR metrics have five key strategic performance attributes. A performance attribute is a group of metrics used to express a strategy. An attribute itself cannot be measured; it is used to set strategic direction.

The five strategic attributes are:

1. **Reliability**: the ability to deliver, on time, complete, in the right condition, and with the right packaging and documentation, to the right customer.
2. **Responsiveness**: the speed at which products and services are provided.
3. **Agility**: the ability to change (the supply chain) in order to support changing (market) conditions.
4. **Cost**: the cost associated with operating the supply chain.
5. **Assets**: the effectiveness in managing assets in support of demand satisfaction.

At level 1 for example, Table 4.4 shows some strategic metrics.

At lower levels of detail, the SCOR model sets a variety of specific, standard measures that can be used by an organization. Some examples under the performance attribute of "supply chain responsiveness" for the "deliver" component of the SCOR model can be found in Table 4.5.

SUPPLY CHAIN DASHBOARD AND KPIs

One way to measure, analyze, and manage supply chain performance is with the use of a *dashboard*. The dashboard can range from data that are

TABLE 4.4

SCOR Model Strategic Metrics

Performance Attribute	Sample Metric	Calculation
Supply chain reliability	Perfect order fulfillment	(Total perfect orders) / (Total number of orders)
Supply chain responsiveness	Average order fulfillment cycle time	(Sum of actual cycle times for all orders delivered) / (Total number of orders delivered)
Supply chain agility	Upside supply chain flexibility	Time required to achieve an unplanned 20% increase in delivered quantities
Supply chain costs	Supply chain management costs	Cost to plan + Cost to source + Cost to deliver + Cost to return
Supply chain asset management	Cash-to-cash cycle time	Inventory days of supply + Days of receivables outstanding – Days of payables outstanding

TABLE 4.5

Supply Chain Responsiveness Delivery Cycle Time Example

Supply Chain Responsiveness
RS.2.3 - Deliver Cycle Time
RS.3.16 - Build Loads Cycle Time
RS.3.18 - Consolidate Orders Cycle Time
RS.3.46 - Install product Cycle Time
RS.3.51 - Load Product & Generate Shipping Documentation Cycle Time
RS.3.95 - Pack Product Cycle Time
RS.3.102 - Receive & Verify Products by Customer Cycle Time

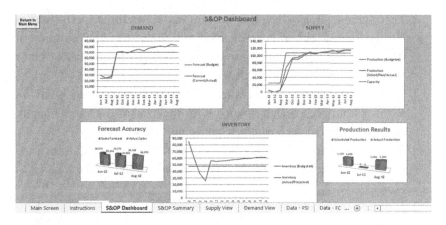

FIGURE 4.3
Supply chain dashboard example. Source: S&OP Excel template, published with permission of Logistics Planning Associates, LLC.

manually collected and put into a spreadsheet with some graphs, to a more automated, visual dashboard generated by an ERP system (Figure 4.3).

A supply chain dashboard helps in decision-making by visually displaying, in real time (or close to it), leading and lagging indicators in a supply chain process perspective. It can help to visualize trends, track performance targets, and understand the most critical issues facing your company's supply chain.

One of the leading-edge type of dashboards used today is known as a "supply chain control tower". A supply chain control tower is defined as a connected, personalized dashboard of data, key business metrics, and events across the supply chain. A supply chain control tower enables organizations to fully understand, prioritize, and resolve critical issues in real time.

Indicators

Metrics used in performance dashboards are typically called *key performance indicators* (KPIs). Having a standardized set of KPIs allows you to review supply chain operations efficiently across regions, business units, and plants, and even across brands and channels.

KPIs usually fall into one of three categories:

1. Leading indicators – have a significant impact on future performance by measuring either current state activities (e.g. the number of items produced today) or future activities (e.g. the number of items scheduled for production this week).
2. Lagging indicators – measures of past performance such as various financial measurements or, in the case of the supply chain, measurements in areas such as cost, quality, and delivery.
3. Diagnostic – areas that may not fit under lead or lagging indicators but indicate the general health of an organization [Myerson, 2012].

BENCHMARKING

Once you have established what KPIs to measure, you need to determine how to gauge yourself against them. This is known as benchmarking, which is the process of comparing one's business processes and performance metrics with industry bests or best practices from other companies. The dimensions that are typically measured are quality, time, and cost. There is both internal and external benchmarking.

Internal benchmarking can be used when the organization is large enough and data are fairly accessible. For example, a company such as General Electric, with over 100 business units, can compare some KPIs across businesses.

External benchmarking is a process where management identifies the best firms in their industry, or in another industry where similar processes exist, comparing the results and processes of those "target" companies with their own results and processes. This allows them to learn how well the targets perform and, more importantly, the best-practice business processes that help to explain why these firms are successful.

The process of selecting best practices to use as a standard for performance involves the following general steps:

1. Determine what to benchmark – what processes are most important to measuring the success of your supply chain? These can be based upon your company's corporate, business and supply chain strategies, goals, and objectives. In some cases, you may want to be "best in class", and, in others, being average may be just fine.
2. Form a benchmark team – select people with some "skin in the game".
3. Identify benchmarking partners – should be a combination of those involved in the day-to-day processes as well as those affected and management (can also include customers and suppliers).
4. Collect and analyze benchmarking information – there are many sources of best-practice metrics. In many cases, companies can pay for this information from consultants or through associations that they belong to.

Now that we have an understanding of what is to be measured to meet our strategic goals, the first longer-term step is supply chain network design (and redesign), which plays a huge role in driving our cost and service performance.

5

Supply Chain Network Design

As the saying goes in retail, the three most important factors for success are location, location, and location. This is true not only in retail but also for manufacturers, as it plays a major role in both the cost and service of the organization.

Unfortunately, it is usually not considered often enough in the case of manufacturers or, in many cases, in enough detail and can potentially lead to catastrophe.

Location is a strategic, long-term decision that is not easily changed in the short term and applies to raw material sourcing, manufacturing, distribution, and retail.

Strategically, the major goal or priority of the location decision for a manufacturer is to minimize cost, while retailers look to maximize revenue where possible.

In the past, it was sufficient to analyze and modify your supply chain network every three to five years if you were a large company, as it was an expensive and complex process.

In today's volatile global world, with constant changes in demand and supply, it has become increasingly more important to have the appropriate supply chain network in place, no matter the size of your company. As a result, this exercise, in one form or another, must be done more often than in the past.

DOI: 10.4324/9781003281078-6

THE IMPORTANCE OF FACILITY LOCATION WHEN DESIGNING A SUPPLY CHAIN

To remain competitive in today's global economy, the efficient movement of goods from raw material sites to processing facilities, manufacturers, distributors, retailers, and customers is critical.

Unlike transportation and inventory decisions, location decisions tend to be less flexible, as many of the costs are fixed in the short term.

Picking the wrong manufacturing or distribution location can have a long-term impact on the total cost of a product. This decision can be heavily influenced by transportation costs as they can average 3–5 percent of sales, with average warehousing costs being 1–2 percent, historically. Customer service, administration, and inventory carrying costs can add another 3 percent or more on top of that.

As this is a supply chain book, we will primarily concentrate on the decision for the location of the finished goods distribution facility, which is important as it is a key driver of the overall profitability of a firm because it directly affects both supply chain cost and what the customer experiences.

The distribution network can be used to achieve a variety of supply chain objectives discussed earlier in this book, such as a cost- or responsiveness-focused strategy.

For example, Dell Computers primarily ships directly to consumers, while other PC manufacturers, such as Asus, sell through retailers. So, while the Dell customer may have to wait several days to get a highly customized PC, a retail customer can take their more standardized PC home the day they buy it locally.

Large household and personal care companies such as Colgate distribute directly to the larger supermarket chains, while small retailers have to buy Colgate products from distributors as they buy in smaller quantities.

SUPPLY CHAIN NETWORK DESIGN INFLUENCERS

Like many aspects of the supply chain, there are a variety of trade-offs involved in the decision-making process. In the case of supply chain network design (also known as "the location decision"), there is the major trade-off of cost vs. service.

From the customer perspective, service may be viewed in a variety of ways, including:

- **Lead time** – the amount of time for a customer to receive an order.
- **Product variety** – the number of different products offered by a distribution network.
- **Product availability** – the likelihood of a product being in stock when the customer places their order.
- **Customer experience** – this may have many dimensions, including how easy it is for customers to place and receive orders, as well as how much the experience is customized.
- **Time to market** – the time it takes to develop new products and bring them to market.
- **Order visibility** – the ability of customers to track orders from time of placement to delivery.
- **Returnability** – how easy it is for a customer to return merchandise and the efficiency of the network in handling these returns.

Types of Trade-offs in the Location Decision

In general, companies selling to customers who can handle a relatively long response time may require only a few locations, far from the customer. In these cases, companies may concentrate on increasing the capacity of each location.

On the other hand, companies that sell to customers who are looking for short response times and maybe even picking up product with their own vehicles need to locate facilities close to them. These companies typically have many facilities, each with relatively low capacity.

So, the trade-off here is that faster response times required to meet customer demand increase the number of facilities required in the network, and, conversely, a decrease in the response time customers desire decreases the number of facilities required in the network (see Figure 5.1).

Changing the distribution network design affects other supply chain costs as well, as seen in Figure 5.2, such as:

Inventory – the more locations there are, the harder it is to accurately forecast demand as there are smaller and smaller demand groupings, making the target smaller and harder to hit. As a result, safety stock requirements go up almost exponentially.

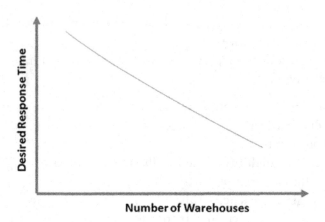

FIGURE 5.1
Relationship between number of warehouses and response time.

This phenomenon is often referred to as "the square root rule", which gives you an estimate of how the number of warehouse locations affects the size of your inventory. It states that total safety stock can be approximated by multiplying the total current inventory by the square root of the number of future warehouse locations divided by the current number of locations. The formula is: $X2 = (X1) * \sqrt{(n2/n1)}$, where $n1$ = number of existing facilities, $n2$ = number of future facilities, $X1$ = existing inventory, and $X2$ = future inventory.

Transportation – ideally, we want a "long in and short out" system to gain economies in transportation on the inbound side (i.e. full truckloads vs. less than truckload – LTL), but this of course can reach a point of diminishing returns as it will increase inventory and warehouse operating costs.

Facilities and handling (i.e. warehouse operations) – there are certain economies of scale that are gained by operating fewer warehouses, whether company-owned or outsourced, by consolidating volume. This can result in lower unit handling and storage costs with fewer facilities and must be analyzed thoroughly. On the other hand, the use of local public distribution centers (DCs) may enable a company to have its products combined with other companies' products to gain some local transportation savings.

There is also the fact that, as the number of distribution facilities increases, the amount of information to manage increases. This can be somewhat mitigated by having efficient and integrated information technology systems.

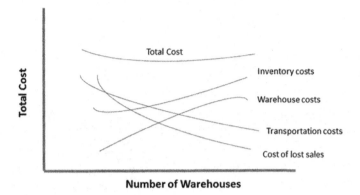

FIGURE 5.2
The number of warehouses and the impact on cost.

TYPES OF DISTRIBUTION NETWORKS

Bearing the aforementioned influences in mind, there are a variety of ways that a company can distribute its products. We will discuss a number of these now.

Manufacturer Storage with Direct Shipping

In this type of distribution network design (Figure 5.3), product is shipped directly from the manufacturer to the end customer, bypassing the retailer or seller (who takes the order and initiates the delivery request). This is also referred to as "drop shipping", where product is delivered directly from the manufacturer to the customer. This tends to work for a large variety of low-demand, high-value items where customers are willing to wait for delivery and accept several partial shipments.

Impact on Costs

In general, this type of network has lower costs because of aggregation, which works best with low-demand, high-value items. Transportation costs are greater because of increased distance and individual item shipping. Facility costs are lower owing to this aggregation of demand, and there

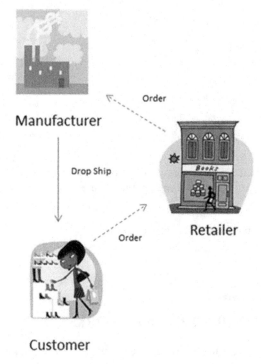

FIGURE 5.3
Manufacturer storage with direct shipping (drop shipping).

may be some saving on handling costs if the manufacturer can directly ship these small orders from the production line. However, this type of design requires a fairly large investment in information infrastructure as the manufacturer and retailer need to be tightly integrated.

Impact on Service

In terms of service, this type of distribution network design requires fairly long response times of one to two weeks because of increased distance and the two stages for order processing. The response time may vary by product, which may complicate receiving. Product variety and availability are relatively easy to provide owing to aggregation at the manufacturer. Home delivery may result in high customer satisfaction, but this can be negatively affected if orders from multiple manufacturers are sent as partial shipments. This type of network can help to get products to market fast, with the product available as soon as the first unit is produced. However, customer visibility and product returnability may be more difficult and expensive.

Manufacturer Storage with Direct Shipping and In-Transit Merge

In-transit merge by a carrier combines pieces of an order coming from different locations so that the customer gets a single delivery (Figure 5.4).

For example, when a customer orders a PC from Hewlett Packard (HP), along with a Samsung monitor, the package carrier picks up the PC from the Samsung factory and the monitor from the HP factory; it then merges the two together at a hub before making a single delivery to the customer.

This type of network works best for low-to-medium-demand, high-value items that a retailer is sourcing from a relatively low number of manufacturers.

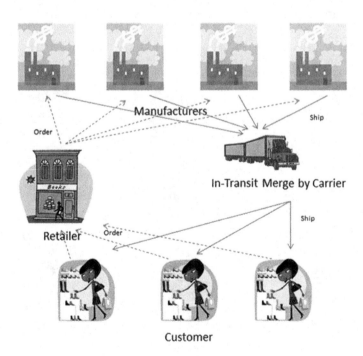

FIGURE 5.4
Manufacturer storage with direct shipping and in-transit merge.

Impact on Costs

The inventory costs associated with this type of distribution network are similar to drop shipping. However, handling and information investment costs may be higher than drop shipping, while transportation costs, as well as receiving costs at the customer, are somewhat lower than drop shipping. As a result of the increased coordination required to combine shipments, the information investment is somewhat higher than for drop shipping.

Impact on Service

The impacts on service, such as response time, variety, availability, visibility, and returnability, are all similar to drop shipping. However, the customer experience may be better than with drop shipping because a single order has to be received rather than multiple orders.

Distributor Storage with Carrier Delivery

When using the distributor/e-tailer/retailer storage with carrier delivery option (Figure 5.5), inventory is not held by manufacturers at factories

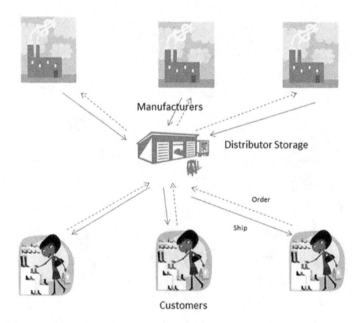

FIGURE 5.5
Distributor storage with carrier delivery.

but instead is held by distributors/retailers in intermediate warehouses, and package carriers are used to transport products from the intermediate location to the final customer. This works well for medium-to-fast-moving items. It also makes sense when customers want delivery faster than is offered by manufacturer storage but do not need it immediately.

Impact on Costs

In this type of configuration, inventory and warehouse operations costs are higher than manufacturer storage with direct shipping and in-transit merge. Transportation costs are lower than manufacturer storage, with a simpler information infrastructure required when compared with manufacturer storage.

Impact on Service

Distributor storage with carrier delivery typically has a faster response time than manufacturer storage with drop shipping, but offers less product variety and higher product availability costs. The customer experience, order visibility, and product returns are better than manufacturer storage with drop shipping.

Distributor Storage with Last-Mile Delivery

Last-mile delivery refers to the distributor/e-tailer/retailer delivering the product to the customer's home instead of using a package carrier (Figure 5.6).

In areas with high labor costs, distributor storage with last-mile delivery is very hard to justify on the basis of efficiency or improved margins and can only be justified if there is large enough demand that is willing to pay for this convenience.

It is always a good idea to group last-mile delivery with an existing distribution network to gain economies of scale and to improve asset utilization.

Impact on Costs

Distributor storage with last-mile delivery inventory costs are higher than those of distributor storage with package carrier delivery. Warehouse operations costs are greater than for manufacturer storage and distributor

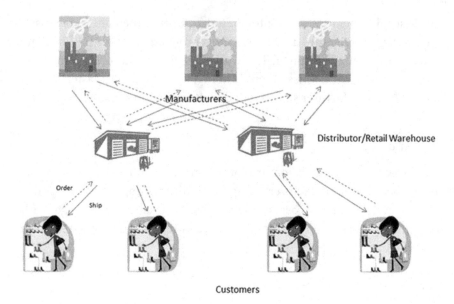

FIGURE 5.6
Distributor storage with last-mile delivery.

storage but lower than the costs of a retail chain. The transportation costs are greater than for any other distribution network option. Information costs are similar to those for distributor storage with package carrier delivery.

Impact on Service

Service response times are very quick and, in some cases, can be same-day or next-day delivery, with a very good customer experience, particularly for bulky items. Product variety is less than with distributor storage with package carrier delivery but greater than for retail stores, with availability being more expensive to provide than any other option except retail stores. There is less of an issue of order traceability than for manufacturer storage or distributor storage with package carrier delivery, and returnability is easier to implement than for other options, except perhaps a retail network.

Manufacturer or Distributor Storage with Customer Pickup

Manufacturer or distributor storage with customer pickup (Figure 5.7) involves inventory being stored at the manufacturer or distributor warehouse,

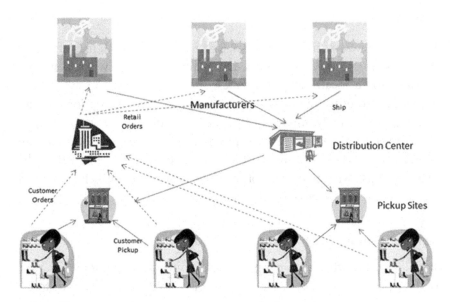

FIGURE 5.7
Manufacturer or distributor storage with customer pickup.

and customers placing their orders online or on the phone and then having to travel to designated pickup points to collect their merchandise. Orders are shipped from the storage site to the pickup points as needed. Such a network is likely to be most effective if existing locations, such as coffee shops, convenience stores, or grocery stores, are used as pickup sites, because this type of network improves the economies from existing infrastructure.

Impact on Costs

Manufacturer or distributor storage with customer pickup is similar to the other distribution configurations in terms of inventory costs. Transportation costs are on the low side as there is not a great use of package carriers, especially if using an existing delivery network (plus customers pick up themselves). Warehouse operations costs can be high if new facilities have to be built, but are lower if existing facilities are in place (and handling costs at the pickup site can be fairly high). Information costs to provide infrastructure in this option can be very high as well.

Impact on Service

Response times are similar to package carrier delivery with manufacturer or distributor storage, with same-day delivery possible when items are already stored locally at pickup sites. Product variety and availability are similar to other manufacturer or distributor storage options. Order visibility is extremely important and can be greatly aided with the help of technology. Product returns are somewhat easier, as pickup locations can typically process returns. The customer experience may be lower than the other options owing to the lack of home delivery but, in densely populated areas the loss of convenience may be small.

Retailer Storage with Customer Pickup

Retailer storage with customer pickup is of course the most common form of distribution network, where inventory is stored locally at retail stores. Inventory can be supplied to the stores from the retailer warehouse in the case of a chain, a distributor/wholesaler warehouse, or even direct to the store from the manufacturer (factory or warehouse) for larger retailers. Customers walk into the retail store or place an order online or by phone and pick it up at the retail store. This option is best for faster-moving items or items for which customers want a quick response.

Impact on Costs

Retailer storage with customer pickup has the highest inventory and warehouse operations costs and lowest transportation costs of all the options. There may be an increase in handling cost at the pickup site for online and phone orders, which may also require some investment in infrastructure as well.

Impact on Service

Response times are the quickest of the options, as same-day pickup is possible for items stored locally at the retail location. Product variety, while great, is lower than the other options, and availability is more expensive to provide than all other options. The customer experience may be considered positive or negative based upon how shopping is viewed by the customer. Order visibility really only applies for online and phone orders, and returnability is easier than other options given that retail locations can handle returns.

Impact of E-business on the Distribution Network

Operating via a purely web-based e-commerce business can have both cost and service impacts on the distribution network.

Cost Impacts

An e-commerce business can reduce its inventory levels and costs by improving supply chain coordination to better match supply and demand. Also, when customers are willing to wait for delivery of online orders, e-business can enable a firm to aggregate inventories remotely from customers.

An e-business can reduce network facility costs (i.e. costs related to the number of facilities in a network) by centralizing operations, thereby decreasing the number of facilities required. Additionally, it can also lower operating costs by allowing customer participation in selection and order placement.

In general, aggregating inventories, often the case with e-commerce, increases outbound transportation costs relative to inbound transportation costs (Figure 5.8). If a firm's product is in a form that can be downloaded, the internet will allow it to save on the cost and time for delivery (e.g. downloadable music and software).

An e-commerce business can share demand information throughout its supply chain to improve visibility more readily than a "brick-and-mortar" business. This can help reduce overall supply chain costs and better match supply and demand.

Service Impacts on the Distribution Network

Response time to customers for products that can be downloaded, such as a mutual fund prospectus or music, is generally very fast. However,

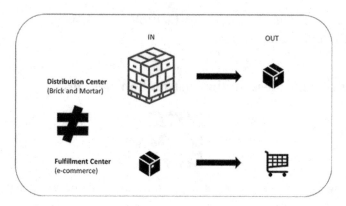

FIGURE 5.8
Distribution vs. fulfillment centers.

e-commerce without a physical retail outlet selling physical products takes longer to fulfill a customer request than a retail store because of the shipping time involved.

E-commerce can offer a much larger selection of products than a brick-and-mortar store as a retail store would require a very large location with a large amount of inventory to offer the same variety.

As e-commerce businesses have greater speed with which information on customer demand is shared throughout the supply chain, they tend to have more timely and accurate forecasts, resulting in a better match between supply and demand.

E-commerce affects customer experience in terms of access, customization, and convenience and allows access to customers who may not be able to place orders during regular business hours as well as to customers who are located far away. The internet is ideal for organizations that focus on mass customization in order to help customers select a product that more closely suits their needs. On top of that, customers have the benefit of not having to leave home or work to make a purchase.

The internet makes it possible to provide visibility of order status, which is especially important for an online order as there is really no way to match the experience of a customer shopping in person.

The proportion of returns for online orders is typically much higher (and expensive as they are usually shipped from a central location) as the customer cannot touch and feel the product before their purchase arrives. To counteract this effect, there is now the fairly common practice of "showrooming", where customers examine merchandise in a traditional brick-and-mortar retail store and then buy it online, sometimes at a lower price.

Having an e-commerce business also allows manufacturers and other members of the supply chain that do not typically have direct contact with customers in traditional channels to increase revenues by skipping intermediaries and selling directly to customers in some cases. However, great caution must be taken by the manufacturers so as not to directly compete with its distribution and retail customers. So, in many cases, this may be used as a way to run out discontinued or excess items or even to sell new/different items.

It is also fairly easy for an e-business to adjust prices at the "click of a button" on its website. In this way, it can maximize revenues by setting prices based on current inventories and demand (e.g. Amazon.com often adjusts book prices, up and down, based upon rankings and other demand criteria). Not to mention that e-commerce businesses can enhance revenues by speeding up collection vs. the 60–90 payment terms found in traditional channels for manufacturers and distributors.

Finally, e-commerce businesses can introduce new products more quickly than organizations that use traditional physical channels as they can rapidly introduce a new product by making it available on the website, vs. a traditional manufacturer who faces a lag to fill its distribution channel pipelines.

SUPPLY CHAINS MUST ADAPT TO OMNI CHANNEL RETAIL

While omni channel retail, which integrates brick-and-mortar, TV, catalog, social media, e-commerce, and m-commerce channels both for purchases and for returns, has rapidly become a source of growth in consumer goods and retail (accelerated by the pandemic, as previously mentioned), few companies are confident about their ability to execute against it and maintain margins.

Omni channel has placed the supply chain front and center, with consumers expecting to shop, purchase, and return goods across a variety of channels, with the supply chain reaching beyond the retail store to the consumer's home and dedicated pickup points. This requires real-time visibility of inventory across the supply chain and a single view of the consumer as they move from one channel to another.

The growing number of channels has increased complexity, especially from a logistics point of view. The fulfillment process is more complicated, because brick-and-mortar retailing is increasingly overlapping with distance e-commerce retail. Before, supply chain management was responsible for delivering goods to a retail store only, as the store was the end point of the transaction. Online retailing has now placed distribution systems at the forefront, since retailers need to offer a variety of options for finding, buying, and returning goods across brick-and-mortar stores and websites. Brick-and-mortar stores today are only one of a multiple set of channels. With the new set of channels, retailers must simultaneously accommodate and anticipate demand and ensure availability, meet varying lead times, and keep costs down for each channel.

An EY survey determined that omni channel is a critical driver for growth for the consumer goods and retail industry, but that traditional consumer goods supply chains are not fit for purpose and must be re-engineered.

The survey concluded that, to remain profitable, companies need to embed an omni channel supply chain into their business strategy, with a goal of transforming their supply chain to be truly agile and responsive, with robust data analytics capabilities.

While there are many benefits to omni channel such as improved consumer insight, strengthened consumer loyalty, and competitive differentiation, omni channel has become a drag on many companies' profits, as many have rushed into it, often bolting on systems and processes without fully considering integration with traditional store fulfillment. As a result, supply chains are inefficient, and there is a lack of visibility across different channels.

Respondents to the survey found the following reasons for, or barriers to, maximizing omni channel benefit in the supply chain:

1. Lack of dedicated resources and capabilities.
2. Level of investment required to succeed.
3. Challenge of supply chain complexity.
4. Limitations of siloed organizational structures.
5. Lack of senior leadership support.

The reason for this is that most consumer goods supply chains were traditionally seen as a cost center to deliver goods to stores. But, in an omni channel world, the supply chain is a consumer-facing front office and ultimately decides if shoppers have a good or bad experience.

The key enablers to be successful with an omni channel strategy are to have:

- Omni channel embedded in the overall company strategy.
- A responsive, combined omni and traditional supply chain infrastructure.
- IT systems and capabilities that enable seamless visibility and offer fulfillment to end consumers.

What Needs to Be Done?

Companies can no longer create strategies in silos or bolt on new channels without integrating them. To succeed, companies must embrace omni channel and ensure that it is fully embedded in their overall corporate strategy and organizational culture.

They must start with understanding what consumers want and how their needs and expectations are changing.

Existing channel silos must be modified, key performance indicators replaced, and new processes and technologies implemented.

Everything must be looked at through an omni channel lens, from the product and packaging design to promotional planning, operating model design, and supply chain.

Omni channel challenges the singular focus on efficiency and requires a new level of responsiveness. A segmented supply chain and inventory model will help to strike the balance between agility and efficiency.

In omni channel, deciding on what inventory to stock where becomes more complex. Companies must now make decisions about the level of stock that is sent to stores vs. that being held back for online availability.

Finally, omni channel is increasing supply chain complexity. The mix continues to shift, with emerging channels such as "click and collect", which is a hybrid e-commerce model in which people purchase or select items online and pick them up in-store or at a centralized collection point and is growing in popularity. Companies will need to adapt their supply chain infrastructure to keep pace with these trends, ensuring that they have the agility to respond to highly complex consumer behavior without this having a negative impact on profits [EY.com, 2015].

DISTRIBUTION DISRUPTION: READY OR NOT, HERE IT COMES

Needless to say, disruptive changes in distribution networks are dramatically reshaping current logistics models.

Sometimes, it seems like things are changing so fast that we can hardly keep up with what is going on around us in the world. For example, does it not seem like smart phones and their current operating systems become "old" almost overnight? Can you imagine the impact of these constant changes on your supply chain? Well, if you cannot imagine it, you may be in trouble.

Chris Caplice, executive director of MIT's Center for Transportation and Logistics, identifies "Four Trends That Could Redefine Distribution in the U.S." to help us organize our thoughts on the subject so that we can try to anticipate some of this. If we don't, they can certainly create lots of inefficiencies in our current distribution networks. The four trends to consider are:

Diversification of sales channels – as discussed, omni channel retailing has grown as e-commerce has taken off, where traditional retailers bundle online, mobile, and traditional channels to compete for sales. This has resulted in omni channel distribution to support this process. Products can be ordered online and shipped directly to the customer or, in some cases, "shipped to store" for customer pickup in contrast to the traditional retail model. In some cases, stores have become distribution centers to supply e-commerce orders directly to customers. This has a significant impact on the distribution network structure and capacity.

Densification of products – back in the early 1990s, household products companies transitioned to concentrated "ultra" laundry detergents, while portable computer storage has gone from floppy disks to thumbnail drives. This evolution has enabled companies to reduce the number of containers, trucks, and railcars used in distribution networks and, in some cases, potentially shift to other, faster modes such as air.

Decentralization of production – in the past, economies of scale were key, where massive manufacturing plants supplied your entire customer base. Now, with the global economy and improvements in technology and processes, production can be decentralized into smaller, regionally based manufacturing facilities (owned or subcontracted) closer to population centers. This has had a significant impact on transportation and shipping patterns as well as lead times.

Digitalization of products – there has been a long trend of movement from physical to information-based products, and not just books, music, and movies, as it is now starting to happen to more traditional products. Think of the potential impact on Crayola of its "Color Alive" line of products, where a special app and crayon transform coloring by activating a virtual experience complete with color effects. This could drastically reshape its distribution needs as there becomes more of a reliance on digital technology and less of one on physical crayons.

So, the disruption from these types of changes in our distribution networks and entire supply chains will dramatically reshape our current logistics models. The real question is: will you be ready for them [Myerson, 2016a]?

OMNI CHANNEL MULTIPLIES THE CHALLENGES FOR DISTRIBUTION-CENTRIC SUPPLY CHAINS

Companies have some big decisions to make about when and how to invest in realigning their supply chains to accommodate an omni channel pipeline.

When e-commerce first emerged, most retailers were able to use a small section of an existing distribution center to fulfill online orders. As demand grew, many retailers opened fulfillment centers dedicated to picking and packing individual orders.

To clarify, a distribution center traditionally ships orders in bulk to retailers or wholesalers, while fulfillment centers are designed for packing single orders shipped to an individual end user. On the surface, each has a much different type of operation (and cost structure) than the other, as a distribution center typically handles pallet and case quantities, and a fulfillment center handles individual piece picking and small parcel orders.

As we know, the goal of an omni channel retail approach is to integrate all of a retailer's channels, creating a seamless shopping experience no matter how the shopper is accessing the product.

So, as a result of an omni channel strategy, some retailers, such as Gap, American Eagle, and now Target, are experimenting with consolidating their distribution and fulfillment centers into one facility, often requiring a new warehouse management system (and material handling systems) intended to better integrate their distribution and fulfillment operations.

In Target's case, at a test facility in Perth Amboy, New Jersey, their goal was to take their replenishment cycle from days to hours and reduce inventory at stores. This required sending shipments to stores more frequently and in smaller lots to more precisely meet demand, rather than shipping big cases of products, allowing Target to expand its use of stores to fulfill online orders, with less inventory held at stores and more room dedicated to digital fulfillment.

Before embarking on such a strategy, one must consider the advantages of traditional separated facilities vs. combined omni channel systems. Some of the advantages of combined facilities include potentially lower operational costs, as fewer facilities generally equate to lower duplication and therefore lower operating costs, shared inventory, and more immediate control and flexibility.

On the other hand, there are many advantages of having separate facilities, such as lower capital costs, since a new shared infrastructure requires significant investment, having more options when dealing with order fulfillment challenges, and the fact that omni channel facilities handle a lot more SKUs than brick-and-mortar retail locations, giving the potential to run out of space due to future rapid growth in omni channel retail.

Obviously, there's a lot to consider here before making such a huge, long-term strategic decision, but it is one that will have to be made at some point in the near future [Myerson, 2018a].

STORE DELIVERY MAY KEEP TRADITIONAL BRICK-AND-MORTAR RETAILERS IN THE (OMNI CHANNEL) GAME

Multichannel retail and fulfillment is typically based on the assumption that customers choose a main way to connect, whether via physical stores or a website. Many retailers manage each channel separately, with different teams, budgets, processes, tools, reporting structures, and revenue goals.

In multichannel retail and fulfillment, stores have their own stock and sell directly to customers, while the website has its own separate stock. Customers purchasing items in stores can make returns only in store and often cannot return online orders in store. Customers' online interactions with the retailer are completely separated from offline interactions.

In an omni channel environment, however, consumers are likely to have multiple touchpoints with a retailer and expect their interactions between each channel to be seamless. Customers can order what they want, when they want, on whatever device they want and have it delivered how they want.

A key difference between multichannel and omni channel is that omni channel joins the touchpoints together so that, whatever method or combination of methods the customer chooses to make a purchase, their experience is consistent, seamless, and unified. But omni channel fulfillment can be tricky. Some companies sell online only, while others have brick-and-mortar stores and added an online channel. Still others started off as online-only companies but are adding some form of showroom-only storefront or pop-up store.

Omni channel customers buying online may take delivery in a variety of forms from one order to the next, in addition to traditional visits to a retail location. Furthermore, e-commerce has complicated the last mile of delivery, making it more difficult for traditional retailers.

Getting Creative

Traditional last-mile delivery involves many challenges, including cost minimization, transparency, and efficiency. Those challenges, along with the growth of e-commerce, are forcing brick-and-mortar retailers to become more creative (Figure 5.9).

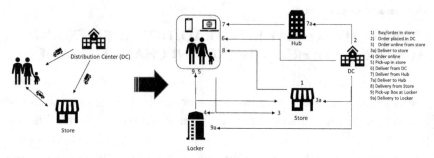

"Traditional" Shopping/Delivery Methods   "Evolving" Shopping/Delivery Methods

FIGURE 5.9
Evolution of shopping/delivery methods.

E-commerce businesses such as Amazon have been exploring air and land drone delivery and lockers in predesignated locations available for customer pickup, among other innovative methods.

Some large retailers, such as Walmart and Best Buy, are using their stores as distribution centers, where employees pick items from the shelves and backrooms to fulfill online orders. They either load the orders into FedEx or UPS trucks, or, as Walmart is testing, deliver packages themselves on their way home.

Stores can potentially cut costs substantially by having employees pick and deliver from stores, as last-mile delivery costs are a significant part of fulfillment costs. Furthermore, in the case of Walmart, two-thirds of the US population live within five miles of a store.

Additional benefits of store last-mile delivery include switching online orders to locations with the most inventory of an item, reducing the need for discounts, and fulfilling orders for items that are out of stock at e-commerce fulfillment centers.

By enabling store delivery, traditional retailers may have found a better way to compete with Amazon's fulfillment network of 100+ distribution centers, using their hundreds, or thousands, of brick-and-mortar locations as DCs [Myerson, 2018b].

E-commerce Looking for Room to Grow

Many activities that were typically carried out within stores are now consolidated into logistics facilities with the advent of e-commerce and omni channel retail, which is also driving the industrial real estate market.

We have all heard about recent retail store closings at successful companies such as Kohl's, Macy's, and Walmart. A major reason for this is the shift from brick-and-mortar stores to the growth of e-commerce as a result of omni channel marketing and distribution. This, of course, has a huge impact on the retail supply chain network.

In fact, in 2021, e-commerce sales for US retailers surpassed $871 billion, which was a 14 percent increase in comparison with the previous year and a 50.5 percent increase over 2019 (no doubt accelerated by the pandemic).

According to an NFI Industries article entitled, "The E-Commerce Effect on the Commercial Real Estate Industry", "As companies are increasingly offering same-day delivery, gift wrapping, ship-to-store and other e-commerce advantages, consumers are opting to do more of their shopping online".

> As e-commerce [and omni channel] continues to grow, industries like commercial real estate are adapting to offer more ideal solutions to support e-commerce goals. E-commerce has shifted what companies look for in their real estate facilities and has evolved what is now expected in today's fulfillment centers.

> **[Myerson, 2016b]**

LOCATION DECISIONS

Strategic Considerations

The first thing you need to think about in terms of the location decision is your particular organization's competitive strategy, which will drive the design of your supply chain network. For example, a strategy of cost leadership will result in a very different supply chain network than one that is primarily based upon responsiveness or product differentiation.

The objective of location strategy is to maximize the benefit of location to the firm. In the case of a manufacturer or distributor, you will want to focus on cost minimization while meeting service goals. For retail, it is more about maximizing revenue.

Other things to consider at a more strategic level are identifying your key competitors in each target market as well as your capital constraints.

As you grow, you will need to consider whether to reuse existing facilities, build new facilities, or partner with other companies (or all of the above).

Selecting a New Facility

When selecting a new facility location, it is important to go through some general steps (Figure 5.10). They are:

Step 1 – identify the important location factors and categorize them as key success factors (KSFs) or secondary factors.

Step 2 – consider alternative countries and then narrow them down to alternative regions and/or communities and, finally, specific sites.

Step 3 – collect data on the location alternatives.

Step 4 – analyze the data collected, starting with quantitative factors.

Step 5 – merge the qualitative and quantitative factors relevant to each site into the evaluation.

Steps 1 and 2 in the location decision can also be accomplished by starting at a predetermined country level, working your way down to the local or site decision.

Location Decisions Hierarchy

An organization's location decision, whether in goods or service, may be at the national (within a continent), regional (within a country), or local

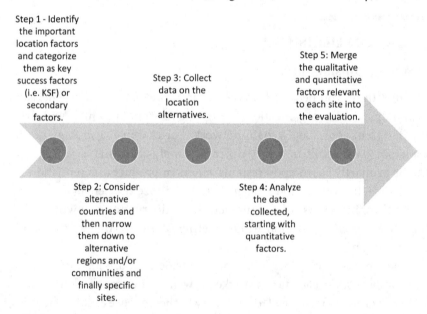

FIGURE 5.10
Steps in a new facility location decision.

selection level [Heizer and Render, 2013]. This will vary, depending on where you are in the location decision for your business. Each decision may be different.

The criteria used to determine the best location, often referred to as key success factors, will vary based upon the levels above.

Country Decision

The country decision, especially in today's global economy, may involve a wide range of factors to consider, including:

- Tariffs and tax incentives.
- Infrastructure factors.
- Exchange rate fluctuations and currency risk.
- Demand and supply risk.
- Competitive environment.
- Political risks, government rules, attitudes, and incentives.
- Cultural and economic issues.
- Location and demand of markets.
- Labor talent, attitudes, productivity, and costs.
- Availability of supplies, communications, and energy.

Regional Decision

Once the country decision has been made, an organization must determine which region is best for its new location.

Factors to consider include:

- Corporate desires.
- Attractiveness of region.
- Labor availability and costs.
- Costs and availability of utilities.
- Environmental regulations.
- Government incentives and fiscal policies.
- Proximity to raw materials and customers.
- Land/construction costs.

We've all seen states competing against each other to land a new large manufacturing facility, offering all kinds of incentives such as tax reductions/postponement, rebates, etc. So some of the factors above may be "artificially" modified to influence this decision.

Local Decision

Once a company has settled upon a location within a relatively small metropolitan area, it must consider which specific site location is best for its needs. Factors in the site decision process include:

- Site size and cost.
- Air, rail, highway, and waterway systems.
- Zoning restrictions.
- Proximity of services/supplies needed.
- Environmental impact issues.

The relative importance of these factors will vary depending on your organization's size and industry. For example, some towns are only zoned for light industry, or your company may need easy access to major highways and airports for inbound and outbound transportation needs.

There are certain types of factors that are more important in the goods vs. services location decision.

Dominant Factors in Manufacturing

The factors most important to the manufacturing location decision include:

- Favorable labor climate.
- Proximity to markets.
- Impact on environment.
- Quality of life.
- Proximity to suppliers and resources.
- Proximity to the parent company's facilities.
- Utilities, taxes, and real estate costs.

Dominant Factors in Services

The major factors to consider in the service location decision include:

- Impact of location on sales and customer satisfaction.
- Proximity to customers.
- Transportation costs and proximity to markets.
- Location of competitors.
- Site-specific factors.

LOCATION TECHNIQUES

Steps 3–5 in the new facility selection decision process, as outlined in Figure 5.10, involve gathering quantitative data and then combining qualitative and quantitative data to determine the specific site location. There are a variety of techniques that can be used to accomplish this, which we will now discuss.

Location Cost–Volume Analysis

A relatively simple location decision tool is known as cost–volume (CV) analysis. It can be represented either mathematically or graphically and is basically the same as a traditional break-even analysis or crossover chart used in a variety of situations in business. The general idea, based upon a future volume forecast with fixed and variable costs known for each location, is to determine which candidate location can be justified by the predicted throughput volume.

CV involves three steps: (1) for each location alternative, determine the fixed and variable costs; (2) for all locations, plot the total cost lines on the same graph; and (3) use the lines to determine which alternatives will have the highest and lowest total costs for expected levels of output.

Additionally, there are four assumptions to keep in mind when using this method (making it rather simplistic, but often giving a "close enough" answer to determine the best facility from a list of candidates):

1. Fixed costs are constant.
2. Variable costs are linear.
3. Required level of output can be closely estimated.
4. There is only one product involved.

The location with the lowest total cost [fixed cost + (variable cost × volume)] is the location selected.

An example of location cost–volume analysis follows. It assumes a selling price of $100/unit with an expected volume of 5,000 units (Table 5.1).

The "crossover point" from Ho Chi Minh City to Singapore (i.e. justifying Singapore) would be:

$$200,000 + 100(x) = 400,000 + 75(x)$$

$$25(x) = 200,000$$

$$(x) = 8,000 \text{ units}$$

The "crossover point" from Singapore to Hong Kong would be:

$$400,000 + 75(x) = 700,000 + 50(x)$$

TABLE 5.1

Location Cost–Volume Example Data

City	Fixed Costs	Variable Costs	Total Costs
Hong Kong	$700,000	$50	$750,000
Singapore	$400,000	$75	$725,000
Ho Chi Minh City	$200,000	$100	$700,000

$$25(x) = 300,000$$

$$(x) = 12,000 \text{ units}$$

Graphically, this can be expressed as shown in Figure 5.11.

Of course, as with many of these tools, this is dependent upon a volume forecast, and so it is wise to do "what if" analysis with different levels of cost and volumes to see the impact on the decision.

Weighted Factor Rating Method

The weighted factor rating method compares a number of locations using both quantitative and qualitative criteria.

The first step is to identify the factors that are key to the success of the facility at the location. Then, you assign a weight as to the importance of each factor (the total of which must sum to 100 percent).

The next step is to determine a score for each factor. Usually, a multifunctional team is involved in this process. At this point, a lot of data has been gathered on the potential sites from research, visits to the sites, and even presentations by the communities, states, or countries extolling the virtues (and incentives) to choose them.

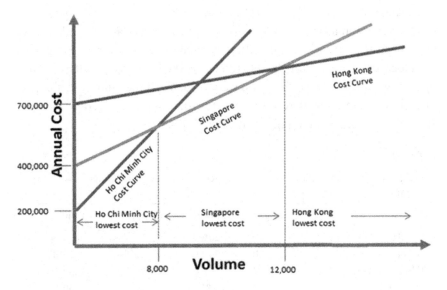

FIGURE 5.11

Location cost–volume analysis example.

You then multiply the factor score by the weight and sum the weighted scores. The location with the highest total weighted score is the recommended location.

This is often a useful tool in whittling down a list of candidates and potentially selecting one. Oftentimes, other factors may come into play, some logical (e.g. extra tax incentives) and some not so logical (the owner of the company has a vacation home in the state or country that came in second).

The example in Table 5.2 illustrates the weighted factor rating method.

Center of Gravity Method

The center of gravity method of location analysis is a technique used in determining the location of a facility which will either reduce travel time or lower shipping costs. Specifically, it determines the location of a distribution center that minimizes distribution costs while considering the location of markets, volume of goods shipped to those markets, and shipping costs (or distance).

In this model, distribution costs are seen as a linear function of the distance and quantity shipped. The center of gravity method uses a visual map and a coordinate system. The x and y coordinate points are placed on an xy chart, with an arbitrary starting point but located in similar positions for each location as they would be on a map, and they are treated as a set of numerical values when calculating averages. If the quantities shipped to each location are the same (rarely the case), the center of gravity is found by taking the averages of the x and y coordinates; if the quantities shipped to each location are different (more typical), a weighted average must be applied (the weights being the quantities shipped).

TABLE 5.2

Weighted Factor Rating Method Example (Scores = weight *100 points maximum)

Factor	Weight	Country A	Country B	Country C
Stability of government	.20	.20*90	.20*75	.20*80
Labor cost	.30	.30*50	.30*80	.30*85
Education and health	.20	.20*70	.20*50	.20*60
Tax structure	.30	.30*70	.30*90	.30*80
Totals:	1.00	68.0	76.0	77.5

Years ago, I'm told, this method was actually demonstrated using strings and weights, and hence the name "center of gravity".

This method is best described graphically using the following example:

If a retailer has four stores located in the following cities with the listed demand, what would be the best location or "center of gravity" for a distribution center that minimizes shipping costs? (See Table 5.3 for demand by location.)

We will first need to determine the x and y coordinates for each of the store locations using an xy chart (see Figure 5.12).

Next, we will use the x and y coordinates, as well as the retail location demand, to calculate the center of gravity for the distribution center location.

The calculation is [(sum of shipping volume * x or y coordinate)/total system shipping volume] and is the same to calculate the center of gravity

TABLE 5.3

Center of Gravity Example

Store Location	Truckloads Shipped to Store/Month
Chicago	5,000
Cleveland	4,000
Cincinnati	3,000
Indianapolis	2,500

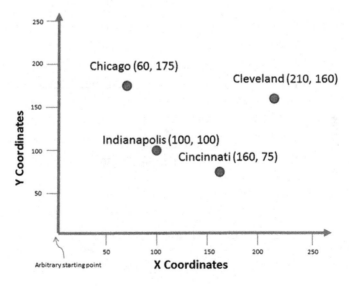

FIGURE 5.12
XY chart for center of gravity method example.

for the x and y coordinates (of course, using the appropriate coordinates each time).

So, in our example, when we solve for x and y, we find:

x coordinate = (60 * 5,000) + (210 * 4,000) + (160 * 3,000) + (100 * 2,500)/

(5,000 + 4,000 + 3,000 + 2,500) = 129.0

y coordinate = (175 * 5,000) + (160 * 4,000) + (75 * 3,000) + (100 * 2,500)/

(5,000 + 4,000 + 3,000 + 2,500) = 137.2

The center of gravity solution can then be placed on the xy chart (Figure 5.13). The actual physical location can be approximated by placing a map over the chart (or using your own geographical knowledge to approximate the location) to get you to the site location decision.

The Transportation Problem Model

The transportation problem is a special class of the linear programming model that deals with the distribution of goods from several points of supply (i.e. sources) to a number of points of demand (i.e. destinations).

Usually, we are given the capacity of goods at each source and the requirements at each destination, as well as a variety of costs for materials, manufacturing, transportation, and warehousing.

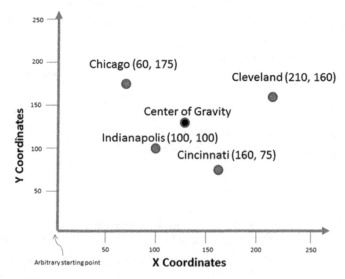

FIGURE 5.13
Solved xy chart for center of gravity method example.

Typically, the objective of the transportation problem with linear programming is to minimize total transportation and production costs while maintaining specified inventory and service level targets.

There are fairly complex software solutions available today which, using this or other algorithms, will provide a solution, which can not only be the optimal solution in terms of the number and location of distribution facilities in your network, but also, through the use of "what if" analysis, test multiple scenarios looking at changes in demand, transportation, and material costs, for example.

In many cases, these types of studies are performed by external consultants for fees of up to $100,000 for medium-to-large organizations. The payoff, however, can be in the tens of millions of dollars, and so it is well worth the cost of doing one of these studies as often as is deemed necessary.

Getting started and gathering information can sometimes be the most daunting task, as there is a lot of data that need to be gathered including material, manufacturing, warehousing, and transportation costs and demand. Once the data are in the model, they must be "validated" against previous periods to make sure that they match actual costs and service. Next, a "baseline" or "base case" model is developed with future projections with the organization's current supply chain network. This baseline is then run against various optimization parameters such as lowest cost, fewest distribution centers, etc. Finally, rather than just running with the revised network, various "what if" scenarios should be run to make sure that a decision, while optimal, is also reasonable if conditions change. This may indicate taking a more gradual "wait and see" approach to distribution consolidation or expansion, for example.

TECHNOLOGY

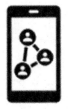

There are a variety of network optimization solutions available today. They range from stand-alone systems to modules of larger supply chain systems and can be installed or on-demand "cloud software" systems.

JDA (now known as Blue Yonder), JD Edwards (Oracle), SAP, and Logility all have network optimization modules that are integrated with their other supply chain planning and execution modules.

Other systems offer a stand-alone system (in some cases, web based and on demand) for lower upfront costs, but, as they aren't integrated with other supply chain planning and execution modules, are perhaps a bit more data intensive.

Once the supply chain network has been updated and is in alignment with the corporate and business strategies, it's important at a more tactical and operational level to make sure things are working to plan while always being looked at in terms of continuous improvement. That is the topic of our next chapter.

6

A Lean, Agile, and Smart Supply Chain to Meet the Volatile Demand and Supply Conditions of the 21st Century

In today's dynamic, global economy with a "buy anywhere, fulfill anywhere" omni channel ideology in the retail marketplace (greatly accelerated by the pandemic), it is beneficial for companies to operate a supply chain that is both lean *and* agile. Using lean and agile in combination is known as having a "hybrid" supply chain strategy.

HYBRID SUPPLY CHAIN

Besides being appropriate for any company that desires to have a blend of efficiency and responsiveness for all of its products, or has a segmented strategy where some products are more on the efficient, "low-cost" side and others on the more responsive, "premium" side, a hybrid supply chain strategy may also be appropriate for a company attempting to become a "mass customizer" – producing progressively smaller batch sizes (sometimes as little as one item) specific to customers' sometimes unique needs, yet still wanting to keep costs down as much as possible.

A lean supply chain focuses on adding value for customers, while identifying and eliminating waste – anything that doesn't add that value – often through standardization of processes and systems (e.g. standard operating procedures, or SOPs, and ERP systems). Being agile and responsive, on the other hand, implies that your supply chain can handle unpredictability – and a constant stream of new, innovative products – with speed and flexibility.

DOI: 10.4324/9781003281078-7

An agile strategy uses a wait-and-see approach to customer demand by not committing to the final product until actual demand becomes known (also referred to as postponement). For example, this might involve the subassembly of components into modules in a lower-cost process, with final assembly done close to the point of demand in order to localize the product.

An agile supply chain must be responsive to actual demand and capable of using information as a substitute (to some degree) for inventory through collaboration and integration with key customers and suppliers.

Either or Both

On some occasions, either an agile or a lean strategy might be appropriate for a supply chain. But many companies will probably face situations where a hybrid strategy is a better fit. If so, they need to carefully plan and execute the combined strategy with excellence, which is often easier said than done, because it involves a lot of moving parts. As in so many aspects of supply chain and operations management, there is more than one way to accomplish this goal.

One example of a company using a hybrid strategy in its supply chain is Zara, a Spanish fashion designer and retailer. Zara directly manufactures most of the products it designs and sells and performs activities such as cutting, dying, labeling, and packaging in-house to gain economies of scale. A network of dedicated subcontractors performs other finishing operations that cannot be completed in-house.

As a result, Zara has a supply chain that not only is agile and flexible, but incorporates many lean characteristics into its processes.

Some semiconductor manufacturers incorporate a hybrid strategy using a flexible manufacturing and distribution model. Subcontractors perform distinct manufacturing processes at separate physical locations. This hybrid approach taps a virtual network of manufacturing partners and requires responsive, flexible, and information-driven sourcing, manufacturing, and distribution functions – in many ways, the opposite of Zara's strategy of shifting processes in-house.

Many organizations can find some form of hybrid supply chain that works well for them. In today's ever-changing, volatile, and competitive global economy, it may often be in a company's best interest to operate a supply chain that is both lean and agile [Myerson, 2014].

THE SMART SUPPLY CHAIN

Furthermore, traditional supply chains are becoming increasingly digital and intelligent, with objects embedded with sensors for better communication, intelligent decision-making, and automation capabilities. The new "smart" supply chain presents huge opportunities for enabling and achieving cost reduction and enhancing efficiency improvement, especially after implementing lean concepts in your supply chain.

Some people refer to this concept as "Supply Chain 4.0", meaning the application of the IoT, the use of advanced robotics, and the application of advanced analytics (including artificial intelligence) of big data in supply chain management: place sensors in everything, create networks everywhere, automate anything, and analyze everything to significantly improve performance and customer satisfaction.

Companies expect their supply chains to deliver more – to be responsive to demand and resilient to change, to optimize costs, and to do good for society. To achieve all this, supply chain leaders must reimagine their supply chains for tomorrow.

Future-ready supply chains are intelligent, self-driving networks of growth. They're built on a foundation of digital, data, and AI to provide the visibility, agility, and new ways of working needed to create 360° value, enterprise-wide.

These intelligent supply networks deliver across three key priorities:

- **Relevant** – agile and customer-centric, addressing demand changes in a cost-effective way.
- **Resilient** – preparing for, mitigating, and responding to disruptions of all scales.
- **Sustainable** – good for society and the planet, enhancing trust with all stakeholders.

So how can we make it happen? Below are five areas to concentrate on:

- Artificial intelligence – transform data-driven decision-making across the supply chain using AI, analytics, and intelligent automation. The most advanced companies understand that, while cloud sets you up with next-level computing power and access to new kinds of data of the right quantity and quality, AI is the bridge to convert those data into business value.

- Cloud computing – the "cloud" refers to software and services that run on the internet, instead of locally on your computer. There is a good chance that the majority of business data will eventually reside in the cloud. Change through custom cloud services and solutions accelerates innovation and increases intelligence and value across the supply chain.
- Ecosystem – navigate a complex partner ecosystem across the supply chain, accelerate digital transformation, and enhance the digital core. The supply chain ecosystem refers to a network of interlinked companies, such as suppliers and distributors, who interact with each other, primarily complementing or supplying key components of the value propositions within their products or services.
- Industry 4.0 – a term coined by consultant Accenture meaning to reimagine the way products, services, and experiences get designed and built in the age of digital disruption to speed up operational efficiency and enterprise-wide growth. Think in terms of how products are designed and engineered, sourced and supplied, manufactured, serviced, returned, and renewed.
- Sustainability – become responsible by design by building sustainable value chains that positively impact business, society, and the planet. For organizations to meet their customers' expectations and be truly sustainable, they must ensure responsible business practices inside their own organization and across their entire value chain.

By starting down this path now, rather than waiting, the smart supply chain can help you manage day-to-day operations, as well as handling global disruptions, and visualize the full picture and respond in real time. Is that not the "smart" thing to do [Myerson, 2022]?

In order to implement a lean philosophy, with its rather unique culture, in today's omni channel retail environment, you first need to understand what it's all about.

HISTORY OF LEAN (FIGURE 6.1)

Early concepts such as *labor specialization* (Smith), where an individual was responsible for a single repeatable activity, and *standardized parts* (Whitney) helped to improve efficiency and quality.

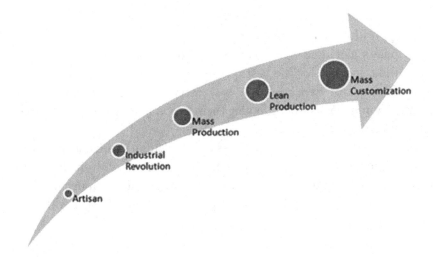

FIGURE 6.1
History of lean.

At the turn of the 20th century, the era of scientific management arrived where concepts such as *time and motion studies* (Taylor) and *Gantt charts* (Gantt) allowed management to measure, analyze, and manage activities much more precisely.

During the early 1900s, the era of mass production had arrived. Concepts such as the assembly line, economies of scale (producing large quantities of the same item to spread fixed costs), and statistical sampling were utilized. Today, this is referred to as a "push" process, which is the opposite of "demand pull" (by the customer) used in a lean philosophy.

Lean, originally applied to the manufacturing industry, was developed by the Japanese automotive industry, largely Toyota, while rebuilding the Japanese economy after World War II. Materials were scarce, and the Japanese realized that, in order to compete with the U.S. auto companies, they would have to work smarter.

The concept of lean was little known outside Japan until the 1970s (generally known as JIT, as the actual term "lean" didn't come about until the 1990s). The United Kingdom had early experience with lean manufacturing from the Japanese automotive plants based there.

Until the 1990s, only the automotive industry had adopted lean manufacturing, and that was primarily on the shop floor. Since then, it has spread into aerospace and general manufacturing, consumer electronics, healthcare, construction, and, more recently, food manufacturing and meat processing, as well as into other processes such as administrative and support functions as well as the supply chain.

In today's global economy, companies source products and materials worldwide, looking for the best quality at the lowest cost. E-commerce and ERP systems have made for easy entry to the global economy for smaller companies as well, allowing them to compete against much larger competitors.

This has led to the concept of "mass customization", which is the ability to combine the low per unit costs of mass production with the flexibility associated with individual customization (e.g. Dell Computers, which can configure, assemble, test, and ship your customized order within 24 hours).

Value-Added vs. Non-value-Added Activities

In order to understand the lean concept of "waste", it is first important to understand the meaning of value-added vs. non-value-added activities (Figure 6.2).

Any process entails a set of activities. The activities in total are known as "cycle" or "lead time". The lead time required for a product to move through a process from start to finish includes queues/waiting time and processing time.

FIGURE 6.2
Value-added vs. non-value-added activities.

The individual activities or work elements that actually transform inputs (e.g. raw materials) into outputs (e.g. finished goods) are known as "processing" time. In general, processing adds value from the customer's standpoint. Processing time is the time that it takes an employee to go through all of their work elements before repeating them. It is measured from the beginning of a process step to the end of that process step.

If we think of a simple example such as taking raw lumber and making it into a pallet of 2×4s, the value added to the customer is the actual processing that transforms the raw lumber into the final pallet of 2×4s. This would include activities such as washing, trimming, cutting, etc. that are a relatively small part of the cycle time (i.e. it may only take one hour to process the raw material into a finished pallet, but the entire cycle time may be one week).

In lean terms, the non-value-added time is actually much greater than just the lead time. We include current inventory "on the floor" (i.e. raw, work in progress, or WIP, and finished goods) and, using a calculated takt time (i.e. the rate at which you need to complete a product to meet customer demand) for a specific "value stream" (a single product, family of products, or service, which will be discussed later in this chapter), convert those quantities to days of supply. Doing so can expand the non-value-added time from days to weeks (or even months).

It is very common for many processes (or value streams) to only have 5–10 percent value-added activities. However, there are some non-value-added necessary activities, such as regulatory, customer-required, and legal requirements that, while they don't add value, are waste. As they are necessary, we can't eliminate them, but we should try to apply them as efficiently as is possible.

It is fairly normal for management to focus primarily on speeding up processes, often value-added ones, such as the stamping speed on a press. From a lean perspective, the focus moves to non-value-added activities, which in some cases may even result in slowing down the entire process in order to balance it, remove bottlenecks, and increase flow.

WASTE

In lean terms, non-value-added activities are referred to as "waste". Typically, when a product or information is being stored, inspected, delayed, waiting in line, or is defective, it is not adding value and is 100 percent waste.

These wastes can be found in any process, whether it's manufacturing, administrative, supply chain and logistics, or elsewhere in your organization.

Below are listed the eight wastes. One easy way to remember them is that their initials spell TIM WOODS (Figure 6.3):

- Transportation – excessive movement of people, products, and information.
- Inventory – storing material or documentation ahead of requirements. Excess inventory often covers for variations in processes as a result of high scrap or rework levels, long setup times, late deliveries, process downtime, and quality problems.
- Motion – unnecessary bending, turning, reaching, and lifting.
- Waiting – for parts, information, instructions, equipment.

FIGURE 6.3
The eight wastes.

- Overproduction – making more than is immediately required.
- Overprocessing – tighter tolerances or higher-grade materials than are necessary.
- Defects – rework, scrap, and incorrect documentation (i.e. errors).
- **Skills** – underutilizing capabilities of employees, delegating tasks with inadequate training.

There are a variety of places to look for waste in your supply chain and logistics function.

One way to consider where waste might exist in the supply chain is in terms of the SCOR (supply chain operations reference) model (Figure 6.4):

Plan: it all starts (and ends) with a solid sales and operations planning (S&OP) process (or lack thereof). If there isn't one in an organization, then there is probably plenty of waste in the supply chain.

Source: as purchasing accounts for approximately 50 percent (or more) of the total expenditures, using sound procurement approaches discussed earlier in this book, such as EOQ and the use of JIT principles (including vendor-managed inventory, or VMI), can go a long way toward reducing waste, especially excess inventory. Partnerships, collaborations, and joint reviews with suppliers can also help to identify and reduce waste.

Make (and store): activities such as (light) manufacturing, assembly, and kitting, much of which is done in the warehouse or by a 3PL these

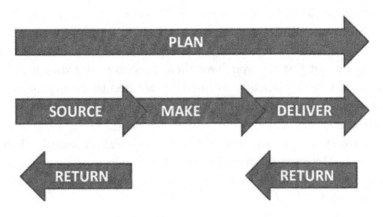

FIGURE 6.4
The SCOR model.

days, can have a huge impact on material and information flow, impacting productivity and profitability.

Within the warehouse, waste can be found throughout the receiving, putting away, storage, picking, staging, and shipping processes, including:

- Defective products which create returns.
- Overproduction or over-shipment of products.
- Excess inventories which require additional space and reduce warehousing efficiency.
- Excess motion and handling.
- Inefficiencies and unnecessary processing steps.
- Transportation steps and distances.
- Waiting for parts, materials, and information.
- Information processes.

Each step in the warehousing process should be examined critically to see where unnecessary, repetitive, and non-value-added activities might be so that they can be eliminated.

Deliver: transportation optimization (especially important with high fuel prices). This would include routing, scheduling, and maintenance, among other things.

Return: shipping mistakes, returns, product quality, and warranty issues, often ignored or an afterthought.

Enable: added in version 11 of the SCOR model in 2012, this includes processes associated with the management of the supply chain. These processes include the management of business rules, performance, data, resources, facilities, contracts, supply chain network management, regulatory compliance management, and risk management. It is important that you do not just say you have these processes, but that you have implemented them efficiently so that they are tied to the organization's lean goals and, as a result, can ensure that you are meeting these goals and objectives.

There are a variety of lean tools available which we will discuss briefly in this chapter. However, it is most important to first have a lean culture and support that are conducive to success, as lean is more of a journey than any individual project.

LEAN CULTURE AND TEAMWORK

In order to be successful for the long term, any type of program has some key success factors. In the case of lean, they include:

- Train the entire organization, make sure everyone understands the lean philosophy, and understand that it may be a cultural change for the organization.
- Ensure that top management actively drives and supports the change with strong leadership.
- Ensure that everyone in the organization commits to make it work.
- Find a good, experienced change agent as the "champion".
- Set a kaizen (i.e. continuous improvement project) agenda, communicate it, and involve operators through empowered teams.
- Map value streams that apply lean tools and begin as soon as possible with an important and visible activity.
- Integrate the supporting functions and build internal customer and supplier relationships.

Lean Teams

Teamwork is essential for competing in today's global arena, where individual perfection is not as desirable as a high level of collective performance.

In knowledge-based enterprises, teams are the norm rather than the exception. A critical feature of these teams is that they have a significant degree of empowerment, or decision-making authority.

There are many different kinds of teams: top management teams, focused task forces, self-directed teams, concurrent engineering teams, product/service development and/or launch teams, quality improvement teams, and so on.

It is no different in lean. As a result, it is important to establish lean teams that can develop a systematic process that consistently defines and solves problems utilizing lean tools.

Lean teams are a great way to share ideas and create a support system helping to ensure better buy-in for implementation of improvements.

Successful teams realize the *power of teamwork* and teamwork culture and that the goal is more important than anyone's individual role. However, teams must be in a *risk-free* environment but have leadership, discipline, trust, and the tools and training to make things happen.

To make teamwork happen, it is important that executive leaders communicate the clear expectation that teamwork and collaboration are expected, and that the organization members talk about and identify the value of a teamwork culture. Teamwork should be rewarded and recognized, and important stories and folklore that people discuss within the company should emphasize teamwork.

Kaizen and Teams

The work *kaizen*, which literally means "improvement" in Japanese, refers to activities that continually improve all functions and involve all employees.

Kaizen events are a big part of a successful lean program. A typical kaizen event involves a team of people for a period of three to ten days. They typically focus on a working (or proposed) process with the goal of a rapid, dramatic performance improvement. Typically, the event starts with training on topic of the event to ensure common understanding.

Team and Kaizen Objectives

Once teams have been established, and basic training has begun to implement a lean philosophy, it is important for any projects undertaken by teams have proper objectives to ensure success. So, you will need to ask questions such as:

- What is the customer telling you in terms of the cost, service, and quality of your products/services?
- What objectives and goals have been established by your company to address market needs?
- What processes immediately impact the performance of these products and services?
- Who needs to support this effort?
- How can the business objectives be used to garner support?

By asking these types of questions, it's not hard to link lean projects to overall functional objectives and metrics for improvement.

VALUE STREAM MAPPING

Before discussing specific lean tools, it is first important to understand the current processes to be examined. Lean has a visual, relatively high-level and broad method, known as a "value stream map" (VSM), for analyzing a current state and designing a future state for the series of activities (both value-added and non-value-added) required to produce a single product, family of products, or services for a customer.

A VSM is typically labeled a "paper and pencil" tool, although it may be constructed digitally, and is a value management tool designed to create two separate visual representations (i.e. "maps").

The *first map* illustrates how data and resources move through the "value stream" during the production process and is used to identify wastes, defects, and failures (Figure 6.5); the *second map*, using data contained in the first, illustrates a "future state map" of the same value stream with any waste, defects, and failures eliminated (Figure 6.6).

The two maps are used to create detailed strategic and implementation plans to enhance the value stream's performance.

Constructing a VSM is usually one of the first steps your company should take to create an overall lean initiative plan.

Developing a visual map of the value stream allows everyone to fully understand and agree on how value is produced and where waste occurs.

VSM Benefits

Benefits of value stream mapping include:

- Highlighting connections among activities and information and material flow that impact the lead time of your value stream.
- Helping employees understand your company's entire value stream rather than just a single function of it.
- Improving the decision-making process of all work teams by helping team members to understand and accept your company's current practices and future plans.
- Allowing you to separate value-added activities from non-value-added activities and then measure their lead time. This provides a way for employees to easily identify and eliminate areas of waste.

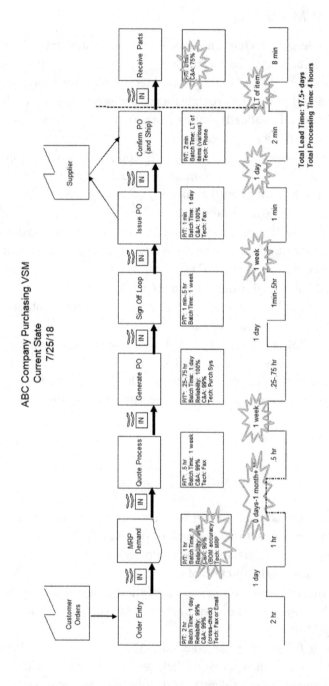

FIGURE 6.5

Current state value stream map.

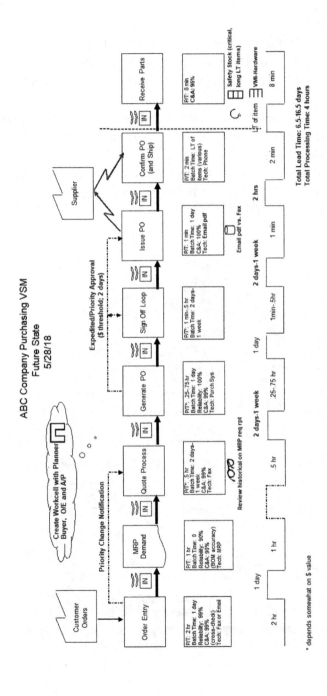

FIGURE 6.6

Future state value stream map.

LEAN TOOLS

As was previously discussed and is displayed in Figure 6.7's "House of Lean", the foundation for a lean enterprise (including the supply chain and logistics areas) is to have a lean culture and infrastructure as well as a way to set and measure objectives and performance.

After performing basic lean training and establishing teams, one or more value stream map studies are typically performed to identify areas for improvement. However, it is not uncommon for teams to "brainstorm" to come up with ideas for future kaizen events in addition to or instead of value stream mapping events (see Figure 6.8 for an example of a kaizen form for brainstorming ideas).

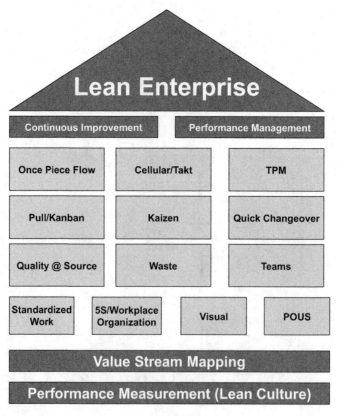

FIGURE 6.7
House of lean.

Cost Reduction Kaizen Implementation		
Department: _____ Process for Kaizen:_____	Kaizen #: _____	
Cost Center: _____	Date: _____	
Approvals: Lean Champion: ____ Maint: ____ Controller: ____	GM: ____	

1) Current Situation	3) Solution Activity	

2) Analysis	4) Cost Reduction	(Total Savings: ___)
	Current	Proposed

FIGURE 6.8
Cost reduction kaizen implementation form.

Next, we will look at some of the tools that can be used by lean teams in pursuit of continuous improvement.

Standardized Work

Standardization refers to best work practices – that is, how the work is actually routinely (and best) performed in real life. The purpose of standardization is to make operations repeatable and reliable, ensuring consistently high productivity and reduced variability of output.

It ensures that all activities are safely carried out, with all tasks organized in the best-known sequence using the most effective combination of people, material, machines, and methods.

It is important, where possible, to make standardized work more of a "visual job aid" that is easy to understand and follow (e.g. a laminated simplified list of standard instructions supplemented with digital photographs).

In the supply chain and logistics function, standardized work (preferably visual) can be applied nearly everywhere. The office and warehouse are the most common places it is found, and it can include order processing, invoicing, and drawings. Out on the warehouse floor itself, most of the basic activities of receiving, putting away, picking, packing, loading, and shipping can benefit from standardized work in the form of visual job aids.

5S Workplace Organization System

5S is a philosophy that focuses on effective workplace organization and standardized work procedures. It is a great general activity to start a lean program with, as it's easy to understand and implement throughout a business.

5S simplifies your work environment and reduces waste and non-value activity while improving quality, efficiency, and safety. It ensures that a workplace that is clean, organized, orderly, safe, efficient, and pleasant results in:

- Fewer accidents.
- Improved efficiency.
- Reduced searching time.
- Reduced contamination.
- Visual workplace control.
- A foundation for all other improvement activities.

A 5S project begins with the selection of a specific area (usually one that is fairly disorganized) and a multifunctional team that includes at least one member from the selected area.

Next, the team goes to the selected area to perform a "workplace scan", which involves activities such as taking "before" pictures, drawing a "spaghetti diagram" showing locations of materials and equipment as well as product flow, and the performance of some kind of 5S audit (various forms are readily available on the internet).

The steps in 5S (and what the actual Ss stand for) are:

- Sort – unneeded items are identified and removed. Only needed parts, tools, and instructions remain.
- Set in order – everything has a place; everything is in its place. Create visual controls to know where items belong and when they are missing, as well as how much to keep to hand in the area.
- Shine – do an initial spring-cleaning. This can include scouring as well as some painting.

- Standardize – routine cleaning becomes a way of life. Preventative maintenance is routinely performed. Standards are created to maintain the first three Ss.
- Sustain – this is perhaps the hardest part of 5S, where it has to become a routine way of life. Root causes are routinely identified and dealt with.

Visual Controls

Simple visual signals give the operator the information to make the right decision. They are efficient, self-regulating, and worker-managed.

Examples include visual job aids mentioned previously, "kanbans", "andon" lights (i.e. green = process working; red = process stopped), color-coded dies, tools, pallets, and lines on the floor to delineate storage areas, walkways, work areas, etc.

Facility Layout

Considering optimal facility layout, like standardized work, is nothing new. However, as a tool of lean, it is focused primarily on maximizing flow and eliminating wastes such as transportation and motion. If used properly it can result in:

- Higher utilization of space, equipment, and people.
- Improved flow of information, materials, or people.
- Improved employee morale.
- Improved customer–client interface.
- Increased flexibility.

Batch Size Reduction and Quick Changeover

The concepts of batch size reduction and quick changeover (sometimes also referred to as "setup reduction") are highly intertwined.

When material is "pushed" through a supply chain and operations process, you produce, store, and ship in large quantities to spread your fixed costs over a large number of items, thus minimizing your costs per unit. In "pull", you schedule what the downstream customer actually wants, using a JIT approach. The goal is one piece flow (or at least a reduction in batch or lot size).

Long changeovers tend to create larger batch sizes, resulting in higher inventory costs, longer lead times, and potentially larger quality issues, and that is why we focus on reducing changeover times through "setup reduction" kaizen events.

In supply chain and logistics processes, we often see the results of batching in production to cover manufacturing wastes, resulting in excess inventory, and in purchasing to obtain economies of scale. Additionally, there is a large amount of batching of paperwork in the office, which, if reduced, can encourage improved flow and getting orders out faster, resulting in a shorter order-to-cash cycle.

In warehouse operations, there are setups everywhere, including receiving, picking, staging, loading, and shipping (especially during shift start-ups).

Quality at the Source

Also known as "source control", the idea with this concept is that the next step in the process is your customer, and, as a result, you need to ensure perfect product to your customer.

One major technique used in source control is known as "poka-yoke", which is the concept of using foolproof devices or techniques designed to pass only acceptable product. Poka-yokes can range from simple tools, such as a "cutout" to ensure proper dimensions, to a scale at a packing station that checks the weight of an item, and, if it is outside the proper range, software would prevent a label from being printed.

Quality at the source can eliminate or reduce final inspections, reduce passed-on defects, eliminate non–value-added processing, increase throughput, and increase employee satisfaction.

Quality at the source helps to reduce the total cost of quality, which looks at the true impact of defective work as it moves toward the customer. This includes:

- Prevention costs – reducing the potential for defects (e.g. poka-yokes).
- Appraisal costs – evaluating products, parts, and services (e.g. quality control sampling).
- Internal failure – producing defective parts or service before delivery (e.g. final inspection).
- External costs – defects discovered after delivery (e.g. returns).

Obviously, the further along a quality issue gets, the greater the impact (cost and otherwise) it has on an organization.

Other techniques such as standardized work, visual workplace, and 5S are all tools for implementing quality at the source.

Point of Use Storage

Point of use storage is the storing of raw materials and supplies needed by a work area that will use them nearby. It works best if the supplier can deliver frequent, on-time, small deliveries. It can simplify the physical inventory tracking, storage, and handling processes.

Total Productive Maintenance

Total productive maintenance (TPM) is often used interchangeably with the concept of preventative maintenance. While preventative maintenance may be involved, TPM is actually a team-based, systematic approach to the elimination of equipment-related waste. It involves the charting and analysis of equipment performance to identify the root cause of problems and then implementing permanent corrective actions.

TPM is a shared responsibility, which involves not only mechanics but operators, engineers, and employees from other functional areas.

Ultimately, in addition to creating countermeasures using techniques such as poka-yokes, TPM develops preventative maintenance plans that utilize the best practices of operators, maintenance departments, and depot service. It also involves the training of workers to operate and maintain their own machines, often referred to as "autonomous maintenance".

While the supply chain and logistics function may not have as many or as complicated pieces of equipment as in manufacturing, there is plenty of equipment that must run at peak performance, including forklifts and carousels in a warehouse, trucks on the road, and office equipment, including computer hardware and software.

Pull/Kanban and Work Cells

As mentioned before, a "push" system produces product, using forecasts or schedules, without regard for what is needed by the next operation, whereas a "pull" system is a method of controlling the flow of resources by indirectly linking dissimilar functions through the use of visual controls (e.g. kanbans), replacing only what has been consumed at the demand rate of the customer.

A pull system is a flexible and simple method of controlling and balancing the flow of resources and eliminates the waste of handling, storage, expediting, obsolescence, rework, facilities, equipment, and excess paperwork. It consists of processing based on actual consumption, low and well-planned work in process (paperwork), and management by sight, with improved communication.

One of the main tools in a pull system is a kanban, in which a user removes a standard-sized container, and a signal is seen by the producing/supplying department as authorization to replenish. The signal can be a card or even something as simple as a line on a wall.

Another lean tool is known as a "work cell", which reorganizes people and machines that typically would be dispersed in various departments into a group so that they can focus on making a single product or group of related items. Work cells are usually "U"-shaped as against a traditional linear assembly-line type of format.

Work cells require the identification of families of products or services and a high level of training and flexibility on the part of employees and, in many cases, utilize poka-yokes at each station in the cell.

Work cells can be found on the shop floor, in the warehouse, and in the office, in a variety of industries. In the warehouse, there may be more limited opportunities than elsewhere, but they are typically found in areas such as packaging or in value-added activities performed by third party logistics (3PLs) such as packaging of kits for a customer or a staging location to organize outgoing shipments.

Lean and Six Sigma

In recent years, lean has often been combined with six sigma to become "lean six sigma" in many companies. The concept of six sigma was originated by Motorola in the early 1980s and is now used in many industries. Six sigma attempts to improve the quality of process outputs by identifying and removing the causes of defects (errors) and minimizing variability in manufacturing and business processes, hence the term "six sigma", which refers to a process which has 99.99966 percent of products produced free of defects.

Lean and six sigma are complementary, as lean uses relatively simple concepts to make improvements and covers the *entire* process or value stream, from the customer end upstream to suppliers, and six sigma is a tool (heavily statistical) that looks at individual steps in the process and attempts to identify and remove defects and variability. In general, lean tries to reduce waste in the production process, and six sigma tries to add value to the production process [Myerson, 2012].

Needless to say, lean retail thrives in an omni channel world, as lean helps streamline a business's retail operations in order to expediently provide excellent goods and services, while maximizing value for the customer.

OMNI CHANNEL REQUIRES AN AGILE AND RESPONSIVE SUPPLY CHAIN

While lean can improve quality and productivity and reduce waste and cost, an agile and responsive supply chain is also important in an omni channel environment as the customer controls not just what to buy, but also when, where, and how.

The demand to reconfigure centers has evolved into demand for the creation of facilities that can handle retail, wholesale, and direct-to-consumer in the same location, pulling from the same inventory.

The changes affect the entire organization – facilities, equipment, technology, people, and agility are critical to supporting omni channel requirements because the environment is constantly changing.

Because of this, the key to achieving an agile supply chain in an omni channel world is orchestration: having the technology and systems in place to move products through the supply chain seamlessly while still being in control at the origin.

Key supply chain challenges are a dynamic demand across channels, high shipping costs, and costs associated with different fulfillment types. These factors add to the complexity in the supply chain process and also impact the lead time and the cost of serving the customer.

THE RETAIL SUPPLY CHAIN NEEDS TO CONTINUOUSLY ADAPT

Omni channel retail is putting a lot of pressure on the supply chain. Retailers need to provide multiple delivery options to multiple destinations, deliver accurately and on time, and be affordable.

The retail supply chain is made up of the processes used to get your products to your consumers and ranges from procuring raw materials to make your product to delivering that product into your consumers' hands. Retail supply chain management then focuses on the need to optimize those processes to maximize both speed and efficiency.

Areas for Change and Improvement

Some areas where you can usually reduce costs are improving your distribution and fulfillment strategy and operations, improving supplier relationships, analyzing customer demand patterns, and turning product faster. This enables retailers to offer lower prices and a better customer experience for a competitive advantage.

It is estimated that the cost of out-of-stocks and overstocks among retailers today, if eliminated, could increase same-store sales by 9.2 percent (not an easy task, for sure).

One benefit of the growth of e-commerce is that it enables retailers to sell to consumers anywhere in the world. However, there are still geographic constraints on the logistics and fulfillment of supply. Supply can still be restricted because of the costs that come with buying and holding inventory.

With consumer-facing omni channel retailing, it is important to provide flexibility so that your items can be purchased at a store, on the web, or on mobile devices, but great technology won't help much if you don't have a supply chain geared for quick and efficient order fulfillment.

Therefore, supply-side innovation, control, and flexibility are key to winning, as seen by Amazon and Walmart.

For small to mid-sized retailers to endure, inventory flow needs to change from a mostly product "push" process based upon forecasts to more of a product pull process and a reactive supply chain with the kind of agility that has been successful for Amazon and Walmart.

As we know, consumers love having an assortment of choices which requires a commitment to optimizing logistics and investing in technology, resulting in a wider assortment of products that may reduce inventory risk. To accomplish this without escalating costs, many retailers have adopted management philosophies such as a lean and agile supply chain along with techniques such as drop shipping, postponement, lean enterprise, and JIT.

Some key benefits and competitive advantages they provide to this streamlined, flexible pull approach are:

- Endless aisle – this term refers to the retailer's ability to sell out-of-stock items to in-store customers or sell online items that are not kept in local inventory. By matching supply and demand in real time, you assist consumers to access what they want, where they want, and from whom they want. That results in selling more products, in more places, more accurately.
- Competitive pricing – more than ever, to succeed you need competitive pricing. Increased visibility of products in your supply chain also helps reduce prices of products by bringing down overhead and fulfillment costs.
- Reduced costs – increasing selling opportunities does not have to result in increased transportation and storage costs. For example, Amazon doesn't have to pay for third-party inventory that it moves through its distribution hubs, as the only cost Amazon incurs when providing third-party fulfillment is money it would have spent on the infrastructure, labor, transportation, and other direct sales operation costs anyway.

Another example can be found with Ocado, the British e-commerce firm that is the world's largest online-only grocery chain and operates 1,100 robots that process 65,000 customer orders per week at its Hampshire, United Kingdom, warehouse.

Ocado has maximized its supply chain efficiencies to deliver product rapidly at the lowest possible cost. Ocado has three automated warehouses, one of which turns over more than $1.2 billion a year, and another turns over $1.4 billion a year. Its three automated warehouses individually pick 1.5 million items a day with over 99 percent item accuracy in its orders. Ocado promises its customers its prices will be cheaper than huge competitor Tesco's, partially as a result of the efficiencies provided by automation which has supported accuracy and reduced costs. It has also optimized the routing of its deliveries, resulting in a typical Ocado van having annual sales of $1.4 million vs. $600,000 for a Tesco's van.

So, in this e-commerce-enabled and highly disrupted world, supply chain improvement and innovation are key to gaining a competitive advantage, as is discussed throughout this book [Hanks, 2013].

LEAN AND AGILE SUPPLY CHAIN PLANNING PROCESS

As this book is about demand and supply chain planning, I think it's important to point out how lean isn't just about operations but can, in fact, have a huge impact on planning as well (which helps to enforce lean operations, supply chain and otherwise).

A lean supply chain organization focuses on providing the best quality within the shortest possible lead time, while minimizing waste throughout its processes. Many tend to think that minimizing waste means minimizing inventory, but time, effort, and people are also resources to be utilized properly. Analyzing how people are used and time is spent is a critical step in minimizing waste, and there is no better place to do this than in the planning processes for an organization.

We can apply lean principles to supply chain planning, the biggest objectives of which are to reduce costs and improve customer service.

Many of the lean conceptual tools evolved from the Toyota Production System (TPS), which is a management system that organizes manufacturing and logistics for the automobile manufacturer, including interaction with suppliers and customers. The system is a major precursor of the more generic "lean manufacturing". TPS and lean principles in general can be applied to supply chain planning.

Let's take a look at a few and see how they can help planning organizations become lean.

Just in time ensures all efforts are directed at providing only the materials, goods, and services required by customers (at any point in the supply chain), both when they want them and in the exact quantity they desire. The goals of JIT are aligned with the goals of supply chain planning.

Value stream mapping, which is unique to lean, involves mapping out all the current steps of your processes for a product or service (or family of products or services), value-added and non-value-added, including the flow, timing of each step, and wait times for all associated activities. VSM identifies and eliminates waste.

Mapping out the various processes in supply chain planning and how they are all connected will lead to a better understanding of the value of each step and how to streamline and eliminate non-value-added activities in a "future state" map, along with an implementation plan.

Kaizen (i.e. continuous improvement), as discussed earlier, is an ongoing process of looking for improvements in every area of the process. This philosophy can be embraced at *all* levels of the organization and applied to any task. Finding ways to do things more efficiently, accurately, and effectively minimizes waste and adds value to supply chain planning processes. Doing more with less is all about finding ways to minimize waste and improve efficiencies.

Lean is about not just identifying waste but getting rid of it. A form of "root cause" analysis that is simple yet effective, known as the "five whys", is the philosophy of always asking questions, in this case five times, until you get to the root cause of a problem or issue. Asking questions leads to an understanding of how things work and to finding potential fixes to problems. This should be a core principle in supply chain planning. Determining why something happened in the supply chain leads to the ability to anticipate and optimally respond.

Lean Supply Chain Objectives

Some objectives to consider when trying to identify and eliminate waste in the supply chain planning process include:

- Collaborate and use process discipline – when all members of the lean supply chain can see they are operating in concert with customer need consumption, they can more easily collaborate to identify problems, determine root causes, and develop appropriate solutions to solve any root cause problems. Lean's VSM helps break down processes and gives you the ability to rebuild your process more effectively. Utilize six sigma's DMAIC – define, measure, analyze, improve, and control – to solve any problems or roadblocks.

Lean's PDCA can also be used – plan, do, check, and act. Any and all members of the lean supply chain should use these tools to solve problems and reduce costs to increase value to the customer.

- Focus on total cost of fulfillment – make decisions that will meet customer expectations at the lowest possible total cost, no matter where the costs occur along the supply chain. This means eliminating decisions that benefit only one part of the stream at the expense of others. This can be achieved when all partners of the lean supply chain share in operational and financial benefits when waste is eliminated.

- Make customer usage visible to all members of the supply chain – flow in the lean supply chain begins with customer usage. Visibility of customer usage for all supply chain partners is critical. This sets the supply chain pace and goes hand in hand with collaboration and integration of systems and processes (both internal and external).

- Reduce lead time – reducing inbound and outbound transportation logistics gets us closer to customer demand, which results in reduced reliance on forecasting, increased flexibility, and reduced waste of "overproduction". When you create your monthly (or more frequent) S&OP, gather input to the S&OP process from your top suppliers and customers. Work in collaboration – interdepartmentally and with customers, suppliers, and partners – to reduce lead times and brainstorm how you can create a lean supply chain that brings value beyond your customers' expectations.

- Create a level flow/level load – leveling the flow of material *and* information results in a lean supply chain with much less waste at all critical points in the system.

- Use pull systems, such as kanbans – kanban pull systems reduce wasteful complexity in planning and overproduction that can occur with computer-based software programs such as enterprise resource planning, which can create a push system with too much wasteful inventory going into the warehouse. Pull systems permit visual control of material flow in the supply chain. You can also use ship-to-use (STU) systems. Quality assurance goes to your suppliers, assures the quality of their systems, and enables them to ship to a point of use on the production floor to avoid wasteful inventory sitting in a warehouse.

- Increase velocity and throughput and reduce variation – planning for, and fulfilling, customer demand through the delivery of smaller shipments more frequently increase velocity and throughput to your customers. This, in turn, helps to reduce inventories and lead times and allows you to more easily adjust delivery to meet actual customer need consumption.
- Consider advancements in technology to improve the supply chain – I always say that technology can enable a good process. The following is a list of great technology investments that should be considered in the quest for the lean supply chain:
  - Workforce management throughout the supply chain.
  - Omni channel fulfillment, RFID.
  - Supply chain management (SCM) systems, electronic data interchange (EDI).
  - Trading partners interface (TPI; Retail Value Chain Federation).
  - Customer order management.
  - Customer relationship management (CRM)/cloud solutions.
  - Transportation's yard management systems (YMS) to manage and track freight in the 3PL's yard outside the warehouse dock doors.
  - GPS for tracking freight.
  - A transportation management system (TMS).
  - And any other technology that streamlines the supply chain and improves communication and value to the customer [Globaltrans, 2015].

A LEAN SUPPLY CHAIN IMPLEMENTATION METHODOLOGY

A lean supply chain defines how a well-designed supply chain should operate, delivering products quickly to the end customer, with minimum waste.

Srinivasan (2007), in his book *Streamlined*, outlined a reasonable seven-step methodology to create a lean and agile supply chain. The necessary steps are:

1. Develop systems thinking – the systems perspective recognizes that, if each element in the supply chain tries to optimize its own operations in isolation, everyone suffers in the long run. The lack of a systems perspective has now made it very difficult to establish long-term partnerships with an organization's suppliers. This has been expanded upon in recent years to be thought of as "outside in" thinking that links the internal decision process with input from your extended supply chain.

2. Understand customer value – understanding what adds value to your (internal and external) customers and what doesn't. What doesn't is waste and should be eliminated.

3. Value stream mapping – once you have an understanding of the basics, you can develop current and future state maps for products and services which include the planning processes such as forecasting and not just the operational aspects.

4. Benchmark best practices – investigate and understand how other best-practice organizations in your industry (and other industries) run their processes and apply improvements that will fit your strategy and culture.

5. Design to manage demand volatility – rather than just covering volatile demand with excess inventory, you need to look at your demand planning process and the source of variability and manage your supply chain accordingly, as was discussed in Chapter 3 ("Supply Chain Performance: Achieving Strategic Fit and Scope"). This may mean changing the structure of your supply chain or predicting and managing demand better, or differently, to minimize the bullwhip effect.

6. Create flow – the concept of "one piece flow" can be applied in the planning and administration processes as well as manufacturing and supply chain operations. In the case of planning, information needs to flow smoothly and quickly in order to support faster, more accurate decision-making.

7. Performance metrics – it is important to set targets and measure the right things. We need to start looking more broadly to help determine how we can design metrics to manage organizations, recognizing that these organizations are components of complex and highly interconnected systems. For example, Sony knows that inventory

of its products at Best Buy ultimately affects its profitability if it remains on the shelf for more than a few days, and so it has changed its delivery metric from "sell-in" to "sell-through".

Srinivasan discusses a case study where a leading Fortune 1000 company applied the seven-step process to enhance its financial performance. This organization has a diverse number of products that it manufactures and distributes worldwide.

It began to apply these steps in early 2006 and realized an increase in its profits (reduction in operating expense) of more than $20 million within 12 months. The organization then extended the concepts across its supply chain, conducting week-long training events for its key suppliers, at least twice each month, with each event generating an increase in profits and/or a reduction in operating expense, ranging from $500,000 to $1 million per year. These events are also generating a reduction in inventory of a similar magnitude.

As has been discussed (and as just shown in the above case study), to enable a lean and agile supply chain and to minimize issues in your supply chain such as we've seen during the pandemic, you need to utilize creative sourcing strategies to survive and thrive. This is the topic of our next chapter.

7

Strategic Sourcing and Procurement

STRATEGIC SOURCING VS. PROCUREMENT

Strategic sourcing should not be confused with simply using centralized procurement to leverage volume buying. In fact, it is a systematic and fact-based approach for optimizing an organization's supply base and improving the overall value proposition and is the process of taking advantage of purchasing opportunities by continually reviewing current needs against purchasing opportunities.

Procurement, on the other hand, involves the process of selecting vendors, strategic vetting, establishing payment terms, negotiation of contracts, and actual purchasing of goods and is concerned with acquiring the goods, services, and work vital to an organization.

In its broadest sense, strategic sourcing expands an organization's focus to the supply chain impacts of procurement and purchasing decisions, with goals being to achieve large and sustainable cost reductions, long-term supply stability, and minimization of supply risk.

The approach, first established by General Motors in the 1980s and now a common business purchasing tool, is founded on a detailed understanding of the spend profile of both the organization and the supplier market. This understanding is continually updated in order to deliver ongoing improvements to the organization's sourcing and procurement performance.

STRATEGIC SOURCING PROCESSES

A seven-step strategic sourcing process developed in 2001 by consulting firm A.T. Kearney has stood the test of time and, with variations, has become best practice. The result of this process may be savings in cash (typical savings range between 4 and 20 percent), greater added value from the suppliers, and/or time and aggravation saved on a previously time-consuming and unwieldy exercise.

The seven steps or processes within this best-practice strategic sourcing process are:

Step 1: profile the category – this helps you to understand your organization's internal spend for categories of products while, at the same time, researching the external market.

A category is made up of a number of products from similar vendors that can be grouped together in a competitive sourcing process. For example, a bicycle company might purchase different tires for different bikes from different manufacturers, in which case it makes sense to group the total spend on tires together into one category to identify savings potentials.

The types of analysis involved in this step include:

Spending analysis – identify your organization's total spending with a vendor(s) in advance of contract negotiations.

Needs analysis – develop an understanding of specifications and needs for the product and, if applicable, the current supplier's performance and any enhancements that they would like to see in the product.

Supply market analysis – it is important to then research the external supply market and the market pressures the supplier faces. This includes understanding your vendor's pricing structures to be potentially used later in the process as a negotiating tool.

Step 2: select the sourcing strategy – it is important to understand how the product (or service) that you are sourcing aligns with your company's overall strategy, especially where you would place the product within a category positioning matrix (Figure 7.1).

This also ties into a lean philosophy through the various approaches used where, for example, a strong relationship and integration with the supplier might be necessary (i.e. strategic items) and, in other cases, a more streamlined purchasing process might be a priority (i.e. non-critical items).

Leverage	Strategic
Characteristics: Competitive market, high expenditure levels, commodity type items **Approach:** Use competitive marketplace to reduce total cost, and consolidate volume as a negotiation tool	**Characteristics:** No true substitutes, usually single sourced, high product differentiation, and key to core business **Approach:** Ensure availability of supply, focus on relationship building, process integration, and innovation
Non-Critical	Bottleneck
Characteristics: Low expenditure, small % of expenses, and not key to core business **Approach:** Simplify and streamline purchasing process, reduce number of suppliers and simplify ordering	**Characteristics:** No true substitute, usually single source, not core to business and lack of availability will cause problems **Approach:** Search for alternatives and strengthen relationships

Business Impact

Supply Market Complexity

FIGURE 7.1

Category positioning matrix Source: A.T. Kearney (2001).

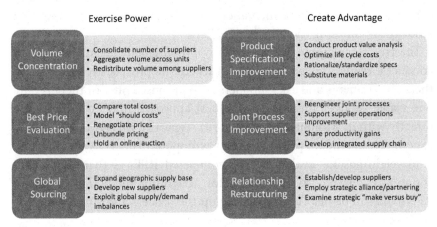

FIGURE 7.2

Sourcing strategies. Source: A.T. Kearney (2001).

Once you have decided how it aligns with your corporate strategy, you are able to decide on which sourcing strategies you wish to utilize (Figure 7.2). These strategies generally fall into two major categories of *exercising power* and *creating advantage*. While the *creating advantage* strategy is more in alignment with a lean strategy, the *exercising power* strategy cannot be ignored in some situations, and, in fact, in some cases, both strategies may work together where a company can gain a competitive advantage through volume leverage (e.g. cost) but still work to develop the supplier in a mutually advantageous way.

Step 3: generate the supplier portfolio – this step uses the needs analysis from step 1 to develop your criteria for supplier selection to widen your supplier base and identify all viable suppliers, including small and/or new ones that might have more favorable contract terms.

A variety of means can be used during this step, such as interviewing key suppliers and industry leaders, which will eventually lead to submitting requests for information (RFIs) to potential suppliers.

It is important for a company to select potential suppliers for its portfolio carefully. A supplier's inability to meet selection criteria can result in significant losses for the organization. The business reputation and performance of the supplier must be evaluated, and financial statements, credit reports, and references must be checked carefully. The use of agents who are familiar with the markets and stakeholders can also be beneficial to this process. Organizations may select more than one supplier to avoid potential supply disruptions as well as create a competitive environment.

Step 4: select the implementation path – this creates an execution strategy for choosing short-listed suppliers.

The traditional route taken by many procurement departments is to conduct a request for proposal (RFP) where the prospective buyer states their requirements and asks suppliers for a proposed offer (if there is only one viable supplier to consider, the best approach may be to negotiate directly with it, without issuing an RFP). Typically, this requires vendors to complete a standard pricing matrix to compare all offers. A set of criteria and weightings for evaluating the completed RFPs is then developed, commonly referred to as the "factor weighting method". Electronic RFP tools can be helpful in speeding up the process and simplifying the analysis of responses.

Suppliers that get through the RFP process will then participate in negotiations, which may be conducted face-to-face or, possibly, via the internet (e.g. reverse auctions and e-auctions). Internet negotiations, which work best when there are at least three suppliers whose products are broadly similar, can compress time in the process. No matter, there are then final contract negotiations to be concluded with the successful bidder.

Step 5: negotiate and select suppliers – one of the keys to successful negotiations is careful, detailed preparation, starting with assembling your negotiations team. You will need to develop the team's objectives and roles. Roles on a negotiations team may include the leader, a senior authority, a technical expert, a user, and an observer (note-taker), for example.

When developing a negotiations strategy, information is key, including information from your RFPs and your needs analysis, as well as current knowledge of the supplier marketplace.

It is important to know your current bargaining position, which includes your most desired outcome (MDO), your least acceptable agreement (LAA), your best alternative to a negotiated agreement (BATNA; which is the most advantageous alternative course of action a party can take if negotiations fail and an agreement cannot be reached), and what concessions you are prepared to make.

Have a contingency plan, including your BATNA, and decide in advance if you are willing to walk away from a deal if it does not meet your LAA. In any case, you should never concede anything without getting something from the supplier in return.

At the end of the negotiations, you need to have everything in writing to avoid future disagreements and to finalize a contract.

Step 6: integrate suppliers – in the case of a new supplier, you will need to:

- Identify transition issues.
- Consider the organizational implications and required changes.
- Create new processes and procedures if necessary (for example, how will charge-backs be handled?).
- Create a transition/implementation plan.
- Communicate changes to users.

Step 7: monitor the supply market and supplier performance – work with the supplier only starts once the contract is signed. It is also important to stay abreast of your supply market conditions, as things may change.

The contract should state performance metrics that you have agreed upon with your supplier, such as joint process improvements, meetings, and reporting. There should be agreement as to what procedures will be put in place to monitor agreed-upon metrics [Clegg and Montgomery, 2005].

LEAN STRATEGIC SOURCING

Lean concepts, discussed in Chapter 6, can also be applied to both the strategic sourcing and procurement processes. As a significant percentage of revenue for most companies is spent on procured goods and services, I believe it is especially important to spend a little time discussing lean strategic sourcing and procurement applications in this chapter.

Kearney's 2011 assessment of excellence in procurement (AEP) study found that corporate procurement functions are becoming a more vital, strategic emphasis and have lots of benefits, with better governance to improve performance both internally and externally. Many of the findings connect directly or indirectly with a lean philosophy by focusing on the top line, not just the bottom line, as well as concentrating more on customer value.

The 2011 AEP study found that leading procurement organizations are playing an active role in developing and executing top-line strategies for growth while still being held accountable for bottom-line efficiencies. Many companies have processes, methodologies, and technologies that take advantage of their power in the supply base.

Many leading companies are starting to develop long-term category management strategies, where collaboration with key suppliers is used to create value. Performance management, knowledge and information, and human resources are key to a successful procurement organization. As a result, it pays to invest in new ways to measure performance, sophisticated technology to embed best practices, and expanded professional skills.

Seven Activities of Lean Strategic Sourcing

The survey identified seven best-practice activities in companies, most of which support a leaner supply chain, demonstrate consistently high levels of procurement performance, and are strategic contributors to their business. They are:

1. Align with the business – leaders in the survey understand that the procurement strategy must align with overall business goals and go beyond the traditional areas (transportation, IT, engineering) to engage with R&D, marketing, finance, customer support, and legal.

2. Contribute to the top and bottom lines – 75 percent of the leaders say they contribute to innovation, integrate suppliers into the new product development process, reduce time to market for new products, and create new business opportunities with suppliers.
3. Manage risk systematically – procurement leaders focus on managing risk as most use risk-impact analysis, financial risk management (such as hedging), and disaster planning as ways to protect against potential threats.
4. Use supplier relationship management consistently – leaders felt that a structured process can increase strategic value by pointing to improvements in innovation and growth, better managed risk, and more agile, flexible, and efficient supply chains. They put a lot of effort into managing strategic suppliers, expanding the supply base into new markets, monitoring compliance and risk management, performing joint initiatives, and developing suppliers' capabilities.
5. Tailor category strategies – leaders in the survey tend to tailor their approaches to each situation, but more complex categories require closer collaboration with suppliers.
6. Adopt technology – procurement leaders have technology that allows for better visibility of spending and supply chain activity. They also tend to be automated and have adopted technology needed to support contact management and compliance.
7. Win the "war for talent" – leaders tend to be more forward-looking in their approaches to recruiting and retaining top talent. They tend to have more sophisticated recruiting approaches, use online collaboration technologies, and offer part-time work and flexible hours for their diverse, dispersed workforces [Blascovich, Ferrer, and Markham, 2011].

LEAN SOURCING JOURNEY

Ultimately, lean sourcing requires a long-term commitment to combining elements of strategic sourcing with lean principles. As it's not a destination but a journey, there are stages of maturity along the way. Figure 7.3 is an example of a lean sourcing maturity model.

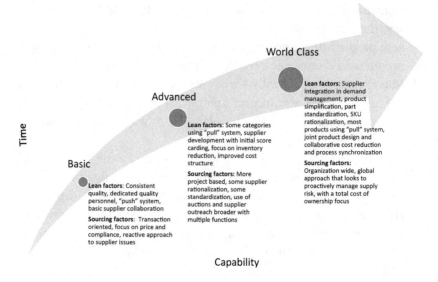

FIGURE 7.3

Lean sourcing maturity model. Source: Aptium Global (2005).

The model shows the progression of developing a lean philosophy that can be integrated and work hand in hand with strategic sourcing over time. Companies that apply basic tools and techniques typically have a "push"-type system and are focused primarily on price. World-class companies, on the other hand, take a more global approach to sourcing, while managing risk, and have a total cost of ownership focus. They typically employ collaborative "pull" systems focused not only on cost reduction but also on process improvement and waste elimination [Aptium Global, 2005].

The following case studies show some examples of how strategic sourcing can be combined with a lean, efficient, and agile philosophy to improve the top and bottom lines.

LEAN STRATEGIC SOURCING MRO: CASE STUDY 1

Challenge

A large, publicly traded mining and minerals processing corporation, with 44 locations across 24 states and Canadian provinces, was trying to preserve profit margins during a turbulent economy and rising supply costs.

While the company had a central reporting system, individual plants made many of the purchasing decisions independently, and so the company found it difficult to leverage its entire spend and to coordinate contracts.

Approach

After an initial cost analysis, an executive committee decided to focus on the maintenance, repairs, and operations (MRO) spend. In the past, the company didn't have the resources to adequately analyze all the purchasing information owing to the inconsistent records of entries from the various plant locations. To overcome this obstacle and gain strategic sourcing expertise, the executive committee engaged Source One, a provider of procurement and supply chain solutions, to help. The goal of the project was to have more competitive pricing by leveraging the corporate spend, strategic relationships, and marketplace competition.

The project included 14 MRO spend categories, including general mechanical supplies, fasteners, electrical/electronic components, safety supplies, and lubrication products. The consultant conducted a spend analysis and created a baseline spend report which identified historical purchasing patterns and revealed possible sourcing strategies that could be examined.

The consultant then proceeded to determine which spend categories presented potential savings opportunities. For each category, Source One conducted a market assessment and spend analysis. The client and consultant agreed that they should conduct a full sourcing project in each of the 14 categories.

RESULTS

Through the introduction of competition, utilization of strategic relationships with supplier conglomerates, and extensive negotiations, Source One managed to produce an average annual saving of 14 percent by helping the client to improve its plant purchasers' ordering, inventory, and reporting methods.

The client, various suppliers, and consultant achieved supplier rationalization, with successful implementation of new pricing and purchasing processes in each category. Improved performance and compliance metrics that were implemented helped the client company to develop better systems for understanding, monitoring, reporting, and controlling its spend for each product category. The consultant continued to ensure the success of the initiative through internal process and supplier auditing well after completion of the implementation phase.

The collaborative team not only reached the initiative's primary goal of creating cost savings without any major disruption of the client's business processes, but also implemented the tools, insight, and relationships necessary to continuously improve its sourcing procedures. As a result, the client company has ongoing cost savings as well as better reporting systems, improved supplier relationships, and better control over their total spend [www.sourceoneinc.com, 2017].

SOURCING AS STRATEGY: CASE STUDY 2

Challenge

An $18 billion manufacturer transformed its procurement process from a transactional cost center to a source of strategic advantage, while saving $500 million at the same time.

The Fortune 200 manufacturing company had grown through an aggressive acquisition policy but did not integrate various businesses. The company's decentralized structure gave it flexibility and an entrepreneurial culture, but without a focus on minimizing costs. The board of directors realized that significant cost savings could be achieved by leveraging the company's $9 billion annual procurement spend, especially with commodities used across its manufacturing operations. However, as they didn't have the expertise to build a consolidated purchasing program on their own, they needed specialized help to develop the processes and create the organizational structure that would make a difference. So, they brought in consultant PwC to assess the value they could achieve with a leveraged purchasing program.

Approach

PwC proposed a three-phased plan to: (1) assess the client's procurement capabilities and potential savings; (2) build new processes and a centrally led procurement organization, including pilot commodity testing; and (3) transfer control of the new procurement operation back to the client.

The first phase assessed the company's global commodity spend to identify opportunities for significant savings and evaluate its procurement capabilities, revealing up to $500 million in savings that could be achieved over five years. Three strategies emerged.

The first was to transform procurement into a strategic function. This meant more than just consolidating purchases; it also meant working with suppliers to innovate and improve end products, develop a strategic understanding of its supplier relationships, and identify opportunities to stay ahead in the commodities marketplace. Secondly, the company would need to build a hybrid centralized procurement division. It had no chief procurement officer (CPO), and so there was no direct input on the topic when executive-level strategic decisions were being made. Procurement would need to be part of the firm's strategy to recognize risks and seize opportunities. Finally, sourcing pilots were set up to demonstrate the savings and build momentum for the cultural change needed for the success of the new sourcing strategy.

The company hired a CPO and brought the executives of its business units on board with the initiative, holding workshops to train key personnel in each business unit to define their sourcing strategy, develop their organizational structure, and identify key sourcing projects and savings targets.

RESULTS

Well into the second phase of its procurement transformation, the client has created a hybrid centralized procurement department, a chief procurement officer has been hired, and a steering committee has been assembled to serve as a strategic sourcing advisory board. Now, all the business units use strategic sourcing to achieve savings and create innovation.

So far, the pilot tests on several commodities have yielded over $50 million in savings, with an overall annualized savings rate of $80 million and a pipeline of more projects to save another $150 million. Tools, templates, and processes have been developed to continue to identify opportunities for savings across the organization, with a culture change from where procurement had been a cost of doing business to the realization that it can be a strategic weapon to achieve product innovation and long-term growth for the company [www.pwc.com, 2014].

PROCUREMENT (AKA SOURCING)

As stated previously, procurement involves the processes of selecting vendors, strategic vetting, establishing payment terms, the negotiation of contracts, and actual purchasing of goods; it is concerned with acquiring the goods, services, and work vital to an organization.

Therefore, we should consider procurement and purchasing as part of the "supply-side planning" function discussed later in the text. It is included in this "supply chain strategy" section of the book, rather than the later "supply-side planning" section, since strategic sourcing, as discussed above, is directly related to procurement (and the line between them is often blurred in organizations). However, it should be noted that procurement, including purchasing, is more tactical and operational in nature than strategic sourcing and is usually an early step in the supply planning process.

Procurement is essentially the overarching or umbrella term within which purchasing can be found and is a defined set of processes that, depending on execution, can be the difference between the success or failure of an organization.

In the remaining section, we will go into some depth to understand the procurement process and its related technologies and then look at the lean procurement concept and some case studies where lean philosophies have been successfully applied.

THE PROCUREMENT PROCESS

The procurement process typically includes the functions of determining the purchasing specifications, selecting the supplier, negotiating terms and conditions, and issuing and administrating purchase orders.

FIGURE 7.4
The procurement process.

There are some general steps involved in the procurement process, which we will now review in some detail (Figure 7.4). The steps to be reviewed are:

1. Identify and review requirements.
2. Establish specifications.
3. Select suppliers, issue quotations.
4. Determine the right price.
5. Issue purchase orders.
6. Follow up to assure correct delivery.
7. Receive and accept the goods.
8. Approve invoice for payment.

Step 1 – Identify and Review Requirements

When discussing requirements, it should be understood that procurement activities are often split into two categories, direct and indirect, depending upon the consumption purposes of the acquired goods and services (Table 7.1).

The first category, direct, is production-related procurement, and the second, indirect, is non-production-related procurement.

Direct Procurement

Direct procurement is generally referred to in manufacturing settings only. It encompasses all items that are part of finished products, such as raw material, components, and parts. Direct procurement, which is a major focus in supply chain management, directly affects the production process of manufacturing firms. It also occurs in retail where "direct spend" may refer to what is spent on the merchandise being resold.

Indirect Procurement

In contrast, indirect procurement activities concern "operating resources" that a company purchases to enable its operations (i.e. MRO inventory, as

TABLE 7.1

Direct vs. Indirect Procurement

		Types		
		Direct Procurement	Indirect Procurement	
		Raw material and production goods	Maintenance, repair and operating supplies	Capital goods and services
Features	Quantity	Large	Low	Low
	Frequency	High	Relatively high	Low
	Value	Industry specific	Low	High
	Nature	Operational	Tactical	Strategic
	Examples	Resin in plastics industry	Lubricants, spare parts	Resin and plastic product storage facilities

well as capital spent on plant and equipment). It comprises a wide variety of goods and services, from standardized low-value items such as office supplies and machine lubricants to complex and costly products and services such as heavy equipment and consulting services.

The source for purchasing requirements can come from material requirements planning (MRP) systems via planners and purchase requisitions from other users in the organization (a purchase or material requisition is a document generated by an organization to notify the purchasing department of items it needs to order, the quantity, and the time frame in which they will be needed in the future).

During this step, purchasing will review paperwork for proper approvals; check material specifications; verify quantity, unit of measure, delivery date, and location; and review all supplemental information.

The topic of MRP and indirect procurement will be discussed in detail in Chapter 13.

Step 2 – Establish Specifications

To establish specifications, one must identify quantity, pricing, and functional requirements, as described below.

Quantity – in the case of small volume requirements, you need to find a standard item. If you are dealing with larger volumes, then it must be designed for economies of scale to both reduce cost and satisfy functional needs.

Price – this relates to the use of the item and the selling price of the finished product.

Functional – there is a fundamental need to understand what the item is expected to do per the user(s). This includes performance and aesthetic expectations (e.g. for a hand can opener: how smoothly does it remove the top of cans, and how ergonomically appealing is the design?).

In general, the description of the item may be by brand or specification. You would use brand if the quantity is too small, the item is patented, or it is requested by a customer. It would be by specification if you're looking for very specific physical or chemical makeup, material, or performance specifications.

The source of the specifications themselves can be based upon buyer requirements or standards that may be set independently.

If the buyer sets the specifications, it can become a long and expensive process requiring detailed description of parts, finishes, tolerances, and materials used, resulting in the item being expensive to produce.

Standards, on the other hand, set by government and nongovernmental agencies, can be much more straightforward to use as they tend to be widely known and accepted, lower in price, and more adaptable to customer needs.

Step 3 – Identify and Select Suppliers

The next step in the procurement process is to identify and select suppliers. Typically, this process involves coming up with a "long list" of suppliers who meet your requirements in general and then whittling the list down to final candidates before selecting the ultimate vendor.

Identification of potential suppliers can come from a variety of sources including the internet, catalogs, salespeople, and trade magazines and directories.

Once you have identified potential vendors, a request for information (RFI) is issued to them that states a bit about your company and its requirements, as well as requesting background on the vendor. It is usually not too difficult to refine the vendors that respond down to a smaller list of candidates (usually between five and ten), and from there it's best to include a multifunctional team of employees to determine the finalist(s).

Once you have it down to a short list, a request for quote (RFQ) or request for proposal (RFP) is issued. An RFQ is an invitation to selected suppliers to bid or quote on delivering specific products or services and will include the specifications of the items/service. The suppliers are requested to return their bids by a set date and time to be considered for selection. Discussions may be held on the bids, in many cases to clarify technical capabilities or to note errors in a proposal. The initial bid does not have to mean the end of the bidding as there may be more than one round.

Vendor Evaluation

I've found what is known as the "factor rating method" (see Table 7.2) to be useful in the task of vendor evaluation.

The factor rating method identifies criteria that need to be considered as part of what you will be buying and assigns weights according to the relative importance of each of these factors. You then score how well each supplier compares on each factor and give them a score which is weighted times the rating.

While this may not be the only decision-making tool used, it can get you close enough to help you make a final decision. There are also intangible

TABLE 7.2

Factor Rating Method for Vendor Evaluation

Criteria	Weights	Scores (1.5)	Weight × Score
Engineering and research capabilities	0.1	4.0	0.4
Production process capability (flexibility/agile)	0.2	5.0	0.8
Delivery capability	0.1	3.5	0.2
Quality and performance	0.2	3.0	0.6
Location	0.1	1.0	0.1
Financial and managerial strength (stability and cost structure)	0.2	5.0	0.8
Information systems capability (e-procurement, ERP)	0.1	2.0	0.2
Reputation (sustainability/ethics)	0.1	5.0	0.5
Total	1.00		3.4

factors that can come into play, such as the personal opinions of executives, prior experience with a vendor, etc.

There are many factors or criteria besides price (and the lowest is not always selected) that are important when selecting a supplier, such as:

Technical ability – as their product will become part of your product, can the potential vendor help you to develop and make improvements to your product?

Manufacturing capability – can they consistently meet your stated quality and specifications?

Reliability – to the best of your ability, you need to determine if they are reputable and financially stable.

After-sales service – do they have a solid service organization that offers technical support?

Location – are they close enough to support fast, consistent delivery and support service when needed?

Step 4 – Determine the Right Price

As was pointed out before, while price may not be the only determinant, it certainly contributes greatly to the bottom line as it can be upwards of 50 percent of the cost of goods sold.

There are three basic models that are used as a basis for pricing. They are:

Cost-based – the supplier makes its financials available to the purchaser.

Market-based – the price is based on published, auction, or indexed price.

Competitive bidding – this is typically used for infrequent purchases but can make establishing a long-term relationship more difficult.

When negotiating price, preparation is the key. On a personal level, if you are buying a house or car, the more research you do, the better idea you have of what is available and what is a "fair" price in the market area (at least to you). Thanks to the internet, there are many sources available to get a good idea as to what's available and a range of pricing based upon recent history. The same goes for business negotiations, where the buyer should have knowledge of the seller's costs to some extent.

Negotiation

For the most part, negotiations are based upon the type of product. General categories of products include:

Commodities – the price is usually determined by the market.

Standard products – the price is set by catalog listings, and there is usually little room for negotiation (other than volume).

Small value items – companies should try to reduce ordering costs or increase volume where possible.

Made-to-order items – prices are based upon quotations from a number of sources, and, as a result, prices are negotiated where possible.

Distributed and Integrative Negotiations

Where negotiations are possible, there are two general types of negotiation that can be used, distributive and integrative.

In distributive bargaining, the goals of one party are in fundamental, direct conflict with another party, resources are fixed and limited, and maximizing one's own share of resources is the goal for both parties. So, in this case, there is usually a "winner" and a "loser".

You need to set a target point and a walk-away point to negotiate a final price that is satisfactory to you. To determine these may take a good amount of research and judgment. The seller may have a listing or asking price, and you will submit an initial offer or counter offer. This type of negotiating usually requires sufficient "clout" to justify lower pricing. Larger companies with multiple locations or business units may have sufficient volume to justify this.

When I was a member of General Electric's corporate sourcing, we were able to leverage over $1 billion spent annually on transportation corporation-wide by collecting freight volumes by mode for the 100+ GE units to negotiate significant savings. This was accomplished not only by collecting and analyzing the annual spend, but also by reducing the number of carriers within each mode to a company-wide group of "core" carriers to maximize negotiation power.

Integrative negotiation, on the other hand, is more collaborative, with a goal for a "win-win" conclusion by the creation of a free flow of information and an attempt to understand the other negotiator's real needs and objectives. This process emphasizes commonalties between the parties and minimizes the differences through a search for solutions that meet the goals and objectives of both sides.

At this point, we move from procurement to more of the day-to-day supplier scheduling and follow-up, which come under the heading of purchasing activities and will be discussed in Chapter 9.

KEY PROCUREMENT METRICS

Price is only one measure of cost and only one element of assessing the attractiveness of a supplier, but it is the most common way the majority of companies view and manage interactions with their suppliers.

Besides price (which is benchmarked against industry standards in many cases), most companies also spend a lot of time and attention on operational dimensions of measurement, which can include quality measures such as parts per million defect rates, service level measures such as time to respond to inquiries, on-time delivery, etc.

Some of the most important key performance indicators (KPIs) to keep an eye on are:

Procurement cycle time – this begins when a company decides to order items and ends when the goods are delivered to the warehouse. If handled properly, the company can benefit from the opportunity to sell its inventory more quickly or take advantage of discounts by paying suppliers sooner. If cycle time lags, time must be spent correcting mistakes or streamlining workflow for faster results.

Quality – one common measurement is the number of defects per thousand or million, used to measure the quality of purchases. High rates of defective merchandise of course limit the amount of quality merchandise in inventory, but also can increase the procurement cycle if items constantly have to be returned.

Procurement return on investment (ROI) – this is measured by comparing the department's costs with the savings it generates. It involves detailed examination of your procurement operations, from the amount of labor and wages involved to the supplies and technology being utilized and even the amount of company space occupied.

Spend under management – this compares strategic sourcing expenditures on products and services against overall expenditures in a given fiscal period. The greater the percentage, the more influence procurement has for savings and optimization. A general rule of thumb is that top-performing companies are around 85 percent, average companies are at 55 percent, and weaker teams are at 35 percent or less.

Implemented cost savings – this measures cost savings realized after implementation. Traditionally, procurement teams have credited savings at the time of negotiation, while this calculation can help to drive organizations to improve the effectiveness of procurement activities.

Contract compliance – this looks at how well suppliers are meeting contract terms and conditions and is usually the ratio of the number of contracts not meeting specifications to the total number of contracts, or the dollar value of spend in noncompliant contracts vs. total contracted spending.

Delivery – this measures whether procurement is obtaining what the organization needs when it needs it, such as the percent of on-time deliveries, percent of shipments arriving in usable condition, and quoted delivery time compared with actual delivery time.

Some forward-thinking companies share information about their strategic business strategies with their key suppliers and have joint discussions about how they can contribute and what metrics can be used to evaluate those contributions. These metrics can be designed to highlight areas for supplier improvement or development, provide early warning of potential problems at suppliers, and ensure the ongoing financial health and sustainability of key suppliers.

LEAN PROCUREMENT

A lean philosophy, when applied to procurement, can:

- Improve the procurement process, workflows, and other activities that add value to the company while reducing time and eliminating waste.

- Reduce costs while simultaneously improving the quality of products and services.
- Increase the performance and response time of suppliers.
- Shift procurement's focus to being more strategic in nature.

It is now apparent that lean has moved beyond the shop floor to include elements of the supply chain such as procurement, which includes the supply base. Lean procurement can be applied in all industries, in manufacturing and service sectors, resulting in impressive operational and financial results.

Lean procurement questions why activities are being done and how to increase procurement's total value. While cost reduction is important in procurement, there needs to be a focus on how it adds value.

Basic lean principles such as value stream, pull, and flow are extremely relevant to procurement. Many lean tools such as value stream mapping, 5S-workplace organization, visual, kaizen, and standard work can be applied to procurement processes.

Supplier proliferation is a major reason for increased transactions and waste in procurement, and companies that go through a supply base rationalization process end up with fewer, higher-performing suppliers.

Focusing on your current supplier base using performance management tools helps to ensure a higher-performing supply base that requires less expediting, resulting in higher quality, improved responsiveness, lower cost, and more value from suppliers, which means a more efficient and cost-effective procurement operation.

In addition, adoption of supply chain technologies such as strategic sourcing software and spend analysis can help make procurement leaner, as pointed out in the next section.

However, to be truly successful for the long term, the focus should be on leadership, overall strategy, people, and culture rather than primarily on the tools. Lean tools are a means to an end, not an end in themselves [www.ivalua.com, 2016].

Core Principles of Lean Procurement

So, with that in mind, there are some general guiding lean procurement core principles derived from demand-driven manufacturing and supply chain initiatives to consider when embarking on this type of strategy:

1. Migrate from "push" to "pull" – strengthen and improve your "pull" supply chain processes by deploying supply chain event management solutions that enhance collaboration with your suppliers. Connecting people (i.e. buyers, suppliers, and partners) directly to their "pull" business processes allows buyers and their suppliers to communicate supply chain "exception-based" signals in real time.

2. Develop a flexible and responsive supply chain – help your procurement professionals eliminate long material lead times by utilizing postponement strategies for a more responsive supply chain. So, when customer demand unexpectedly goes up, your supply chain can meet that increase, and, when forecasts go down, you are not left with excessive levels of inventory. This type of strategy will also help to reduce long lead times normally associated with offshore procurement and can help to proactively manage potential shortages through automated forecast collaboration solutions and proactive alerts when suppliers cannot support requirements.

3. Eliminate all waste in the procurement cycle – without lean procurement, buyers spend a lot of their time on non-strategic processes such as tracking order status, purchase order entry, and maintaining individual spreadsheets for analysis. As a result, they miss opportunities for mutually beneficial supplier negotiations and process efficiencies. By being connected with suppliers to respond electronically with critical business process information and automate their purchase order acknowledgment approval processes, companies can end overreliance on phone, fax, and e-mail and spend more time on more strategic activities [Oracle, 2006].

PROCUREMENT TECHNOLOGY

Most ERP and accounting systems have at least some purchasing features, if only to create purchase orders directly or from an material requirements planning (MRP) system, which will be discussed in Chapter 15 ("Information Technology in a Supply Chain").

There are also internet applications such as e-commerce, exchanges, and auctions for e-procurement.

Additionally, procurement platforms are online marketplaces (like an e-commerce experience) that support the sale and purchase of supplies, commodities, technology, or services. Procurement platforms are often used to facilitate business-to-business or business-to-government sales.

Web-based platform applications such as SAP Ariba software, for example, enable companies to facilitate and improve the procurement process by providing solutions which help companies analyze, understand, and manage their corporate spending to achieve cost savings and business process efficiency. Ariba started with the idea of purchasing staff buying items from vendors who provided their catalogs online, as the typical procurement process can be labor-intensive and often costly for large corporations. Customers are offered a large number of supplier catalogs from which to purchase.

Today, Ariba software allows a company to automate, monitor, and control the complete purchasing life cycle from requisition to payment. Users can create requisitions that are approved according to preconfigured business rules that each company decides upon. Purchase orders can be automatically generated and sent directly to suppliers, while order acknowledgments and ship notices are sent back to the original requester.

The invoicing process is relatively easy for suppliers using a tool such as Ariba, as they can create an invoice directly from the requester's purchase order. Invoices are then pre-matched with the purchase order line items as well as any receiving information, so that the requester can reconcile and pay without any delay.

Technology to Enhance Lean Procurement

New technologies can make your various procurement processes leaner and more efficient, especially in what has now become known as "e-procurement". For our purposes, we will define e-procurement as *business-to-business purchase and sale of supplies and services over the internet which can be integrated with internal computerized procurement processes and systems.*

In procurement, which may sometimes include e-procurement functionality, there are two types of software vendors: (1) ERP providers offering both internal procurement and e-procurement as one or part of their modules, and (2) services or vendors focused specifically on e-procurement.

Procurement software itself is a computer program or suite of products that helps to automate (and thereby improve) the processes of purchasing materials and inventory maintenance of goods. Following the typical procurement process, it can generate purchase orders, execute the ordering process online, match invoices to materials received, and pay bills electronically.

Again, more often than not, systems today include e-procurement functionality as well as leveraging the benefits of the internet. As a result, the benefits of using procurement software include ease of administration and potential cost savings, as well as having a single interface for procurement to monitor its company's spending.

Procurement software helps to efficiently manage a variety of activities. Specifically, it includes the ability to:

- Create a purchase order based on need.
- Verify a purchase order.
- Submit a pending purchase order for approval or rejection.
- Automate an electronic purchase order transmission.
- Confirm or cancel purchase orders.
- Help to execute financial and inventory transactions when ordered materials arrive.
- Gather data and analyze to improve profitability.
- Streamline and standardize administration. For example, procurement systems generally offer multi-currency support as well as tools that can automate purchases and purchasing approvals.

These systems can also connect users with large networks of qualified suppliers, which is a critical capability for supply chain professionals who are trying to identify the most reliable raw material suppliers at the best price, wherever they might be located.

As opposed to procurement modules internal to ERP systems such as SAP and Oracle, there are also stand-alone procurement solutions coming in a variety of forms. Dominick identified ten types of stand-alone procurement software systems:

1. Spend analysis – allows you to find purchasing patterns within categories, by suppliers, etc. that might offer cost savings, performance improvements, and overall efficiencies. Most spend analysis vendors have been acquired by other types of procurement software vendors.

2. Supplier discovery – allows you to search for suppliers that meet specific criteria, such as capabilities, location, supplier diversity, etc. Examples are ThomasNet and Ariba.

3. Supplier information management – allows you to efficiently collect and maintain accurate supplier information, including contact information and certification status, directly from suppliers. Examples are HICX Solutions and Hiperos.

4. e-Sourcing – allows you to get electronic quotes and proposals from suppliers quickly. This can be done privately or can allow suppliers to see their rank among bidders to increase competitive pressure. Examples are WhyAbe, K2Sourcing, and Trade Extensions.

5. Contract management – enables you to prepare contracts using various templates. It can electronically route contracts for approval, track revisions, notify of contract expirations, and store executed contracts. Examples are Selectica and Prodagio.

6. e-Procurement – allows end users to search catalogs of preapproved products and services from contracted suppliers, create requisitions, and have some requisitions turned into purchase orders (either manually by buyers or automatically). Examples are ePlus and eBid.

7. e-Invoicing (also known as e-payment) – enables you to receive accurate supplier invoices electronically and efficiently. It may include "dynamic discounting", allowing suppliers to reduce the amount your organization owes in exchange for faster payment. Examples are Taulia and Tradeshift.

8. Supplier management – enables you to track and/or rate supplier performance using manual or scorecard-style ratings. This also integrates with other systems to gather actual performance and may include risk assessment capabilities. Examples are Aravo and BravoSolution.

9. Combination solutions – a type of e-procurement system allowing for direct payment to suppliers, commonly referred to as "procure-to-pay" or P2P. Ones that offer the option of soliciting quotes from suppliers are called "source-to-pay solutions". Examples are Coupa and Puridiom.

10. Complete suites – there are some software vendors that have many or even all of the solutions listed above. They are referred to as "suites". Examples are GEP, Zycus, SciQuest, and iValua [Domonick, 2015].

Lean procurement, when aided by the appropriate technology, can:

- Remove the obstacles to the free flow of information to a supply chain.
- Create real-time visibility of inventory.
- Transition your supply chain from "push" to "pull", consumption-based replenishment models.
- Manage by exception by providing your buyers and planners with proactive, real-time exception messages that strengthen replenishment processes.
- Eliminate the long lead times for critical materials and assemblies.
- Make sure you are covered for the upside of your material forecast.

What follows are some applications of a lean philosophy in a procurement process.

ERSKINE LEAN REVIEW OF PROCUREMENT – CASE STUDY 1

Challenge

Erskine Hospital Limited is the leading care organization in Scotland. Erskine provides nursing, rehabilitation, and dementia care for residents in care homes throughout Scotland.

Erskine has a dedicated procurement function responsible for negotiating contracts with suppliers, ordering, receiving and issuing goods and products for the West Coast care homes, and maintaining the stock room.

In 2014, Erskine's procurement manager left the organization, giving the organization an opportunity to review its existing processes and determine if there were opportunities for savings and/or improvements. Erskine asked consultant Scott-Moncrieff to carry out a lean review of its procurement function.

Approach

After careful observation and analysis, the consultant identified that the existing procurement function was not appropriate for the size of

Erskine (the function had been designed and developed for a much larger organization) or the skills mix and level of staff required. The existing process was designed to identify and procure the required products and services, receive them in the stockroom, and process purchase invoices. In a larger organization, these activities are split across teams within the procurement function, where no one person is responsible for purchasing, receiving, and paying for all the goods received. In Erskine's smaller organization, the procurement function was required to perform all these activities.

Erskine's procurement IT system did not effectively satisfy the needs of the procurement function, and staff found themselves often identifying ways in which they could make the system work better by putting in place "work-around" arrangements.

It was found that the existing stock control systems were not sufficiently robust and did not represent an effective use of resources. Stockroom staff time was wasted owing to the inability to find goods, and the systems in place for distributing goods between the main hospital and other sites were not consistent. In addition, as the stockroom held goods for multiple sites, there was limited room for deliveries to be received and processed, resulting in large deliveries being left outside until they could be unpackaged and processed, risking damage from possible adverse weather conditions.

RESULTS

By applying lean tools and techniques, the review identified the following recommendations for Erskine:

- Realign responsibilities for procurement functions – procurement staff would now be responsible for ordering the necessary goods, the stock controller would log receipt of the goods, and finance staff would process the payments, bringing them in line with procurement best practices. By transferring an existing temporary procurement post to the current finance function, the recommendations had no resource implications for Erskine.
- Fulfill the identified need for the current software provider to deliver specific training sessions to Erskine's procurement and finance staff

on the new finance system being introduced – this training should prevent staff developing "work-around" options as they had done under the current system and would also remove the need to enter the data twice (i.e. once into their work-around arrangement and once into the IT system), freeing up staff time that could be better utilized on other duties.

- Deliver stock directly to the care homes, reducing the volume of items to be held at the main hospital stockroom and enabling Erskine to reorganize its stockroom to deal with the weekly deliveries. Goods would no longer have to be left outside, reducing the amount of money lost reordering items that had been damaged.
- The lean review has empowered Erskine staff to take greater ownership of the use of stock and the delivery of the procurement function and delivered a more efficient procurement process. The organization has made annual savings of at least $52,000 per annum from a review that cost the organization less than a tenth of this [Thomson, 2015].

SCAPA – CASE STUDY 2

Challenge

The Scapa Group is a global supplier of bonding solutions and manufacturer of adhesive-based products for the healthcare and industrial markets.

Too much time was being spent on managing small, low-value items such as janitorial, packaging, safety, and office supplies. Scapa was ordering these products (313 items in total) from multiple suppliers and receiving multiple deliveries and invoices. The overload of ordering put pressure on the buyers and receiving, and the excessive number of invoices resulted in the accounts payable department spending a lot of time on relatively low-value items, with frequent stock-outs ultimately becoming a problem.

Approach

The Consumers Interstate Consulting (CIC) group implemented a lean procurement strategy. CIC did a full audit of the products currently used throughout the facility. CIC then organized all 313 items and created a unique list of products for all eight departments, where they could place their orders using the CIC website (www.supersupplies.com), with a CIC manager taking charge of ordering and consolidating deliveries.

RESULTS

As a result, the ordering process became streamlined, spending was controlled, and a large amount of time was given back to the procurement team and accounts payable. Scapa now receives 1 invoice a month instead of 25 and has much more time to spend on more value-added activities [www.leanprocurement.com, 2017].

To enable an extended, harmonized demand and supply chain process takes a lot of integration, coordination, and collaboration, the topic of our next chapter.

8

Integration, Coordination, and Collaboration in the Supply Chain

Supply chain integration refers to the degree to which the firm can strategically collaborate with its supply chain partners and collaboratively manage the intra- and inter-organization processes to achieve the effective and efficient flows of product and services, information, money, and decisions (Figure 8.1). The objective of this integration is to provide the maximum value to the customer at low cost and high speed, so as to achieve a harmonized, integrated, "outside-in" demand and supply process.

Integration is not the same as collaboration, as integration is the alignment and linking of business processes and includes various communication channels and connections within a supply network. Collaboration, on the other hand, is a relationship between supply chain partners that is developed over time. Integration is possible without collaboration, but it can also be an enabler of collaboration.

There are two general categories of business integration, internal and external, which we will now explore.

DOI: 10.4324/9781003281078-9

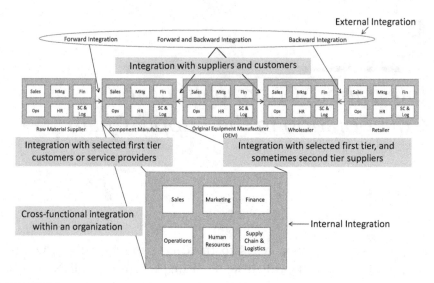

FIGURE 8.1
Major types of integration.

INTERNAL AND EXTERNAL INTEGRATION

Internal Integration

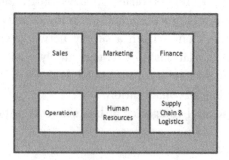

Understanding the entire supply chain of an organization begins with understanding its internal processes, as an integrated firm presents a united front to customers, suppliers, and competitors.

As the saying goes, a chain is only as strong as its weakest link, and so it is critical that there are good communications, policies, and procedures that link the internal supply chain processes not only with each other but also with the other major functions within the organization.

In general, purchasing, operations, and logistics are responsible for delivering the product to the customer. Purchasing is a gatekeeper for process inputs, operations transforms raw materials into final product, and logistics is responsible for physical transfer and delivery.

Internal supply chain integration, therefore, is a process of interaction and collaboration in which manufacturing, purchasing, and logistics work together in a cooperative manner to arrive at mutually acceptable outcomes for their organization.

It is important to integrate communications and information systems so as to optimize their effectiveness and efficiency, and this can be achieved by structuring the organization and the design and implementation of information systems, where non-value-adding activity is minimized, costs, lead times, and functional silos are reduced, and service quality is improved.

Many organizations today use process improvement tools such as lean and six sigma (and the combination of the two, known as "lean six sigma", to be covered later in this book) to analyze existing organizational structures, eliminate non-value-adding activities, and implement new work structures so that the organization is optimally aligned.

An integrated enterprise resource planning (ERP) system (software that manages a company's financials, supply chain, operations, commerce, reporting, manufacturing, and human resource activities) is a key enabler of internal integration, often exposing remaining non-value-added activities in the organization and allowing for better communication and collaboration through a common database.

Internal integration needs more than a system and proper organization. It also needs:

- Shared goals – which refer to the extent to which the manager of each key function (purchasing, operations, and logistics) is familiar with the strategic goals of each of the other two focal functions.
- Cooperation – measured by the frequency of requests from other focal functions fulfilled by the members of each focal function.
- Collaboration – defined as the frequency with which a member of a key function actively works on issues with members from the other key functions.

External Integration

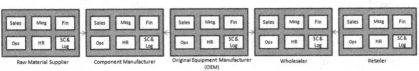

Raw Material Supplier   Component Manufacturer   Original Equipment Manufacturer (OEM)   Wholesaler   Retailer

External or inter-organization integration involves the sharing of product and service information and knowledge between organizations in a supply chain. Like internal integration, it also requires shared goals, cooperation, and collaboration to work successfully.

This enables all stages of the supply chain to take actions that are aligned and increase total supply chain surplus (i.e. the difference between revenue less cost to produce and deliver product to the customer).

It requires that each stage in the entire supply chain share information and take into account the effects of its actions on the other stages.

If the objectives of the different stages conflict with each other, or information moving between stages is delayed or distorted, lack of coordination will result, resulting in the bullwhip effect.

Successful collaboration relies on the development of mutual trust between you and your partners, as well as the willingness to share information (electronically and manually) that can benefit all the members of your collaborative team. The goal is to treat all suppliers, outsourcing partners, customers, and service providers as an extension of your organization.

Supply Chain Collaboration by Industry

Many industries are experimenting with supply chain collaboration, adapting the concept to fit their specific needs.

For example, consumer products and retail companies are implementing safety stock levels across their entire supply chains. Using POS and other information sources, these companies have increased service levels all the way to the store level.

Pharmaceutical and automotive industries have used collaboration to prevent counterfeit products from getting into their supply chains. And pharmacies are using RFID to better manage the shelf life of perishable, coded products.

The high-tech industry is looking to get production visibility beyond purchase-level response, to better control quality, cost, and availability and to improve measurements of customer service such as customer request date.

Capital equipment and manufacturing companies are leveraging collaboration technologies to extend lean supply chain principles across the enterprise by extending electronic kanban processes (i.e. a lean technique to visually replenish inventory based on downstream demand) to suppliers.

Levels of External Collaboration

Across all industries, supply chain collaboration operates at the strategic, tactical, and execution levels:

- Strategic – at this level, organizations and their partners make joint decisions on strategic issues such as production capacities, product design, production facility and fulfillment network expansion, joint portfolio marketing, and pricing plans.
- Tactical – this level involves sharing information with partners on topics such as forecasts, production and transportation plans and capacities, bills of material, orders, product descriptions, prices and promotions, inventory, allocations, product and material availability, service levels, and contract terms, such as supply capacity, inventory, and services.
- Execution – at this level, organizations and their partners engage in an integrated exchange of key transactional data such as purchase orders, production/work orders, sales orders, POS information, invoices, credit notes, debit notes, and payments [www.sap.com, 2014].

Types of External Collaboration

External collaboration can range from relatively simple to very complex, based upon the amount of dependency and information sharing between parties (Figure 8.2).

The simplest form of collaboration would be contracting, which adds a time dimension to traditional buying and selling (i.e. having price, service, and performance expectations over a specific period).

The next level of collaboration is outsourcing, which shifts the focus from just buying materials to actually performing a specific service or activity.

After that come what could be referred to as "managed" types of collaboration where a dominant company uses a command-and-control system to direct the partner, and there is limited sharing of strategic

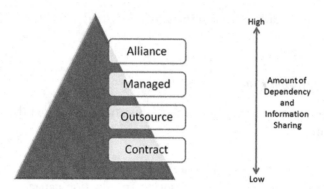

FIGURE 8.2
Range of external supply chain relationships.

information and limited joint planning. This type of relationship has no specific time frame to it (i.e. termination and/or rebid).

The most advanced forms of collaboration are alliances such as we've seen with Dell and its suppliers in a JIT environment, where the parties voluntarily work together both strategically and operationally, and there is some integration of human, financial, operational, and technical resources. There is an extensive amount of joint planning as well as expectation of a long-term relationship.

As companies move along this path toward alliances, trust is a key component. Trust doesn't occur overnight, requiring ongoing interaction between organizations. It is necessary to first see reliability in operations and then a gradual sharing of all information for the relationship to function properly. Trust can be maintained by being open and honest in regard to key decisions (often referred to, somewhat tongue in cheek, as "opening your kimono").

It is helpful to look at the types of external collaboration in terms of those with both suppliers and customers as well as the importance of integrating the S&OP process to include information from both sources.

Supplier Collaboration

Some of the types of supplier collaboration include:

- **Kanban** – a signal-based replenishment process used in lean or JIT production that uses cards or other visual signals, such as a line on a wall, to signal the need for replenishment of an item.

Using collaborative technologies, the kanban process allows customers to electronically issue the kanban replenishment signals to their suppliers who can then determine requirements and see exceptions.

- **Dynamic replenishment** – this is a process where suppliers compare customer forecasts or production schedules with their own production plans to match supply and demand. It allows suppliers to adjust to changes in customer requirements or supply shortages.
- **Invoicing processes** – automating invoicing and related processes makes the entire supply side visible to the vendor, including purchase orders, releases, supplier-managed inventory, kanbans, and dynamic replenishment.
- **Outsourced manufacturer collaboration** – when managing outsourced manufacturing relationships or contract manufacturers, you must shift your focus from owning and organizing assets to working collaboratively with partners.

The collaborative efforts should help simplify processes such as product development, reduce manufacturing costs, and improve responses in reaction to customer demand.

Any efforts to automate these processes should support information sharing, collaboration, and monitoring activities that are needed to effectively manage the relationship with a contract manufacturer.

Customer Collaboration

Customer collaboration involves receiving demand signals and automatically replenishing the customer's inventory based upon actual demand. This is seen primarily in consumer products and other industries that have downstream distribution systems that extend to retailers.

This type of integration and collaborative effort enables manufacturers to shift from a "push" system to a demand "pull" supply chain while combining both forecasts and actual customer demand.

Collaborative replenishment processes are more responsive than purely forecast-based processes as they are driven largely by actual customer demand and also provide visibility in out-of-stock situations so that manufacturers and retailers can react more quickly. Several of these processes will be discussed later in the chapter and go by the names "quick response" (QR) and "efficient consumer response" (ECR). POS information can add visibility across the entire supply chain as well when included in a collaborative replenishment process.

Another type of customer collaboration, which focuses on forecasts, is known as collaborative planning, forecasting, and replenishment (CPFR, which is a trademark of the Voluntary Interindustry Commerce Standard – VICS – Association). It is an outgrowth from some of the earlier customer replenishment initiatives such as QR and ECR.

In general, CPFR is an attempt to reduce supply chain costs by promoting greater integration, visibility, and cooperation between trading partners' supply chains. It combines intelligence from multiple trading partners in the planning and fulfillment of customer demand.

Figure 8.3 shows collaborative or vendor-managed inventory configurations in terms of the level of sophistication or complexity. Levels 1 and 2 have been implemented in various industries and would include programs such as QR and ECR. Levels 3 and 4 are more advanced and would include CPFR-like programs.

Sales and Operations Planning: Bringing the Outside In

S&OP is an integrated business management process through which the executive/leadership team continually achieves focus, alignment, and synchronization between all functions of the organization and is the topic

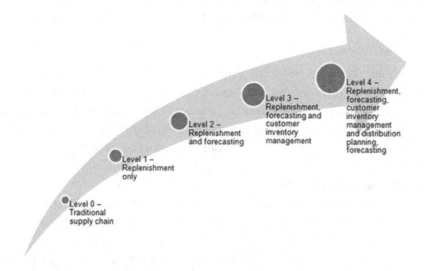

FIGURE 8.3
Types of collaborative systems in supply chains.

of Chapter 12; it allows you to introduce collaborative information into the decision-making process and, when used as part of your collaborative efforts, enables better communications between cross-functional groups and trading partners, both customers and suppliers.

Globalization and outsourcing generate a lot of information, externally to the enterprise, that can impact an organization's decision-making process. As a result of this, a comprehensive S&OP process is even more important. The S&OP process makes sure that your business is continually managed to meet organizational strategies, goals, and commitments, despite ongoing changes in your environment.

Benefits to Collaboration

Increased connectivity and collaboration between companies and their trading partners create many benefits for both suppliers and customers, such as:

- Higher inventory turns.
- Lower fulfillment (transportation and warehousing) costs.
- Lower out-of-stock levels and improved customer service.
- Shorter lead times.
- Early identification of changes to demand and improved market intelligence.
- Visibility into customer demand and supplier performance.
- Earlier and faster decision-making [www.sap.com, 2007].

SUPPLY CHAIN COLLABORATION METHODS – A CLOSER LOOK

There are a variety of supply chain collaboration methods or models that have been used during the past 30 years or so. There is some overlap between some of them and confusion as to the (somewhat subtle) differences.

We'll now describe some of the major methods.

Quick Response

QR was an apparel manufacturing initiative that started primarily in the United States during the mid-1980s. The main objective of QR was to drastically reduce lead times and setup costs to allow the postponement of ordering decisions until right before, or during, the retail selling season, when better demand information might be available.

QR is typically implemented in conjunction with information technologies such as EDI (a standardized format for businesses to exchange data electronically), bar codes, and RFID (the wireless use of radio frequency signals to transfer data to identify and track tags attached to objects).

A QR strategy can result in efficiencies such as maximized diversity of offering, quicker deliveries, faster inventory turns, fewer stock-outs, fewer markdowns, and lower inventory investment.

This type of strategy can also reduce the time between the sale and replacement of goods on the retailer's shelf as it places an emphasis upon flexibility and product velocity in order to meet the changing requirements of a highly competitive and dynamic marketplace.

Efficient Consumer Response

ECR, launched in 1984, is a grocery sector joint trade and industry organization with the goal of making the industry more responsive to consumer demand and removing unnecessary costs from the supply chain.

The thinking is to improve the efficiency of a supply chain as a whole, beyond the wall of retailers, wholesalers, and manufacturers, so that they can all gain larger profits than if each pursues its own business goals.

One of the main practices used in ECR is to place smaller orders more often to shorten lead times, improve inventory turns, and reduce stock-outs (Figure 8.4). ECR is similar to QR, except that it is targeted toward the grocery industry, where the supplier takes responsibility for monitoring and replenishing the retailer's distribution center inventories with the approval of the retailer.

In the 1990s, when I was with Church and Dwight (Arm & Hammer products), we successfully implemented an ECR program to both place orders for, and manage the inventory of, our products at the distribution centers of a number of our grocery clients, including Wakefern (i.e. Shop Rite) and H.E. Butt.

Like QR, ECR is highly dependent upon technology, using tools such as EDI, forecasting, and distribution requirements planning (DRP) software, and POS data to manage the process.

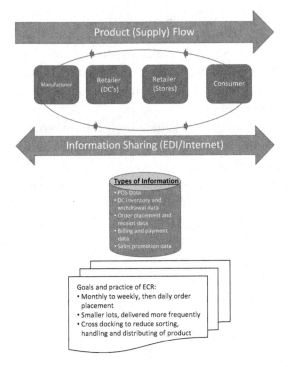

FIGURE 8.4
Efficient consumer response.

The use of sophisticated technology such as this, as well as the lack of capabilities (both skill- and technology-related), the resistance of wholesalers, retailers, and manufacturers to collaboration, and the attitudes of company personnel can all be barriers to successful implementation of an ECR- (or QR)-type program. It is well worth the effort, however, and can prove to be a "win–win" for all involved, as forecast accuracy tends to improve for the manufacturer, and the retailer is relieved of managing the replenishment of some of its 50,000+ SKUs while reducing stock-outs and inventory and ordering costs.

Collaborative Planning, Forecasting, and Replenishment

CPFR is a form of collaboration that combines knowledge and information from multiple trading partners to reduce supply chain costs and improve efficiencies by linking sales and marketing best practices to supply chain planning and execution processes. Its overall objective is to increase customer service while reducing inventory, transportation, and logistics costs.

CPFR has its roots in ECR and is an attempt to improve marketing, production, and replenishment functions, resulting in increased value to the consumer and, at the same time, improving supply chain performance for producers and retailers.

The VICS Association has defined both a framework and guidelines for CPFR, including elements for strategy and planning used for the development of joint business plans and forms of collaboration, supply chain management focusing on forecasting and order planning, execution for the fulfillment of replenishment orders, and analysis for exceptions and performance metrics.

The benefits of CPFR can include:

- Improved forecast accuracy.
- Smoother ordering patterns.
- Increased sales revenues.
- Higher order fill rates.
- Decreased safety stock inventory levels.
- Reduction in cost of goods sold (COGS) as a result of improved visibility of end consumer demand, more accurate forecasts, and more stable production schedules.

Similarly to QR and ECR, CPFR requires the use of technology, which can be shared technology for planning, execution, and measurement.

As in most cases of intercompany integration and collaboration, besides having sophisticated supply chain processes and technology, the key is to have proper organization alignment and training (Figure 8.5).

On the supplier side, there will need to be CPFR teams made up of supply chain, sales, and customer service employees. On the customer side, which can be either the distributor or retailer, representatives from the purchasing, marketing, and merchandising functions will also need to be organized into a focused CPFR team.

Internal processes such as S&OP will have to be integrated with the CPFR process, and education initiatives are needed in order to make sure everyone understands and buys into CPFR and its processes, as well as the implications of the coming change, benefits of CPFR, and the strategic importance of this type of initiative [www.sdcexec.com; 2008].

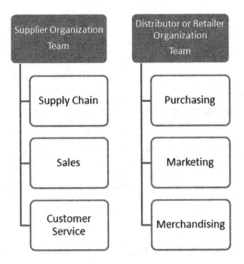

FIGURE 8.5
CPFR teams.

In the 21st century, we are truly in a new phase of the industrial revolution that focuses heavily on interconnectivity, automation, machine learning, and real-time data which can supercharge collaboration in the extended supply chain. This stage is often referred to as "Industry 4.0".

INDUSTRY 4.0 AND SUPPLY CHAIN 4.0 FOR FURTHER INTEGRATION AND COLLABORATION

Industry 4.0 is the realization of the digital transformation of the field, delivering real-time decision-making, enhanced productivity, flexibility, and agility. Manufacturers are integrating new technologies, including the IoT, cloud computing and analytics, and AI and machine learning into their production facilities and throughout their operations.

This has led to the concept of "Supply Chain 4.0", leveraging the same technologies to significantly improve performance and customer satisfaction in the supply chain.

Integrated Process Optimization

With firms along the supply chain using digital technologies, digitalization can facilitate data and information exchange across company borders and enable better collaboration between supply chain partners. As of today, this is really a work in progress.

Many companies have started to implement an integrated planning process, but in many cases this is still done in silos, and not all information is leveraged to achieve the best planning result possible.

Beside intracompany optimization, process optimization between companies has not been fully leveraged yet, and the potential for improvement created by increased transparency has not yet been realized.

To get to the next level of integrated process optimization, the organizational and governance processes and incentives need to be aligned within and between partners in the supply chain.

Collaboration through the Cloud

The supply chain "cloud", which refers to software and services that run on the internet instead of locally on your computer, forms the next level of collaboration in the supply chain.

Supply chain clouds are supply chain platforms shared between customers, the company, and suppliers, providing either a shared logistics infrastructure or even joint planning solutions. Especially in noncompetitive relationships, partners can collaboratively work on supply chain tasks to reduce administrative costs, implement best practices, and, in general, learn from each other.

Another major field within collaboration is end-to-end/multitier connectivity. For example, some automotive companies have already started collaborating throughout the entire value chain (e.g. from the cattle farmer to the finished leather seat in the car), while other companies still need to catch up.

Successful collaboration along the value chain can lead to much lower inventories through an exchange of reliable planning data, a significant lead time reduction through instantaneous information provision throughout the entire chain, an early-warning system, and the ability to react fast to global disruptions [McKinsey & Company, 2016].

Now that we've sufficiently covered various types of supply chain strategies throughout the first section of this book, it is time to take a closer look at demand and supply planning processes, starting on the demand side in the next section.

Section II

Demand-Side Planning

9

Demand Planning: The Art and Science of Forecasting

It has only been in the past 30 years or so that businesses have truly come to realize the importance of forecasting. If you think about it, forecasting is usually the first step in the planning and scheduling process for most goods and service organizations, and forecasts for demand drive everything in an organization, from longer-term decisions (three or more years out) as to new facilities and products to medium-term decisions (months to years out), such as production planning and budgeting, and the short-term decisions (months to a year, at most), where we need to know what to produce (or purchase) and deploy (see Figure 9.1).

The function itself has evolved from being an almost "dreaded" responsibility of sales and marketing to where operations took control to produce stable production requirements and on to today, where it is most typically part of the supply chain function, where it can rise to the level of importance in an organization to the point where there may be a director of forecasting or demand planning. In fact, there is now a professional organization dedicated to the profession, the Institute of Business Forecasting & Planning (www.ibf.org).

FORECASTING USED TO BE STRICTLY LIKE "DRIVING AHEAD, LOOKING IN THE REARVIEW MIRROR"

Historically, manufacturers forecasted sales based upon shipments to customers only, which was less than optimal as (1) what we sold may not have been what was ordered (or where it was supposed to ship from) and

DOI: 10.4324/9781003281078-11

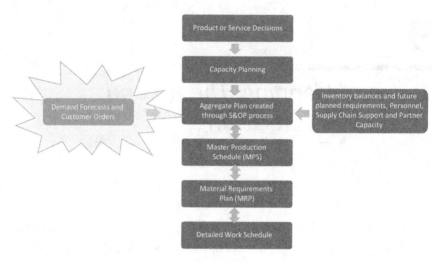

FIGURE 9.1
Generic best-practice planning and scheduling process.

(2) the true "driver" of most businesses and services is the consumer, not necessarily our distribution channels.

These limitations were due primarily to companies working in more of a "vacuum", as data was hard to get and limited to internal sources and storage space was expensive and limited.

Many companies also operated under a "two-number" system, where sales and marketing budgeted one number (which might only be changed once per quarter), and manufacturing developed its own SKU forecast based upon more current sales. In some cases, there was even a third number, used by those responsible for finished goods' deployment to distribution centers, which in many cases was based upon percentage allocations of one of the two aforementioned national or global forecasts.

As technology became more readily available (and eventually more affordable) in the mid-1980s to early 1990s, many businesses were able to begin to get a better handle on the forecasting process. Using the "pyramid" approach to forecasting (see Figure 9.2), organizations were able to develop a bottom-up/top-down "one number" forecast, often using a consensus forecast process requiring collaboration, as described in the previous chapter, which used various statistical methods as well as other sources of information at various levels of detail. These one number forecasts were able to drive budgeting, production, and deployment simultaneously and were updated typically on a monthly (or more frequent) basis.

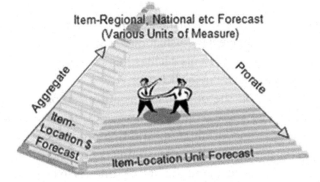

FIGURE 9.2
The pyramid approach to forecasting.

Forecasts are often required or better managed at multiple levels of detail/aggregation (and built by "consensus"). The most common methods are:

- Top-down forecasts:
  - Forecast by product family/groups.
  - Fair-share disaggregation to SKU.
  - Strategy-/budget-focused.
  - Greater visibility to seasonality or trends.
- Bottom-up forecasts:
  - Sum SKU history/forecasts to family/groups.
  - Operationally or customer-focused (by customer location/ warehouse).
- Middle-out forecasts:
  - Blended method.

DEMAND SENSING AND SHAPING

Today, with the advent of readily available and affordable web-based technology making available massive amounts of data, the idea of "demand sensing" has come into vogue.

Demand sensing is a forecasting method that leverages new mathematical techniques and near real-time information to create an accurate forecast of demand, based on the current realities of the supply chain. Demand sensing uses a much broader range of demand signals (including current data from the supply chain) and different mathematics to create a more accurate forecast that responds to real-world events such as market shifts, weather changes, natural disasters, consumer buying behavior, etc.

Demand shaping, on the other hand, is an operational supply chain management strategy where a company uses tactics such as price incentives, cost modifications, and product substitutions to entice customers to purchase specific items (as well as alter timing of demand when desirable). Companies can also use demand shaping techniques to help meet product development projections.

The increasing volatility of the global supply chain requires increased use of both demand sensing and shaping techniques to remain competitive.

One example of a combination of demand sensing and shaping, partially due to the availability and sharing of POS data from either paid services or larger customers, has also been integrated into the forecasting and replenishment process using collaborative programs between manufacturers and retailers, such as QR and ECR (discussed in the previous chapter), to be able to reduce the bullwhip effect.

Artificial Intelligence and Forecasting

As the amount of data available today can at times seem overwhelming, not to mention the ongoing volatility in the global demand and supply chain, as has been mentioned, the time has finally come for the use of AI systems in the forecasting process. In fact, the overall market for AI-related systems is growing rapidly. At present, the United States accounts for over 60 percent of an estimated $900 million global AI market.

AI, simply put, is a computer-based analytical process that exhibits behavior and actions that are considered "intelligent" by human observers. It attempts to mimic human thought processes, including reasoning and optimization.

One purpose of AI is to help organize and supply information for the management decision-making process in such a way as to improve overall efficiency and performance.

The key difference between traditional business forecasting and a machine learning-based solution (an application or subset of AI) is that AI can be fed as many business metrics and KPIs as you may have.

An AI-based forecasting solution uses an assortment of machine learning algorithms to optimize forecasts. The system then selects a model that's uniquely suited for the particular business metric that is being forecast.

Machine learning can find patterns and correlations in data that a traditional (or human) system simply would never be able to find.

Not only can AI-based forecasting provide the accuracy you need by taking into account all these factors, it is also fully autonomous, continuously reconfiguring projections as patterns change to better inform your decisions [Anodot, 2022].

FORECASTING REALITIES

There are certain realities about forecasting that one has to understand before getting into the details of the process. They are:

- All forecasts are wrong – it's very rare that a forecast is 100 percent accurate. The idea is to have an integrated, collaborative process that minimizes variance of actual vs. target. We'll talk later about the process and importance of setting and measuring forecast accuracy targets.
- The more "granular" the forecast, the less accurate it is – a national forecast for a family of items is likely to be more accurate than a weekly forecast for an SKU at a distribution center that handles a region of the country. We can compensate for some of the inaccuracy through proper inventory planning, factoring in scientific safety stock inventory based upon desired service levels, reduced lot sizes, and cycle times included in lean, as covered in Chapter 6.
- We can forecast next month more accurately than next year – if we know what we sold yesterday, then we typically have a better idea of what we'll sell today, whereas, 12 months from now, a lot of things can have happened that affect sales.
- You will get a more accurate forecast using demand (or order) history than sales (or shipment) history – years ago, when data storage costs were high and capacity was lower, most companies only stored sales information. Nowadays, most store order or demand information as well. Unless your company has a 100 percent service level, there

will be occasions where you ship short, late, or from the "wrong" location. If you only used sales history, you would be forecasting to repeat yesterday's failure. That's why you should always use demand history to drive statistical forecasts.

- Forecasting really is a blend of "art and science" – as we will discuss, there are both qualitative and quantitative methods of forecasting. Today, the best practice is a combination of both, as well as collaboration with supply chain partners providing better visibility downstream in the "demand chain".

TYPES OF FORECASTS

There are various forecasting needs in an organization. The major ones are as follows:

- Marketing requires forecasts to determine which new products or services to introduce or discontinue, which markets to enter or exit, and which products to promote.
- Salespeople use forecasts to make sales plans, since sales quotas are generally based on estimates of future sales.
- Supply chain managers use forecasts to make production, procurement, and logistical plans.
- Finance and accounting use forecasts to make financial plans (budgeting, capital expenditures, etc.). They also use them to report to Wall Street in regard to their earnings expectations.

Demand Drivers

In general, demand can be driven by a number of internal and external factors which need to be identified and understood.

Internal Demand Drivers

These types of drivers of demand include sales force incentives, consumer promotions, and discounts to trade. It was only in the past 20–30 years that some manufacturers and retailers began to get a better understanding of the full impact of these drivers on the supply chain, resulting in the bullwhip effect we discussed.

For example, starting in the late 1980s, Procter & Gamble and Walmart began a channel partnership that eventually led to the "every day low pricing" (EDLP) concept to reduce costs and improve service. At one point, P&G went as far as stationing 200 employees at Walmart's headquarters in Bentonville, Arkansas. Over the years, the resulting supply chain channel has become much more efficient because channel activities are better coordinated.

Previously, supply chain and operations were at the mercy of these internal drivers and had to live through the consequences. Of course, they will always exist to some degree.

External Demand Drivers

These drivers, while not controllable to any great degree, can be managed better through best-practice techniques, with a structured methodology in place that employs improved communications and integration with other departments within an organization as well as with customers. These drivers can include events in the environment that are mostly unpredictable, such as terror attacks and stock market crashes, and others that are due to a lack of good communication and visibility, such as new distribution and larger than anticipated orders.

FORECASTING PROCESS STEPS

While everyone does things a little differently, it's always a good idea to develop a standard methodology for a process. In the case of demand forecasting, there are certain general steps that should be included, and they are [Heizer et al., 2013]:

1. **Determine the use of the forecast** – this varies by industry and company. In the case of manufacturing, it might be to drive production and deployment; in the case of retail, it might be to determine purchasing requirements; and for pure service companies, it might be used primarily for labor staffing.
2. **Select the items to be forecasted** – will we be forecasting by individual items in various granulations, and what levels and units of

measure will be needed for us to be able to aggregate forecasts and demand history?

3. **Determine the time horizon of the forecast** – do we need to look at it in the short, medium, or long term (or "all of the above"), and what type of time planning buckets are appropriate (e.g. 30 days or less: daily buckets; one to three months out: weekly buckets; and four or more months: quarterly buckets).

4. **Select the forecasting model(s) and methods** – based upon a number of things we will be discussing, such as where a product is in its life cycle, will we use qualitative, quantitative, or a blend of models? To what degree will we integrate externally supplied information (e.g. customer forecasts, POS data, CPFR, etc.), and what weight will we give it?

5. **Gather the data needed to make the forecast** – when using forecasting software, the initial integration will consider much of this, such as using demand vs. sales, as mentioned previously, eliminating data errors, etc. Once this integration has been created, and data have been validated, it becomes more of a maintenance issue for things such as new and discontinued items.

6. **Generate forecasts** – typically, statistical methods are used to generate a "baseline" forecast, possibly at different levels of detail. The planner will then usually "audit" the results and, if needed, try other statistical models. They will then factor in management overrides based upon their experience and knowledge as well as promotional plans, sales estimates, and externally supplied information mentioned in step 4.

7. **Validate and implement the results** – during the demand part of the S&OP process that we will discuss in Chapters 10 and 12. forecasts are reviewed by cross-functional teams at various levels of detail and units of measure to ensure the highest level of accuracy possible. This will ultimately lead to the one number system that was discussed earlier so that everyone is on the same page.

During this time, recent forecast accuracy will be evaluated as well to help target improvement.

It is also during this step that the new forecasts are saved to be measured later for accuracy against predetermined variance/error targets, which we will be discussing later in the chapter.

Many companies cycle through this process on a monthly basis (again, this will vary by industry and how the forecasts will be used); although forecasts are typically adjusted on an "as needed" basis owing to over-/underselling, new demand information, changes to promotions and discounts, etc.

QUANTITATIVE VS. QUALITATIVE MODELS

There are two general types of forecasting models, quantitative and qualitative.

Qualitative Models

The qualitative method is typically used when the situation is somewhat vague and only a small volume of data exists. It is useful for creating forecast estimates for new products, services, and technology. Generally, it relies heavily upon intuition and experience.

Qualitative methods include knowledge of products, market surveys, jury of executive opinion, and the Delphi method, described below.

Knowledge and Intuition of the Products

A forecast can come from the experience of a planner/forecaster who has years of experience with the product and can look over historical and forecast statistical estimates to make adjustments based upon his or her judgment. This same method can be used with other people in the organization such as sales and marketing personnel to gather their estimates.

However, one must always be aware of biases that may result from different individuals' "motivation". For example, sales personnel may be incentivized to hit a high target to reach a bonus.

In my experience as a senior forecaster at Unilever, after a while, I was able to determine that sales estimates were typically 50 percent too high and, once that had been factored in, they were fairly useful (at least to start a dialogue). It is also very important to be able to share forecast and historical data in units of measure and levels of aggregation that are meaningful to others. For example, the sales department thinks more in terms of revenue dollars, customers, and product categories. So a good forecasting process and software system should be able to convert data back and forth to both present the data and receive feedback.

Market Surveys

Market surveys involve the process of gathering information from actual or potential customers. I am sure most of us have experience of being asked to answer a survey in a mall. When I was an employee at Burger King Corporation at their headquarters in Miami, Florida, we would be asked on occasion to visit the "test kitchen" upstairs. We would then try different versions of current and new/test items. Usually, we were asked to compare items that might have subtle differences, such as different brands of catsup.

Another example is focus groups, where people are asked about their perceptions, opinions, beliefs, and attitudes toward a product, service, concept, advertisement, idea, or packaging. Questions are sometimes asked in a group setting, and participants can talk with other group members.

Jury of Executive Opinion

In the jury of executive opinion forecasting method, managers within the organization get together to discuss their opinions on what sales will be in the future. These discussion sessions usually revolve around experienced guesses, and the resulting forecast is a blend of informed opinions with some use of statistical methods.

Delphi Method

In the Delphi method, which is a bit more formal than the jury of executive opinion method, the results of questionnaires are sent to a panel of "experts". Through an iterative process, multiple rounds of questionnaires are sent out, and the anonymous responses are aggregated and shared with the group at the end of each round. The experts are allowed to modify their answers for each round. The Delphi method seeks to reach the "correct" response through consensus.

Both the Delphi and jury of executive opinion forecasting methods are usually a bit more strategic in nature and are used more in developing higher-level, longer-term forecasts.

Quantitative Models

As opposed to qualitative methods, quantitative methods are typically used when the situation is fairly stable and historical data exist. As a result, they are used primarily for existing and/or current technology products and involve a variety of mathematical techniques we will cover in some detail later in this chapter, under the two major categories of time series and causal models.

Time Series Models

Time series forecasting uses a set of evenly spaced numerical data that is obtained by observing a response variable at regular intervals. The forecasts are based on past values and assume that factors influencing past, present, and future will continue. Relatively simple and inexpensive methods such as moving averages and weighted moving averages are used to predict the future.

Associative Models

Associative (often called "causal") models forecast based upon the assumption that the variable to be forecast (i.e. the dependent variable) has a cause-and-effect relationship with one or more other (i.e. independent) variables. Projections are then based upon these associations. Models such as linear and multiple regression are used in this case.

A Blended Approach: Collaboration and Consensus Forecasting

As noted earlier in the chapter, a consensus (and collaborative) "one number" forecast approach tends to result in a best single number to drive the downstream (and upstream) planning process. This approach can really be looked at as a combination of the quantitative and qualitative approaches just mentioned; it is very common today and considered best practice.

PRODUCT LIFE CYCLES AND FORECASTING

Before we delve into the various quantitative forecasting models in more detail, it is worth discussing the relationship between forecasts and a product's life cycle, as it is somewhat useful to understand where a product is in its life cycle when determining whether to rely more heavily on qualitative or quantitative models.

It should be noted that the product life cycle also has an impact on the supply side, which we will cover in the next section.

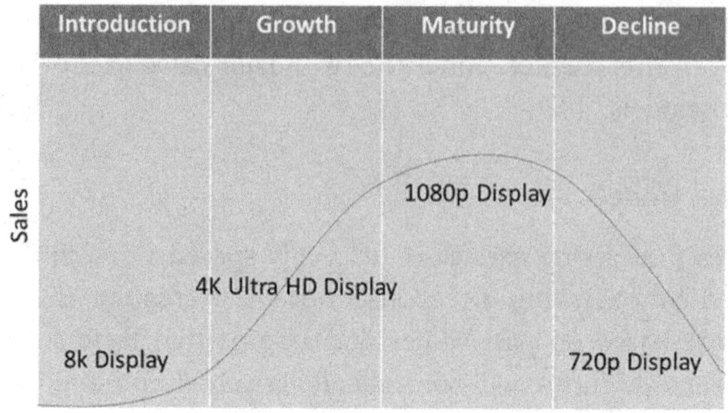

FIGURE 9.3
Product life cycle (flat screen TV example).

The phases in the life cycle of a product or service are introduction, growth, maturity, and decline (Figure 9.3).

Introduction Phase

During the introduction phase, there is very little history, if any, to go on, and so forecasters tend to rely more on qualitative estimates that are generated both internally and externally. This information can come from sources such as market research, test markets where that information can be extrapolated, similar items that you've sold before, which may or may not cannibalize other existing items, sales and customer estimates, advance orders to fill the distribution pipeline, etc.

Growth Phase

As a product gains momentum through expanded marketing and distribution, some of the simpler time series methods may be used as minimal demand history becomes available.

A general "rule of thumb" in forecasting is that, to generate a decent statistical forecast, one needs at least 12 months of history. So, during this growth phase, forecasting is truly a blend of "art and science", as both quantitative and qualitative methods are used to create a blended forecast.

During the growth phase, it can be very easy to over- or underestimate forecasts, which can have dramatic effects on cost and service, and so great care must be taken, and all lines of communication must be established and open, both internally and externally, to avoid surprises where possible (which, in some cases, such as new distribution, may be hard to avoid).

Maturity Phase

When a product reaches maturity, forecast accuracy tends to improve. For example, when I was in charge of forecasting at Church and Dwight for Arm & Hammer, a 1-pound box of baking soda was relatively easy to forecast demand for as it had been around for over 150 years. So, we could rely on simple models to forecast and didn't need much field information, as the item wasn't gaining many new customers. However, once a product reaches maturity, there are opportunities for brand extensions, which is just what happened with baking soda. Baking soda actually has hundreds of applications, and so, starting with refrigerator and freezer "packs", baking soda gained new life (and new products). This carried on to baking soda toothpaste, baking soda deodorant, etc. in the years that followed.

Decline Phase

Once a product goes into its decline phase, besides sales having a general downward trend, the demand locations start to shift, as the trend is not uniform. On top of that, other channels not previously used, such as dollar stores, discount chains, export, etc., may now be used.

Eventually, the product may be discontinued. However, forecasts must still be generated to run out existing inventory, and so, similarly to in the introductory phase, the forecaster relies more on qualitative than quantitative methods.

TIME SERIES COMPONENTS

Time series models can contain some or all of the following components (Figure 9.4):

- Trend – an ongoing, overall upward or downward pattern, with changes due to population, technology, age, culture, etc., that is usually of several years' duration; for example, a fashion trend toward smaller bikinis.

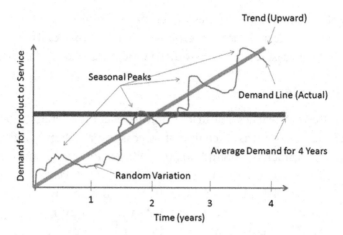

FIGURE 9.4
Components of demand.

- Cyclical – repeating up and down movements, typically affected by business cycle, political, and economic factors, which may vary in length and are usually between two and ten years in duration. There are often causal or associative relationships. Examples include economic recessions.
- Seasonal – a regular pattern of fluctuations due to factors such as weather, customs, etc. that occur within one year. Examples can be natural occurrences such as climatic seasons or artificially created ones such as the school year or seller promotional plans.
- Random – erratic fluctuations that are due to random variation or unplanned events such as union strikes and war, which are usually relatively short in nature and non-repeatable.

As these components can be combined in different ways, it is usually assumed that they are multiplicative or additive.

TIME SERIES MODELS

The most common quantitative time series models are:

- Naive approach – the last period's actual demand is used as this period's forecast, without adjusting them or attempting to establish causal factors (e.g. if January sales were 100, then February forecasted sales will be 100). It is simple, yet cost-effective and efficient.

- Moving average – this is the simple average of a demand over a defined number of time periods and is used if there is little or no trend as it tends to smooth historical data. Typically, more recent history is averaged to create the estimate (e.g. January–March sales are averaged to create an April forecast).
- Weighted moving average – an average has multiplying factors to give different weights to data at different positions in the sample window. This is typically used when some trend might be present, as it usually treats older data as less important. The weights are based on experience and intuition and can be used to minimize the smoothing effect if desired.

  For example:
  Weighted moving average forecast for April = 0.6 * March sales + 0.3 * February sales + 0.1 * January sales

  In this example, more weight has been given to March demand than to January and February to generate the April (and onward) forecast.

- Exponential smoothing – a smoothing technique is used to reduce irregularities. It is a form of the weighted moving average model where weights decline exponentially, with the most recent observations given relatively more weight in forecasting than the older observations. Exponential smoothing requires an alpha smoothing constant (ranges between 0 and 1 and is denoted by the symbol α) which is subjectively chosen.

  For example:

  New forecast = last period's forecast + .7 * (last period's actual demand – last period's forecast)

  In this example, the smoothing constant used of .7 will give a relatively high weighting or "smoothing" factor to an over- or undersell during the most recent month of history when generating the new forecast.

- Holt–Winters (aka "triple exponential") smoothing – a model of time series behavior that can be used to forecast data points in a series, provided that the series is "seasonal", i.e. repetitive over some period. It is a way to model three aspects of the time series: a typical value (average), a slope (trend) over time, and a cyclical repeating pattern (seasonality).

CAUSAL OR ASSOCIATIVE MODELS

There are more sophisticated models known as "associative" (or causal) models, such as linear regression (also known as the least squares method) and multiple regression analysis, which use the relationship of an independent variable(s) (*x*) to predict a dependent variable (*y*).

Associative forecasting models include identifying variables that can be useful in estimating another variable where they have some type of association with each other.

The reason linear regression is called the least squares method is that the formula draws a "best fit" line through the historical data over time (i.e. with the least deviation; see Figure 9.5). That formula can then be used to predict future values of *y*.

In linear regression, the relationship is defined as: $y = a + bx$, where $a =$ the *y*-axis intercept, and $b =$ the slope of the regression line.

A simple example of linear regression would be to derive and use this equation to predict future sales (*y*) by plugging in the sales budget (*x*) that we plan on using (with *n* being the total number of observations). If we know that the two variables are strongly correlated, we can easily derive the equation using historical sales personnel employment numbers along with historical sales.

To come up with this equation, we must solve for *b* and then *a*. The formula used to derive each are:

$$b = \frac{\sum xy - n\overline{x}\overline{y}}{\sum x^2 - n\overline{x}^2}$$

$$a = \overline{y} - b\overline{x}$$

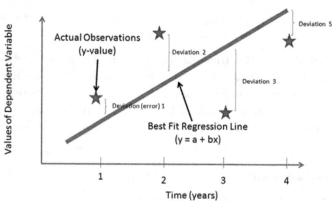

FIGURE 9.5
Least squares method.

Once we have solved for *a* and *b*, we have our regression formula and can plug in future sales personnel employment estimates to predict future sales.

Correlation

To measure correlation (i.e. the mutual relation between two or more things), we calculate a correlation coefficient, also known as r, which is a measure of the strength and direction of the linear relationship between two variables that is defined as the (sample) covariance of the variables divided by the product of their (sample) standard deviations.

$$r = \frac{n(\sum xy) - (\sum x)(\sum y)}{\sqrt{\left[n\sum x^2 - \left(\sum x\right)^2\right]\left[n\sum y^2 - \left(\sum y\right)^2\right]}}$$

The range of correlation is 0–1. A perfect correlation between two variables would result in an r of ±1. The lower the correlation between the two variables, the closer to 0 the result.

R squared, on the other hand, is the square of the correlation coefficient (r) and indicates the percentage of variation explained by the regression line out of the total variation. The value for r squared ranges between 0 and 1. The closer the value is to 1, the stronger the relationship between the predictor variable(s) and the response variable.

Note that a correlation between x and y can be positive or negative. An example of positive correlation would be if y = sales and x = sales budget as in the example above. A negative correlation example (somewhat harder to find) would be if y = sales of new refrigerators and x = mortgage rates. If mortgage rates are going up, there will typically be lower home sales.

Seasonality

In all of the aforementioned time series methods, as well as linear regression (or any forecast for that matter), we can apply what is known as a seasonality index, which is a measure of how a particular season in some cycle compares with the average season of that cycle. As mentioned, this may reflect actual seasonal sales of an item (i.e. we sell more snow shovels in the winter) or can be artificially created (e.g. a promotional calendar).

A seasonality index is relatively easy to create and can be applied to any of the aforementioned forecasting methods to give the forecast more realistic "peaks and valleys".

To create a seasonality index, you must:

1. Calculate an average for all item history (for all years and periods).
2. Average each period's historical data.
3. Divide each period's average by the overall average.
4. Apply the period index to the existing time series or linear regression forecast.

For example, a snow shovel that we sell has historical quarterly sales, as shown in Table 9.1.

We can create a seasonality index to apply to a "flat" moving average quarterly forecast of 100, for example. To do this, we first calculate an average for each period and then calculate an overall average of 268. From there, we can calculate indices for each quarter by dividing their period averages by the overall average of 268.

If we had a quarterly forecast for next year of 100/quarter, we could apply the seasonality index for each quarter to that forecast. The resulting quarterly forecasts would be: Q1 = 2.07 * 100, or 207 shovels; Q2 = 0.42 * 100, or 42 shovels; Q3 = 0.09 * 100, or 9 shovels; and Q4 = 1.42 * 100, or 142 shovels.

As mentioned previously, seasonality can be natural or induced. In either case, over time, it can change and needs to be recalculated on an ongoing basis.

TABLE 9.1

Seasonality Index Example

Year	Q1	Q2	Q3	Q4	
2010	500	100	25	350	
2011	550	125	15	400	Overall average = 268
2012	625	95	30	325	
2013	550	130	20	450	
Period Average	556	113	23	381	
Index	2.07	0.42	0.09	1.42	

Multiple Regression

When more than one independent variable is going to be used to develop a forecast, linear regression can be extended to multiple regression, which allows for several independent variables (e.g. discounting, promotions, advertising, etc. may all have an impact on sales to one degree or another). The formula for this is: $y = a + b1x1 + b2x2 \ldots$ (similar to the least squares formula, except with multiple independent variables). This is quite complex and is generally done with the help of statistical software.

In the end, you will want to arrive at the best combination of independent variables for the best possible forecast. The statistic mentioned above called r squared, or the coefficient of determination, which is the square of the correlation coefficient mentioned earlier and is a measure of the strength of the correlation between y and the various combination of xs, is calculated. The closer the r squared is to 1, the better the correlation and, hopefully, the more accurate the forecast.

There are many other statistical methods used which range from simple to very complex. The "best in class" methods of forecasting use a blend of qualitative and quantitative methods which include collaboration both internally, with staff from various departments including sales, marketing, and finance, and with customers and suppliers.

Box–Jenkins

The Box–Jenkins model is a forecasting methodology using regression studies on time series data.

The methodology is predicated on the assumption that past occurrences influence future ones. The Box–Jenkins model is best suited for forecasting within time frames of 18 months or less.

It applies autoregressive moving average (ARMA) or autoregressive integrated moving average (ARIMA) models to find the best fit of a time series model to past values of a time series.

Estimations of the parameters of the Box–Jenkins model can be very complicated. Therefore, similarly to other time series regression models, the best results will typically be achieved through the use of programmable software.

Focus Forecasting

Another forecasting technique worth mentioning is "focus forecasting".

It is a forecasting approach that has gained some popularity in business. It was developed by Bernie Smith, who believed that complex statistical methods do not work well for forecasting. He believed that simple rules that have worked well in the past are best used to forecast the future. The idea behind focus forecasting is to test these rules on past data and evaluate how they perform (using another technique referred to as "backwards forecasting"). New rules can be added at any time, and old ones that have not performed well can be eliminated.

Focus forecasting requires a computer simulation program that evaluates the forecast performance of a number of rules on past data. The program keeps track of the rules and evaluates how well they perform. The following are some examples of rules:

- We will sell over the next three months what we sold over the last three months.
- What we sold in a three-month period last year, we will sell in the same three-month period this year.
- We will sell over the next three months 5 percent of what we sold over the last three months.
- We will sell over the next three months 15 percent of what we sold over the same three-month period last year.

These rules use commonsense concepts. In focus forecasting, managers can come up with any new rules that they believe reflect accurate forecasts in their business and then test their value on historical data.

In fact, in a forecasting tool that I developed had some basis on focus forecasting (I called it "best method", using the same backwards forecasting idea), we blended simple time series methods, such as averages and the naive approach, with other methods, such as linear regression, to see which method would give the most accurate forecast for the most recent period of history and used that going forward. It was quite accurate in most cases.

No matter which forecasting process, tools, and methods you use (qualitative, quantitative, blended, consensus, AI-assisted, etc.), it is critical to set reasonable and sometimes aggressive forecast accuracy targets. When exceptions are found, tools such as root cause analysis can be used to try to improve future forecasts.

FORECASTING METRICS

You can't control and improve a process if you don't measure it, and so it is very important to both establish targets and to then track and measure forecast accuracy. There are many ways to establish forecast targets, including historical data, contribution, etc. The one I prefer is the "ABC" method which is a way to classify items based upon their sales velocity or contribution to profits, and can be used not only to set forecasting targets but also in inventory planning and control, which will be discussed in Chapter 11.

To explain the ABC method, one needs to understand a phenomenon known as the "Pareto principle" or the "80/20 rule". It states that a relatively small number of your items generate a fairly large percent of your sales or profits and are referred to as "A" items (e.g. whopper, fries, and Coke are "A" items at Burger King).

In forecasting, these "A" items require more time and effort put into them and typically have better accuracy as a result. The slower movers, known as "B" and "C" items, are somewhat less important, require less forecasting time and effort, and typically have more variability [Myerson, 2014].

Forecast Error Measurement

Forecast accuracy is the difference between what was forecasted for a period and what was actually sold or shipped. It can be measured in whole units or as a percent.

There are a number of methods used to measure and monitor accuracy. The main ones are:

Mean Absolute Deviation (MAD)

Simplistically, the MAD is a way to measure the overall forecast error in units over periods of time.

The actual calculation for the MAD is the sum of the absolute error in units divided by the number of occurrences and is represented as:

$$\frac{\left(\sum |\text{Actual} - \text{Forecast}| \right)}{n}$$

Mean Squared Error (MSE)

The MSE is the average of the squared differences between the forecasted and actual values. Its formula is the sum of the square forecast errors divided by the number of occurrences and represented as:

$$\frac{\sum \left(\text{Forecast Errors} \right)^{2}}{n}$$

Mean Absolute Percent Error (MAPE)

As opposed to the MAD and MSE, which can vary in size based upon the volume sold of an item, the MAPE calculates the absolute percent error. From my experience, this is the most common way for businesses to measure and control forecast accuracy.

Typically, targets are set by ABC code or other methods that highlight relative importance of items with "A" type items generally having a smaller variance as they are major, everyday items and thus more predictable. "C" items, as there are more of them with much smaller volume, tend to be more volatile and thus tend to have greater forecast variance.

The MAPE is calculated as:

$$\frac{\sum \left((100 * |\text{Actual} - \text{Forecast}|) / \text{Actual} \right)}{n}$$

Tracking Signal

Over time, forecasts can tend to get out of control fast. As a result, it is a good idea to utilize what is known as a tracking signal.

The tracking signal is used to determine the larger deviation (both plus and minus) of error in a forecast and is calculated by the following formula:

$$\frac{\text{Acculumated Forecast Errors}}{\text{Mean Absolute Deviation}}$$

Usually, there are upper and lower control limits (UCL and LCL) for the number of MADs that the tracking signal represents. There are no "magic" numbers for the UCLs and LCLs, as they are somewhat subjective, but one should keep in mind that 1 MAD = 0.8 standard deviations.

In a normal distribution, 3 standard deviations (or ±4 MADs) should include 99.9 percent of the occurrences. So, if your tracking signal starts exceeding those levels, it's a good indication that something isn't right.

Before delving into the topic of inventory management in Chapter 11, it is worth briefly discussing order management and customer service, a kind of crossroads between demand and supply, as net inventory requirements are directly impacted by open customer orders and not just forecasts.

ORDER MANAGEMENT AND CUSTOMER SERVICE

Order management refers to the set of activities that occur between the time a company receives an order from the customer and the time a warehouse is notified to ship the goods to fill that order. There is another term, "order fulfillment", which includes the steps involved in receiving, processing, and delivering orders to end customers. In many cases, they are used interchangeably.

The actual time that it takes to perform these activities is often referred to as the "order cycle" or "lead time" (Figure 9.6), and some organizations expand upon this to include customer payment, which is referred to as the "order to cash cycle". So, the shorter the order to cash cycle, the sooner a company gets paid, which is directly impacted by the efficiency of the order management process as well as other functions including inventory planning and warehouse management.

The supply chain and logistics function is a critical part of the marketing mix as it has a significant impact on all four of its components of product, price, promotion, and place. The supply chain provides a place and time

FIGURE 9.6
Customer order cycle.

utility to the customer as provided by the logistics or physical distribution variables of product availability and order cycle time.

Order management or fulfillment and customer service are usually part of supply chain or operations functions, as they are intimately related.

Order management is primarily made up of four stages (Figure 9.7):

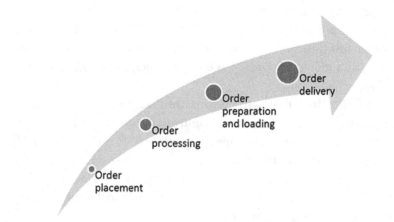

FIGURE 9.7
Order management process.

- Order placement – the series of events that occur between when a customer places or sends an order and the time the seller receives the order. There are a variety of methods of order placement, including in person, mail, telephone, fax, or electronically via EDI or the internet.
- Order processing – the time from when the seller receives an order until an appropriate location (e.g. warehouse) is authorized to fill the order.
- Order preparation and loading – includes all activities from when an appropriate location is authorized to fill the order until goods are loaded aboard an outbound carrier.
- Loading and order delivery – the time from when a carrier picks up the shipment until it is received by the customer. It is important to closely coordinate picking and staging of orders with carrier arrival as docks and yards can get congested very easily, and charges apply when carriers are made to wait too long before loading.

Wrapped around this process is customer service, which has expanded to be known as customer relationship management. CRM refers to focusing on customer requirements and delivering products and services resulting in high levels of customer satisfaction; it also refers to automated transaction and communication applications to support this function (discussed a little in the next chapter, on demand planning technology).

In general, customer service is a means by which companies try to differentiate their product, sustain customer loyalty, increase sales, and improve profitability. Its main elements are price, product quality, and service.

Looking at customer service in terms of its multifunctional dimensions, logistics can provide benefits to the customer in terms of:

- Time – meaning the entire order fulfillment cycle time.
- Dependability – can offer guaranteed fixed delivery times of accurate, undamaged orders.
- Communications – offers ease of order taking, and queries response.
- Flexibility – provides the ability to recognize and respond to a customer's changing needs.

Good customer service extends from before the customer purchases the product to after the purchase transaction has been completed. It can be

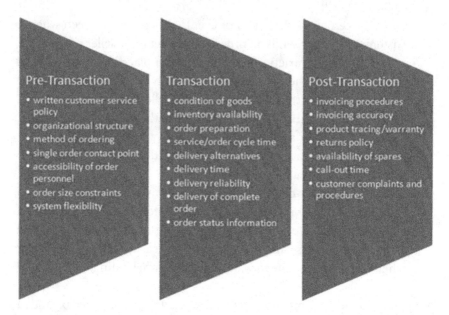

Pre-Transaction
- written customer service policy
- organizational structure
- method of ordering
- single order contact point
- accessibility of order personnel
- order size constraints
- system flexibility

Transaction
- condition of goods
- inventory availability
- order preparation
- service/order cycle time
- delivery alternatives
- delivery time
- delivery reliability
- delivery of complete order
- order status information

Post-Transaction
- invoicing procedures
- invoicing accuracy
- product tracing/warranty
- returns policy
- availability of spares
- call-out time
- customer complaints and procedures

FIGURE 9.8
Components of customer service.

looked at as having three transactional components (Figure 9.8), which include:

1. Pre-transaction elements – customer service factors that arise prior to the actual transaction taking place.
2. Transaction elements – the elements directly related to the physical transaction which are those most commonly concerned with logistics.
3. Post-transaction elements – those elements that occur after the delivery has taken place.

Now that you have a firm grasp of some of the art and science of the demand planning process, we will take a look at the type of technology needed and available to enable the demand planning process.

10

Information Technology in Demand Planning

Technology impacts velocity, accuracy, and efficiency within the supply chain. By implementing new technology, supply chain managers are able to use more data, automation, and other tools to make decisions faster, forecast demand more accurately, and prepare for unexpected events throughout the supply chain.

While hardware such as robotics, RFID, etc. is critical to an integrated, flexible, and real-time supply chain, and is touched on in various places in this book, we will limit this chapter (and supply planning in Chapter 15) to the discussion of information technology that is primarily software related.

DEMAND FORECASTING TECHNOLOGY AND BEST PRACTICES

Computerized forecasting software has been around for a long time. It has evolved from the mainframe to the PC to the web, from installed applications to cloud-based on-demand "software as a service" (SAAS). The systems range from simple spreadsheet calculations to sophisticated packaged software systems utilizing a variety of forecasting methods and are, in some cases, integrated with customers' and suppliers' systems for improved visibility and collaboration. Today, they have even been enhanced with artificial intelligence and machine learning.

Historically, at least in the case of "best of breed" forecasting functionality, forecasting software has been licensed from a separate vendor and integrated

DOI: 10.4324/9781003281078-12

with the accounting or enterprise resource planning software system, and integrated applications are used to manage business and automate back-office functions for all facets of an operation, including product planning, development, finance, human resources, manufacturing processes, sales, and marketing.

More recently, however, through development and acquisition, accounting and ERP vendors are increasingly adding this and other non-traditional functionality to their systems.

Yet, with all of these packaged software options, according to a KPMG advisory global survey of 544 senior executives [KPMG, 2007], nearly all organizations still use spreadsheets for some parts of the process, and similarly, per the Aberdeen Group in 2013, 89 percent of organizations continued to use spreadsheets in the planning, budgeting, and forecasting processes. More worryingly, however, 40 percent of those surveyed rely solely on spreadsheets to produce the forecast. As a result, this leaves major chances for losses in efficiency, accuracy (due to errors), and redundancies in work processes.

However, what the KPMG advisory found that separated the "best in class" from the rest regarding forecasting was that they:

- Tend to take forecasting more seriously, as they hold managers accountable for agreed-upon forecasts, incentivize managers for forecast accuracy, and use the forecast for ongoing performance management.
- Look to enhance quality beyond the basics by incorporating scenario planning and using external market reports and data more often.
- Work harder at it by updating and reviewing forecasts more often and more formally and tend to use packaged forecasting software systems more often rather than just spreadsheets.

FORECASTING TECHNOLOGY OPTIONS AND REQUIREMENTS

Like most technology in the supply chain, there are a range of options when it comes to forecasting demand. They can range from simple

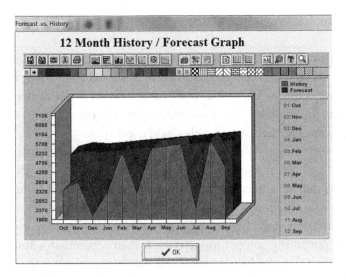

FIGURE 10.1
Demand forecasting item graph example.

spreadsheets, statistical forecasting tools more for analytical use, "point solutions" which allow for the efficient processing of large numbers of items (see example in Figure 10.1) and can be integrated with other more comprehensive ERP applications, to actually being one of many integrated modules in a packaged ERP solution.

There are also installed client–server and desktop solutions as well as SAAS, "on demand" modules, and applications found on the web, also known as "cloud software".

Why Use Forecasting Technology?

From a lean perspective, this type of software attempts to minimize waste by tracking trends that will affect future demand and accomplishes the task by improving the forecasting process in order to eliminate errors or biases in the data and also by reducing data latency, which makes real-time (or, at least, closer to real-time) demand planning possible.

Demand planning tools help an organization to reach two core objectives:

1. Improved demand forecast accuracy.
2. Greater control over demand "shaping" (i.e. influencing of demand to match planned supply).

Demand forecasting systems attempt to accomplish the following:

- Historical analysis – cross-functional or multidimensional statistical and judgment-based forecasting processes that analyze the historical demand for an individual product at various levels of detail (often factoring in broader macro- and micro-economic trends) to deliver an accurate forecast to supply chain executives.
- Data separation – the software gathers a wide range of data to improve past and future demand analysis. Often, the data are filtered and separated by product, customer, seasonal, and market information.
- Demand shaping – the software factors in data that are related to promotions, advertising, planned introductions of new products, and upcoming competitor activity. It then accumulates and displays detailed plans for future marketing campaigns as well as the projected effects on demand and revenue that may occur.
- "What-if" analysis – the software can perform a series of scenarios and simulations based on what-if factors. The results of these what-if simulations can suggest potential deviations from planned demand which can then be communicated to other areas of the supply chain to adjust shipments or production.
- Supply chain communication – demand planning systems are typically integrated with other elements of the supply chain management system to drive and change replenishment scheduling as part of the supply or capacity planning process, preventing excess inventory, reducing inventory carrying costs, and, at the same time, helping to meet targeted customer service levels.

When deciding upon specific forecasting software, you need not only to consider your functional requirements but also to be able to assess the potential system's functionality and its value to the planning process. It also requires an understanding of the efficiency, accuracy, and relevance of the data that are provided, since those data are key to the effectiveness of the system.

When selecting demand planning software, you should consider:

- What specific, detailed data does it collect and interpret?
- How often are the data collected (and how often does the system need to be updated)?

- Will the system be used by itself as more of an analytical tool or be integrated with supply chain planning or a comprehensive SCM system? You must also determine if it is compatible with legacy systems [Harris, 2015].

HOW TECHNOLOGY HELPS THE DEMAND FORECASTING PROCESS

Every enterprise has the need to quickly and accurately anticipate the demand for a product (see lean forecasting discussed later in this chapter) as this ability is essential for every company that intends to be competitive and, ultimately, successful.

Demand forecasting techniques have evolved over the past 30 years or so, as traditional methods of predicting market demand have advanced to newer and better means of understanding customers, their purchasing patterns, motivations, etc.

The introduction and evolution of demand forecasting software have enabled businesses to make accurate demand forecasts at a faster pace, and now, many years after first hearing about it, we finally are seeing the emergence and integration of artificial intelligence and other recent technologies.

Listening to Social Media

Today, social media can be the difference between the success or failure of a business. One post from a significant influencer can generate huge revenue opportunities for your product, and a negative post can severely hurt a business.

A best-practice example of using social media in the forecasting process is by PepsiCo, one of the world's leading beverage manufacturers, which uses social media to sense and predict demand. A 2019 *Martech Zone* article discussed how PepsiCo used econometric demand forecasting with data from unconventional sources, social media included, to identify specific consumer demands [Intuendi, 2020a].

Social media help your business anticipate demand and cope with changes in demand for your product. As a result, social media analytics can help you gather and analyze social media comments on posts mentioning your product, giving you an idea of social media users' attitudes toward your brand, and can help you make adjustments to optimize your supply chain by taking the appropriate course of action in real time.

Improve Demand Forecasting with the IoT

What is known as the internet of things occurs when physical objects that are embedded with sensors, processing ability, software, and other technologies connect and exchange data with other devices and systems over the internet or other communications networks.

Using the IoT as a supplement to demand forecasting is still relatively new but has a lot of potential.

Currently, the IoT plays a large role in managing inventory, including tracking assets and the status and location of inventory.

In terms of forecasting, IoT can help analyze and sense demand as well as shifts in demand by factoring in variables such as seasonal purchases, weather conditions, historical trends, etc. This can enable you to schedule stock purchases on a per need basis, reducing the risk of stocking in excess or too low.

Streamline and Improve Forecasting Processes with AI and ML

Around 2016, companies started to inject AI into the demand forecast picture with probabilistic forecasting. It was a method that combines machine learning with high-dimensional statistics.

AI-assisted demand forecasts are generated in minutes using real-time data, increasing the speed and accuracy of forecasts.

Today, organizations use AI to improve upon popular demand forecast methods, including deep learning and differentiable programming. With AI, companies are now gathering and leveraging business intelligence from an assortment of sources enabling them to create forecasts based on historical data, market trends in the past, social media chatter, and even the weather [Intuendi, 2020b].

In point of fact, using AI and ML to improve demand forecasting is one of the most promising applications of AI for supply chains.

As mentioned in Chapter 9, the technology "learns" from past experience and can analyze the multitude of complex relationships and factors that influence product demand.

However, even today, AI-enabled demand forecasting is still in a relatively early stage of development.

Typical AI-based Forecasting System

A typical process that an AI-based forecasting system uses usually entails the following steps:

1. Connect the data – this involves providing your internal data sources and external data that may be beneficial to the forecast.
2. Select forecast metrics – the customer then selects which metrics to forecast and the time horizon desired.
3. Perform automatic data preparation – historical data are preprocessed using various algorithms to remove factors that aren't relevant to the forecast.
4. Train the machine learning model – the preprocessed data are sent to a variety of algorithms for forecasting and to test the accuracy of each result.
5. Create a customized model – only the most accurate models are used to create a custom model for the forecasts.
6. Review the custom model – frequent reviews of the accuracy of the customized models are conducted, and the previous training steps are repeated if necessary.
7. Generate a forecast – the custom model and the data provided are used to make a real-time forecast, and the results are stored for future use.
8. Consume the forecast insights – forecasts are displayed in dashboards, reports, or alerts so that anyone can make use of them, regardless of their technical expertise [Anodot, 2022].

As a result of the increasing use of AI systems, key questions for supply chain professionals today are "How do the non-traditional methods compare in performance with established forecasting practices" and "To what extent does it affect supply chain efficiency"? A research project at the Malaysia Institute of Supply Chain Innovation (MISI) made this comparison as described below [Feizabadi and Shrivastava, 2018].

Accuracy in Demand

The subject of the research at MISI was a steel-making company that operates globally and offers a wide range of products, such as coated and painted steel coils for roofing applications, produced in a make-to-stock (MTS) manufacturing environment. In this relatively short-term operating mode, demand forecasting has to be accurate at both the product family and individual SKU levels.

So, it is important to know how much to manufacture as precisely as possible, resulting in its interest in improving the demand forecasts that drive production.

Traditional Solution Drawbacks

The company was using two traditional time series forecasting methods, the Holt–Winter method and the damped trend method of exponential smoothing to generate monthly product demand forecasts. A limitation of using these common methods is that they account for a small range of demand-influencing factors such as seasonality. In reality, demand moves up and down in response to market and macro-economic forces.

As a result, the limitations cause traditional solutions to produce poor forecasts, which in their case is reflected in the company's forecast accuracy with a mean absolute percentage error (i.e. MAPE) ranging from 25 to 71 percent.

Demand Uncertainty and Existing Method Forecast Performance

This also highlights the reasons why the company is focused on improving its demand forecasting performance in its retail market segment.

Retail is the largest segment, with 40 percent of total volume sales and with significant volatility compared with their project market segment which has demand driven by large construction projects that are visible years in advance and have predictable demand.

In addition to being the company's fastest-growing market segment, retail also displays significant volatility and demand forecasting error.

Knowledge Gaps Filled by Machine Learning

Machine learning-based forecasting could help the company address these challenges and improve both supply chain efficiency and more accurate customer forecasts as these non-traditional solutions combine AI learning algorithms with big data to analyze an unlimited number of causal factors simultaneously. Also, by learning from data on past and current performances, AI-enabled approaches continuously refine and improve the demand forecasting process.

However, these applications are relatively new, and more information on how they perform in practice is needed. Even though the technology has been applied in various areas of the supply chain such as transportation management, sourcing, and demand forecasting, the results, at least in forecasting, are inconsistent, as some have concluded that traditional demand forecasting methods such as exponential smoothing can yield results that are at least comparable with results when using machine learning.

This has led to research on hybrid solutions that combine traditional and non-traditional methods. Research has looked at how a steel manufacturer might deploy the technology, focusing on two common machine learning techniques: ARIMAX, which bundles time series and causal factors, and neural networks (NNs), which are based on the architecture of the human brain and comprise many densely interconnected processing nodes.

The performance of these methods was compared with the two traditional solutions used currently to help the manufacturer decide how it might adopt machine learning in its demand forecasting process.

Food for Thought

The comparison shows that a machine learning approach to demand forecasting that captures a complex mix of historical data and market variables can perform better than traditional time series and linear models for the functional products studied, as the accuracy of demand forecasts improved by around 6.4 percent on average when machine learning technology was applied.

The project also generated some general observations about the use of machine learning in demand forecasting; for example, applying the technology can mitigate the bullwhip effect to some degree, especially in industries such as steel manufacturing where demand is not seasonal, although a more realistic approach to this issue is to improve collaboration and communication across the supply chain.

The research offers some useful insights for practitioners who may be considering the use of AI-enabled demand forecasting such as developing an algorithm that utilizes NN-based demand forecasting in general and the ARIMAX model when the forecast strays beyond a certain predetermined threshold.

The ARIMAX technique turned out to be better at predicting peaks in demand, while the NN method generated more "smoothed" and more accurate predictions. So, a hybrid solution can yield better forecasts in terms of reduced MAPEs at an aggregate level.

The findings are likely not applicable in markets such as fast fashion and consumer electronics where product life cycles are short and demand patterns are erratic. However, as these types of markets rely much more on expert opinion to drive demand predictions, more research is required to help understand how such decisions can be "learned" by AI-based solutions and incorporated into forecasts.

A LEAN APPROACH TO FORECASTING

While technology can be a true enabler of a lean and agile supply chain, overlaying a bad forecasting process with technology can lead to no improvement or even disaster. So, it is worth discussing here that forecasting, perhaps more than other administrative processes, can drive waste throughout an organization in the short, medium, and long term, if it is not lean and efficient.

For example:

- Strategically – its accuracy (or inaccuracy) can wreak havoc on a supply chain network in terms of locations, functions, layouts, inventory and operating costs, and, ultimately, customer service levels.

- Tactically – it can affect budgeting and production and deployment planning.
- Operationally – it affects purchasing, job scheduling, workforce levels, job assignments, and production levels.

Ultimately, forecast inaccuracy (at any level), can lead to either: (1) waste to the customer in terms of short, late, or no delivery (and, hence, lost sales); (2) larger amounts of safety stock (and costs) to compensate for forecast inaccuracy; or (3) potentially any of the other eight wastes, in addition to excess inventory, as described in Chapter 3 of this book.

The first step in lean forecasting is to have a forecasting process in place.

To review, the typical steps found in a best-practice forecasting process are (as previously discussed in Chapter 9):

1. Determine the use of the forecast.
2. Select the items to be forecasted.
3. Determine the time horizon of the forecast.
4. Select the forecasting model(s).
5. Gather the data needed to make the forecast.
6. Make or generate the forecast.
7. Validate and implement results.

Assuming that is the case, you need to look for opportunities to improve the process. It should focus on minimizing the use of company resources to maximize customer value by creating meaningful, accurate forecasts as efficiently as possible.

Lean Forecasting Process

Kahn and Mello [*Journal of Business Forecasting*, 2004–05] arrived at five steps to lean forecasting:

1. Specify value that channel partners get from forecasting. Primarily, this involves getting the product delivered to them at the right time and price and in the right place and quantity, as well as helping to reduce their supply chain costs through reduced inventory.
2. Identify the value stream and focus on eliminating waste such as excess data collection and reporting, long queue times for information,

overanalysis of data, too many or the wrong people involved in the forecasting process, and high system costs.

3. Create flow especially by reducing the time between receiving information and making decisions, by focusing on reducing the time between creating a baseline forecast, making adjustments, and final approval.
4. Facilitate pull by creating a procedure to initiate when a forecast should be made. Pull can also refer to which items will be forecasted and which will be managed more through inventory control policies such as relying more on reorder points with safety stock or kanbans.
5. Strive for perfection to create the most meaningful forecasts from the customer perspective.

They also pointed out a framework of focal elements to assist in lean forecasting initiatives. The elements are to:

1. Clarify the forecasting objective and the value that customers obtain from the process.
2. Measure the value the customer receives from a leaner forecasting process.
3. Identify the flow behind the delivery of value to the customer.
4. Determine the pull of the elements for efficiency.
5. Establish a continuous improvement process that serves customers best.

So, what if you don't have a good forecasting process in place?

According to an SAS white paper entitled "The Lean Approach to Business Forecasting" [SAS, 2012], the lean approach to forecasting is motivated by the fact that many existing forecasting process activities are not adding value. The failure can be due to failed systems, flawed forecasting models, or inadequate organization processes, often due to internal politics and management opinions.

A lean approach consists of gathering data, conducting analysis to add value, communicating the results to management, and streamlining and improving the overall forecasting process.

As the objective is to eliminate non-value-added processes or waste, you need to identify where you are spending resources in the existing process. Figure 10.2 is a typical generic forecasting process found in goods or service industries.

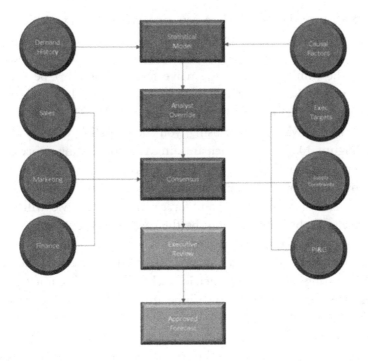

FIGURE 10.2
Typical forecasting process (goods or service industry).

Demand history and other causal variables are fed into statistical models to create an initial statistical forecast.

A forecast analyst may then enter a manual override based upon knowledge of the market and products or information from sources such as sales and customers. Then, the forecast, aggregated by family or class of products or services, is discussed in a consensus, collaborative sales, and operations planning process (the topic of Chapter 12).

As part of the consensus process, members of various functions such as marketing, sales, finance and accounting, supply chain and logistics, etc. give their input to the forecasts. This is not limited to the internal supply chain. Many companies have programs with larger customers such as collaborative planning, forecasting, and replenishment, part of which includes collaboration on forecasts with major customers, as was covered in Chapter 8.

A last step in the process, after supply constraints have been considered, is the executive approval of the forecast and subsequent supply requirements.

The SAS Institute (SAS) white paper suggests starting with a "naive" forecast, which takes little effort and basically assumes that actual demand for an item the previous month will be the forecast for the upcoming period. The thinking is that the naive forecast shouldn't be nearly as good as your existing fairly elaborate process. If it is, then something is extremely wrong with your current process.

Whatever software you are using, you should gather data on all steps (from Figure 10.2) and participants in your forecasting process. It is human nature to assume that, by applying more sophisticated forecasting methods, developing a more elaborate process, and including more management participation in our forecasting process, we will achieve more accuracy, but this may not be the case, and to determine that we require supporting data and analysis.

SAS suggests using a forecast value-added metric to measure the change in a forecasting performance metric (such as forecast accuracy, positive or negative bias, or MAPE) that can be attributed to a particular step or participant in the forecasting process.

The forecast value-added metric allows you to see if each additive change has improved accuracy through added effort (i.e. demand history → statistical model → statistical forecast → management override) by comparing the results of each process activity with the results that would have been achieved without doing the activity.

Forecast accuracy can't be unrealistic, as perfection is seldom achieved, because unpredictable outside factors may impact the forecast. Other realities of forecasting include that product family and aggregated forecasts are more accurate than individual product forecasts, and, the further out the time horizon is, the harder it is to forecast, compared with forecasting tomorrow's demand. It's really more about minimizing variance by setting meaningful targets and putting the appropriate time and number of resources into the development of the forecasts.

As touched on earlier, one fairly common way to do this is using the Pareto principle or 80/20 rule, which states that a fairly small number of items generate the majority of your revenue or profits. These fast-moving products are considered "A" items, and, therefore, considerable effort should be invested in determining their forecasts, with tighter (i.e. smaller) variance targets. The other items ("B" and especially "C" items, of which there are typically many and which usually generate a much smaller amount of revenue or profits) generally have less accurate forecasts and, as they don't contribute that much to the bottom line, deserve less attention in the forecasting process.

Targets may also be tied to where an item is in its product life cycle (i.e. introduction, growth, maturity, or decline). Typically, new or declining items are more volatile (and rely more on "qualitative" approaches to forecasting) than growth or mature items, which tend to rely more on statistics for forecasting demand.

PLAN AND DELIVER

Having had many years of experience in forecasting for companies such as Unilever and Arm & Hammer, as well as consulting and training with many more organizations, I have come to appreciate the "art and science" of the forecasting process, the need to have it integrated internally and externally, as well as how much the "right" technology can help improve the process.

A study by the Aberdeen Group, "The Best-in-Class Leverage Forecast Accuracy across the Organization", documents that those companies that integrate demand planning as part of a larger S&OP process can get even more benefits than the 18 percent improved forecast accuracy at the product family level as documented in a previous survey.

For those of you not familiar with S&OP (to be covered in detail in Chapter 12), it is a process that gives management the ability to strategically direct its business to achieve a competitive advantage on a continuous basis. The S&OP planning process includes an updated, collaborative forecast that leads to a sales plan, production plan, inventory plan, customer lead time (backlog) plan, new product development plan, strategic initiative plan, and resulting financial plan. Ultimately, S&OP is a set of decision-making processes to balance demand and supply, to integrate financial planning and operational planning, and to link high-level strategic plans with day-to-day operations.

The added benefits beyond improved forecast accuracy keyed on the best-in-class companies' ability to leverage that advantage all the way through their supply chain processes as well as the use of technology to ensure its success. The Aberdeen Group found the following key success factors:

Executive sponsorship is critical – the best in class are 25 percent more likely to have executive sponsorship.

Infrastructure in place – the most successful had a supporting cast framework for the demand planning process including dedicated S&OP support and best-in-class forecasting systems that integrate with their ERP systems.

Collaboration and integration are critical – the best in class have master scheduling systems in place that are integrated with suppliers (and I would hope, their demand planning systems are integrated with customers as well!).

Technological investments – these are seen at all levels of the S&OP process including forecasting, scheduling, and collaboration [Myerson, 2014].

ORDER MANAGEMENT AND CUSTOMER RELATIONSHIP SYSTEMS

As mentioned in Chapter 9, order management and customer relationship management are part of the demand management process. Not surprisingly, there are systems for these two critical processes.

An order management system (OMS) is a computer software system used in many industries for order entry and processing. In most cases, it is part of a larger ERP or accounting system (see Figure 10.3).

Order Management Systems

OMS applications manage processes including order entry, customer credit validation, pricing, promotions, inventory allocation, invoice generation, sales commissions, and sales history.

A distributed order management (DOM) system is different from an OMS in that it manages the assignment of orders across a network of multiple production, distribution, and/or retail locations to ensure that logistics costs and/or customer service levels are optimized.

An OMS is usually deployed as part of an enterprise application such an ERP system as its sales engine is integrated with the organization's inventory, procurement, and financial systems.

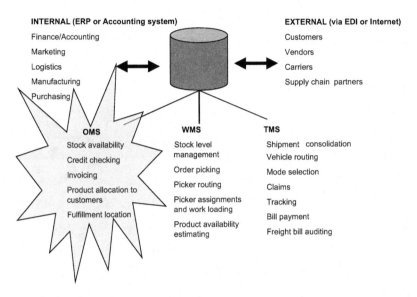

FIGURE 10.3
Order management system (OMS).

Customer Relationship Management Systems

A CRM system manages a company's interactions with current and future customers and involves using technology to organize, automate, and synchronize sales, marketing, customer service, and technical support. This includes the management of business contacts, clients, contract wins, and sales leads within the sales function, sometimes referred to as "sales force automation" (SFA) software.

Perhaps the biggest benefit to most businesses when moving to a CRM system comes from having all their business data stored in and accessed from a single location, whereas, before CRM systems, customer data were spread out over office productivity suite documents, email systems, mobile phone data, and even note cards and Rolodex™ entries.

To conclude, I think that the Aberdeen Group's "The Best-in-Class Leverage Forecast Accuracy across the Organization" survey reinforces the idea that, in order to attain an overall competitive advantage (and to ensure lean and agile processes), it is important not only to have a solid forecasting process in place, enabled by the right technology, but also to have it integrated with the supply side through robust "outside-in" S&OP and solid production and inventory planning processes. Both of these will be covered in the next two chapters, in the supply-side planning section.

Section III

Supply-Side Planning

11

Supply Chain (Independent Demand) Inventory Management and Control

In most goods and many service organizations, such as restaurants, after arriving at a short-to-medium-term forecast, we need to figure out *how much* we want to produce or purchase and *when* to order or produce it (Figure 11.1).

This decision is reached by determining the current inventory position which measures an SKU's ability to satisfy future demand. The current inventory position includes scheduled receipts, which are production (or purchase) orders that have been placed but have not yet been received, plus on-hand inventory (note that a somewhat similar term used for different purposes, "available to promise", or ATP, refers to the projected amount of inventory a business has in stock, ready to sell and not yet allocated for existing customer orders).

The current inventory position is then netted against actual and forecasted demand to create future period (i.e. day, week, month, etc.) inventory requirements, commonly known as "planned orders". A planned order is the same as a planned receipt with the lead time offset, which eventually becomes a scheduled receipt. These planned orders/receipts are then refined using a variety of methods discussed later in this chapter to meet facility SKU capacity, cost, service, and lead time constraints.

Unconstrained SKU requirements are further solidified through a process known as aggregate planning, covered in the next chapter, which considers various material, manpower, and machine supply constraints, at a less granular level, needed to meet aggregate demand at the lowest total cost.

DOI: 10.4324/9781003281078-14

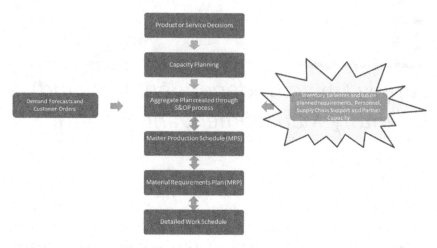

FIGURE 11.1
Typical planning and scheduling process.

INDEPENDENT VS. DEPENDENT DEMAND INVENTORY

There are two general categories of inventory, "independent" and "dependent" demand inventory. In this chapter, we will be discussing independent demand inventory primarily.

Dependent demand inventory is represented by an item the demand for which is linked directly to the demand or production level of another item. Dependent demand items, and the systems for managing them, are typically used in manufacturing. An example of dependent demand inventory requirements would be tires that go on a bike: the production of one bicycle would require two tires of a specific size, and thus the demand for the tires is dependent on the number of bicycles being produced. Material requirement planning (MRP) systems, to be covered in Chapter 13, are planning mechanisms to determine requirements for dependent demand.

By independent demand inventory, on the other hand, we are referring to inventory requirements for "finished goods", which are products ready for the consumer to purchase and use. Finished goods do not just exist in a retail store displayed as individual items, but start their journey upstream in the supply chain after production and are typically packed in groups in corrugated containers (e.g. 12 bottles per container) as that is more economical for warehouse storage and shipping purposes than storing and shipping one unit of an item.

Manufacturer   Wholesaler   Retailer/e-tailer   Consumer

FIGURE 11.2
Channels of distribution.

Prior to ending up in the consumer's hands, finished goods travel through a company's distribution channel, which typically consists of manufacturers, distributors or wholesalers, and retailers/e-tailers (Figure 11.2).

A manufacturer produces in lots or batches to gain economies of scale (i.e. producing in larger quantities to spread fixed costs over many units so that the cost per unit is lower). Unless it is large enough – like Target or Walmart– to buy in bulk direct from the manufacturers, a retailer buys from wholesalers or distributors in smaller quantities.

As product makes its way through the supply chain, both value and cost are added to product.

The value-adding feature of the supply chain was discussed in Chapter 2 when describing value as a utility.

In Chapter 6, we discussed "lean" concepts for reducing non-value-added activities which have a major impact on cost and efficiency as well. Suffice it to say, all forms of inventory have cost components, which we will cover shortly.

First, it is important to define the main types of inventory.

TYPES OF INVENTORY

There are four major types of inventory. They are:

1. Raw materials and components – inventory is usually classified as raw materials if the organization has purchased them from an outside company or if they are used to make components. This category also includes goods used in the manufacturing process, such as components used to assemble a finished product.
2. Work in process (WIP) – these are materials and parts that have been partially transformed from raw materials but are not yet finished

goods and can include partially assembled items that are waiting to be completed.

3. Finished goods – products that are ready to be shipped directly to customers, including wholesalers and retailers. (Note that one company's finished goods maybe be another's raw material or component, as in the case of a business-to-business, B2B, relationship.)

4. Maintenance, repair, and operations (MRO) – these are the items a business needs in order to operate, such as office equipment, packing boxes, and tools and parts to repair equipment.

COSTS OF INVENTORY

As inventory works its way from raw material to finished goods, value is added as well as cost. As it's an asset, inventory not only shows up on a financial balance sheet but also goes straight to the bottom line on income statements through components of what is known as "holding" or "carrying" costs.

Carrying or Holding Costs

Whether inventory is purchased or produced, there are costs involved in the acquisition and holding of it. The components of holding costs are:

- **Capital or opportunity cost** (depending on current interest rates, can range from 5 to 25 percent) – money either has to be borrowed, in which case interest must be paid, or is capital from internal sources which has an "opportunity cost" associated with it (i.e. the money would generate a return if invested in other things, such as capital equipment).
- **Physical space occupied by the inventory** (3–10 percent) – includes building rent or depreciation, utility costs, insurance, taxes, etc.
- **Handling of inventory** (4–10 percent) – includes labor cost such as receiving, warehousing, and security, and material handling costs, which include equipment lease or depreciation, power, and operating costs.

- **Pilferage, scrap, deterioration, and obsolescence** (2–5 percent) – the longer inventory sits around, the more (usually bad) things can happen to it.

In total, holding costs can range from 15 to 40 percent, and, as you can see, many of the costs are ongoing operating expenses which can have a significant impact on a business's profitability.

In addition to holding costs, there are two other major costs associated with inventory: ordering and setup costs.

Ordering Costs

When placing an order to purchase additional inventory, there are both fixed and variable costs involved.

Fixed costs are incurred no matter what and include the cost for the facility, computer system, etc.

Variable costs associated with purchase orders include preparing a purchase request, creating the purchase order itself, reviewing inventory levels, and receiving and checking items as they are received from the vendor, and the costs to prepare and process payments to the vendor when the invoice is received.

Many businesses tend to ignore these costs, especially the variable ones, but those who do take them into account calculate them to be in the range of $50–150 per order.

Setup Costs

If you are a manufacturer as opposed to a wholesaler or retailer, then there are costs associated with changing production over known as "setup", which includes labor and parts as well as downtime.

It should be noted that a full "changeover" includes more than just the equipment changeover and is thought of in lean terms as "last good piece to first, next good piece", which we will discuss later in the book.

As with ordering costs, setup costs involve both fixed and variable costs. The fixed costs of setups include the capital equipment used in changing over the production line used for the old items for the new items.

The variable costs include the employee costs for any consumable material used in the teardown and setup. The longer the setup takes, the greater the variable costs.

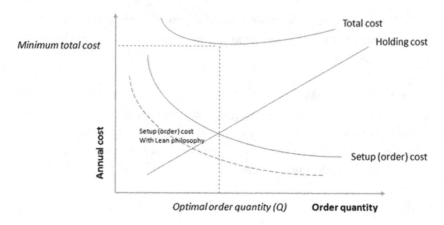

FIGURE 11.3
Holding vs. setup/order cost trade-off.

Total Cost Minimized

The goal is to minimize total costs. Graphically, that occurs at the intersection of holding costs, which go up as lot size quantities increase, and setup costs, which go down as the number of orders/setups decrease (see Figure 11.3). So, in effect, holding and setup costs are inverse, resulting in a trade-off between the two of them. The point where those costs intersect is where total costs are minimized and it is calculated by the simple economic order quantity (EOQ) inventory model.

As was mentioned earlier, it should be noted that there is a lot of pressure to lower inventory costs in an organization. As a result, this pressure ends up falling on the shoulders of the supply chain organization to a great degree. We discussed procurement tactics to minimize some of these costs in Chapter 7, but ultimately, process improvement techniques such as lean (Chapter 6) need to be utilized to effectively create a "paradigm shift" of sorts, as shown in Figure 11.3.

ECONOMIC ORDER QUANTITY MODEL

The order quantity that minimizes total inventory costs by optimizing the trade-offs between holding and ordering costs is known as the EOQ. It is one of the most common inventory techniques used to answer the "how much" question.

The EOQ has some assumptions. They are:

1. The ordering cost is constant.
2. The rate of demand is known and spread evenly.
3. The lead time is known and fixed.
4. The purchase price of the item is constant.
5. The replenishment is made instantaneously, and the entire order is delivered at one time.

These assumptions can be visualized in terms of inventory usage over time, as seen in Figure 11.4, which has come to be known as the "saw tooth model" for obvious reasons.

There are actually three basic EOQ models; we will mainly discuss the first, known as the basic or simple EOQ model.

The other two are the:

1. Production order quantity model – as opposed to the basic EOQ model, the production quantity model assumes that materials produced are used immediately and, as a result, lowers holding costs (i.e. no instant receipt as in the basic model). As a result, this model takes into account daily production and demand rates.
2. Quantity discount model – this is a version of the simple EOQ where pricing discounts are factored into the model based upon reaching certain minimum purchase quantities. This then compares the effect of buying more than perhaps is needed but at a lower price, which

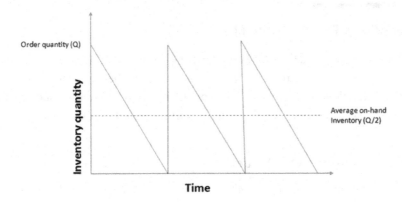

FIGURE 11.4
Sawtooth model.

may offset the impact on holding costs which, in part, are based upon the price of the product, as we shall see in the basic EOQ model.

Basic EOQ Calculation

In order to calculate the EOQ as well as annual setup, holding, and total inventory costs, we need the following information:

Q = optimal number of pieces per order (EOQ)
D = annual demand in units for the inventory item
S = setup or ordering cost for each order
H = holding or carrying cost per unit per year

Once we have that information, we can solve for:

Annual setup costs = (number of orders placed per year) * (setup or order cost per order) or (D/Q) * S
Annual holding cost = (average inventory level) * (holding cost per unit per year) or (Q/2) * H
Total annual cost = setup cost + holding cost or (D/Q) * S + (Q/2) * H

$$\text{Economic Order Quantity (EOQ)} = \sqrt{\frac{2DS}{H}}$$

REORDER POINT MODELS

Now that we've used the EOQ to determine "how much" we need, the next question is "when" to replenish, also referred to as the "reorder point".

Basically, there are two types of models that are commonly used in this regard: fixed quantity ("Q") models and fixed period ("P") models.

Fixed Quantity ("Q") Model

The fixed quantity, or "Q", model has a reorder point (ROP) that is based upon inventory reaching a specific quantity (Q), at which point inventory is replenished based upon the calculated EOQ (Figure 11.5).

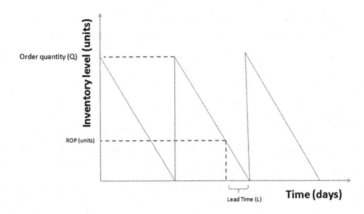

FIGURE 11.5
Fixed quantity (Q) ROP model.

The calculation for the ROP = demand per day × lead time for a new order (in days), or d × L.

In a simple example, if our demand is 10 units per day and our replenishment lead time is 3 days, our ROP would be 30 units (i.e. 10 units × 3 days).

Min/Max and Par Methods

Min/max ordering is a specific generic example of this approach. When the inventory level of an item goes down to a prespecified minimum level (sometimes arbitrary, sometimes calculated using the ROP calculation described above), an EOQ is ordered to replenish the system (or, in some cases, rather than an EOQ, reorder quantity can simply be the difference between an arbitrary maximum and the quantity on hand).

Another twist on this concept is what is known as "par" inventory. This is a method of inventory tracking primarily used by restaurants. Decision-makers will establish a "par", a minimum amount of supply required in-store after each food inventory delivery.

Standard par is the amount you expect to have in-house on a given day, and so pars can and do change according to factors such as seasonality, day of the week, weather, parties, events, and more.

When calculating, they take into account regular stock usage between deliveries and any other emergency stock requirement, to plan when and how much to order.

The "simple" EOQ combined with an (Q) ROP model assumes that demand and lead time are constant, which does not reflect reality. So, typically, extra "buffer" inventory is included in this calculation to compensate for this variability, which is known as "safety stock".

Safety Stock

There are a variety of ways to calculate required safety stock. Many are "rule of thumb", and some are statistically based.

In general, the safety stock quantity that is arrived at is "additive" in nature, and thus the ROP calculation becomes: $d \times L + ss$.

Probabilistic Safety Stock

The idea behind a probabilistic safety stock calculation is that we would like to keep a certain quantity of safety stock to meet a desired service level to compensate for demand variability. If we assume a normal distribution, we can assign a service (or confidence) level as meeting $\times$ percent of demand during the lead time (Figure 11.6).

To calculate this, we can associate the number of standard deviations around the mean with a confidence level (defined as the number of standard deviations extending from the mean of a normal distribution required to contain $\times$ percent of the area), which is contained in a

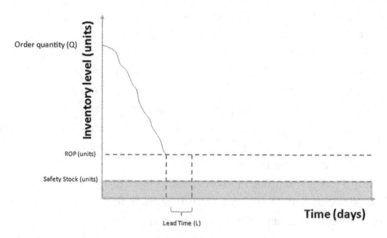

FIGURE 11.6
ROP with probabilistic safety stock model.

commonly available standard normal (Z) table (see some commonly used samples in the table below).

Z	Confidence Level
1.0	85%
1.3	90%
1.6	95%
3.0	99%

To use this method, we also need to calculate the mean and standard deviation of demand for our item, as demand is variable in this case.

Let's take an example where we have a mean demand of 100 units per day, a one-day lead time, a standard deviation during lead time of 15 units, and a desired service level of 99 percent (Z = 3.0).

In this type of calculation, the reorder point is the expected demand during lead time plus safety stock.

So, in our example, the ROP with safety stock calculation would then be: $100 + (3.0 \times 15)$ or 145 units.

While this model considers demand variability during lead time only, there are also other models that compensate for:

- Variable demand with constant lead time.
- Variable lead time with constant demand.
- Variable lead time and demand.

Rule of Thumb Safety Stock Calculations

Besides probabilistic safety stock models, some in industry prefer to use "rule of thumb" models instead (which are sometimes referred to as "safety time", as they are expressed in days of supply), which, while perhaps not as scientific, are easier to understand and calculate. Some "rule of thumb" examples include:

1. Half of demand during lead time – if demand is 10 units per day, and replenishment lead time is 3 days, then the calculated safety stock would be 15 units (i.e. $(10 * 3)/2$).
2. Maximum sales less average sales – provides coverage on the "upside" for the occasional large oversell.

3. Statistical safety stock converted to days (i.e. "safety time") – uses the safety stock probabilistic models' unit calculation above converted to a days of supply inventory target.

Fixed Period ("P") Model

The use of "periods of supply" targets (aka "safety time") such as in the third example above can be advantageous when you tend to have seasonality with your products, which is one of the main features of fixed period or P models (Figure 11.7).

In this type of model, inventory is "continuously" monitored. Typically, faster-moving items are reviewed more often, and slower movers are reviewed less often.

As opposed to an ROP quantity, individual SKU inventory targets (usually in terms of periods of supply) are the trigger point for replenishment.

Fixed period models work well where vendors make routine visits to customers and take orders for their complete line of products, or when it is beneficial to combine orders to save on transportation costs, such as shipments to a distribution center. A tool known as distribution requirements planning (DRP), which enables the user to set inventory control parameters such as safety stock and calculate the time-phased

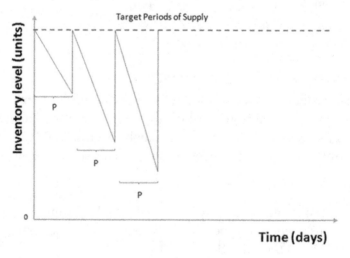

FIGURE 11.7
Fixed period (P) ROP model.

inventory requirements and will be discussed later, is commonly used in the case of managing a network of distribution centers.

Single Period Model

A single period model is used by companies that order seasonal or one-time items. The product typically has no value after the time it is needed, such as a newspaper or baked goods. There are costs to ordering both too much and too little, and the company's managers must try to get the order right the first time to minimize the chance of loss.

A probabilistic way of looking at this is most helpful. We do this by estimating both the cost of a shortage (sales price/unit – cost/unit) and of an overage (cost/unit – scrap value/unit).

We can then determine a service level (i.e. probability of not stocking out) by dividing the cost of shortage by the combined cost of shortage and overage.

The calculated service level percentage can then determine a reorder quantity using the same method as was outlined for the (Q) ROP model.

ABC METHOD OF INVENTORY PLANNING AND CONTROL

Many companies treat inventory planning and control with a "broad brush" when, in fact, they should treat items, or least classes of items, differently. A method used in many inventory systems to stratify or classify items is called ABC analysis.

ABC analysis is based upon the Pareto principle or "80/20" rule, which states that a relatively small number of items typically generate a large percentage of sales or profits (e.g. Burger King's Whopper, fries and Coke vs. everything else; Figure 11.8).

So, in terms of inventory planning, the "A" items, as they are the biggest sellers, have a relatively small days of supply inventory target as a result of their high volume and inherently better forecast accuracy, as well as the fact that they are manufactured or ordered more frequently. "C" items typically sell in small amounts and are more volatile, and so their

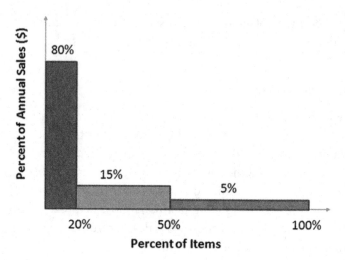

FIGURE 11.8
Pareto principle or 80/20 rule.

inventory target is usually many days of supply of inventory, which might not really amount to much anyway as they are small sellers.

From an inventory control aspect, the more important A items should have tighter physical inventory control, and the accuracy of inventory records for them should be verified more frequently.

Realities of ABC Classification

A couple of other thoughts as to the use of ABC analysis in regard to inventory are as follows:

- It's not necessarily a "volume thing" – it's best to use sales (or cost) dollars or margin vs. units when determining ABC codes, as you may sell a high volume of small, inexpensive parts and fewer units of much more expensive items. If you used units in that case, the high-volume inexpensive items would be given A codes, which is the reverse of what you would want to happen.
- It's not always exactly the "80/20" rule – it's somewhat subjective as to the cutoffs for the assignments of A, B, and C codes, although it's usually not hard to determine the best cutoff from A to B etc.
- An A is not always an A – when you have multiple locations (retail, warehouse, etc) that stock the same item, it's best to run the ABC analysis by location.

- History vs. forecast for ABC analysis – history or forecasts can be used to determine ABC codes. Again, it's somewhat subjective, but, if the items have history, it's usually best to use that (although don't go too far back, as a B can become an A, and vice versa), and, for new items, you may be forced to use a forecast, at least for the time being.

Other Uses for ABC Classification

Besides ABC classification's application in forecasting and inventory planning and control, it is also a useful tool for:

- SKU rationalization – an analysis whereby ABC codes are assigned to determine candidates to be discontinued, scrapped, written off, or sold at a large discount.
- Quality control – Pareto charts are one of the tools of quality and are used to analyze quality issues where resources are limited and there are a variety of quality issues found that need to be resolved.

INVENTORY CONTROL AND ACCURACY

Think of an inventory system in business as being similar to your checking account where you try to maintain a "perpetual" inventory of your money in a checkbook. Once a month, you get a statement of the "physical" count of your money and then reconcile the two. If there is a discrepancy of any significant size, you have to investigate, find out the reason, and make the adjustment to your checkbook.

Similarly, businesses usually have a software system that keeps a perpetual count of inventory in their factory, warehouse, or store (believe it or not, some still do this manually). Similarly to your checking account, system inventory counts can become inaccurate owing to inadequate procedures, lost paperwork, and lack of training.

I'm sure we've all gone into a store at one time or another and found the item you are looking for is out of stock, despite the employee telling you that the system shows there are plenty in inventory at that location.

It is also critical to manufacturing and sales that inventory counts are accurate in terms of incoming and outgoing record-keeping and security.

To ensure system accuracy, historically, once per year (or more often) companies would perform a "physical inventory" count where everything stops for two to three days or more (i.e. nothing comes in and nothing goes out) while employees (usually from another location, or temporary workers) go out and physically count the inventory. This is usually done with what is known as a "blind count", where a person is sent out without knowing the current count and return their count, and someone else then reconciles the system's perpetual count to the physical count. If it's off, a second person may be sent out to do a "double blind count".

Cycle Counting

In recent years, the concept of cycle counting has taken hold. Cycle counts use ABC codes to determine when items should be counted and what the target level of accuracy should be (also referred to as the "ranking method" of cycle counting). As there are fewer, higher-volume/profit A items, they should be "cycled" through more often with extremely high accuracy targets. Cycle counting has the added benefit of not shutting the entire operation down, unlike physical inventory counts.

Table 11.1 shows an example of a cycle counting schedule.

Other benefits of cycle counting include:

- It is less disruptive to daily operations as it is performed during regular hours with "business as usual".
- It provides an ongoing measure of inventory accuracy and procedure execution (requiring less safety stock as a result).
- Accuracy issues are corrected on a timelier basis than with an annual physical inventory.
- It is tailored to focus on items with higher value or higher movement volume, or that are critical to business processes.

TABLE 11.1

Cycle Count Example

Item Class	Number of Items/Class	Cycle Count Policy	Accuracy Target	Number of Items Counted/Day
A	400	Every 20 working days	99%	400/20 = 20
B	1,000	Every 60 working days	96%	1,000/60 = 17
C	4,000	Every 120 working days	90%	4,000/120 = 33

- Trained cycle counters perform the work and usually report to an inventory control manager.
- Root cause analysis is used to ensure that, once counts are corrected in the system, they don't keep occurring. One method is to determine the cause of the discrepancy and then take counts daily for that item until there are no issues.

Another method of cycle counting is the geographic method. In this method of cycle counting, you start at one end of your facility and count a certain number of products each day until you reach the other end of your the building. In this method, you end up counting all of your items an equal number of times per year.

While most companies these days do some take on cycle counting, there are some who still do an annual count (or more often), usually at the insistence of the company's auditor for public financial reporting requirements.

KEY METRICS

There are a number of metrics that are important to inventory. The most commonly used is inventory turnover. This reflects the velocity at which inventory is flowing through your business and is used both as a budgetary and planning target and benchmark against best-in-class companies for all forms of inventory. The calculation for inventory turnover is: cost of goods sold/current inventory investment, where inventory investment can be represented a number of ways, including the average of several periods (i.e. (beginning plus ending inventory)/2) or current on-hand inventory.

For example, if we have $100 million in sales, with a cost of goods sold of $50 million, and currently have $20 million invested in finished goods inventory, we "turn" our inventory five times per year. This may be good or bad, and that is where benchmarking comes in. If we have a low-cost strategy, and the best in class in our industry turn their inventory ten times per year, we have to attempt to turn our inventory faster. We will look at ways to do that when we discuss lean thinking later in this book.

A high inventory turnover reflects faster-moving inventory and, thus, lower holding or carrying costs. The inverse of this, which is commonly used as a target for production and deployment planning, is "periods of supply" (POS), which can be stated in days, weeks, or months of supply. In the example above, where our $20 million in finished goods inventory is turned five times per year, we translate that to an average of 2.4 months of supply on-hand (i.e. 12 months/5 turns). Again, depending on our POS target, that may be good or bad for our business.

In many cases, a true "depletion" formula is used for POS instead, where current on-hand inventory is run out against future requirements in order to catch peaks and valleys in demand (i.e. a month of supply for an item may be 100 units in the winter and 1,000 units in the summer). This is more accurate, but harder to calculate manually.

There are many other relevant measures used as well, such as "assets committed to inventory" (total inventory investment as a percentage of total assets), "current ratio" (current assets divided by current liabilities), "quick ratio" (current assets less inventory divided by current liabilities), and "gross margin return on inventory" (GMROI; gross margin divided by average inventory cost), which is heavily used in retail.

In this chapter, we have laid out the basic concepts of inventory planning and control for a location's SKU requirements; we next move on to a more strategic and tactical process of aggregate or sales and operations planning.

12

Sales and Operations (Aggregate) Planning

After we've made our best estimate of a demand forecast for goods or services and netted it against our current and targeted inventory position to determine our future inventory requirements, it becomes necessary to make sure that we have enough capacity to meet the anticipated demand in terms of what I refer to as the three "Ms" – machine, manpower, and material.

When we think of planning the capacity for a goods or service business, we typically think in terms of three general time horizons:

- **Long range** (1–3+ years) – where we need to add facilities and equipment that have a long lead time.
- **Medium range** (roughly 2–12 months) – we can add equipment, personnel, and shifts; we can subcontract production and/or we can build or use inventory. This is known as "aggregate planning".
- **Short range** (up to 2–3 months) – mainly focused upon scheduling production and people, as well as allocating machinery, generally referred to as production planning. It is hard to adjust capacity in the short term since we are usually constrained by existing capacity.

The supply chain and logistics function must actively support all of the above by supplying material and components for production and product to the customer and in fact has many of its own capacity constraints in terms of its distribution and transportation services.

In many service organizations, the actual work of capacity and supply planning for the production of inventory may be partially or totally performed in another organization, as is the case of retailers or wholesalers.

DOI: 10.4324/9781003281078-15

But even in those instances, retail and wholesale supply chain organizations are intertwined with the vendor's manufacturing process, and so they should participate in and support vendor production plans and integrate them into their own processes when possible. Additionally, service organizations have capacity constraints in terms of various resources that are impacted by inventory levels (e.g. labor, warehouse capacity, backroom retail storage, shelf space, etc.). So, it is well worth understanding the aggregate planning process, no matter where you are in the supply chain.

THE PROCESS DECISION

Stepping back for the moment, it should be understood that all organizations, offering both goods and services, have to make what is known as the "process decision". That is, how the goods or services are to be delivered. This will, of course, have a major impact on future planning and execution of all types.

In most established organizations, there is already an existing process that is usually based upon the industry and management's competitive strategy.

Goods and Service Processes

Process choices in goods and service industries can be defined and delineated by what has come to be known as the "product-process matrix" [Hayes and Wheelwright, 1979] (Figure 12.1). In this model, an organization's process choices are based upon both the volume produced and variety of products. At the upper left of the chart, companies are considered process-oriented or focused, and those at the lower right are considered product-focused. The ultimate decision about where a firm is located on the matrix is determined by whether the production system is organized by grouping resources around the process or the product.

Project Process

Some industries, such as construction or pharmaceutical, are for the most part project-oriented, where they typically make "one-off" types of products. They are usually customer-specific and too large to be moved;

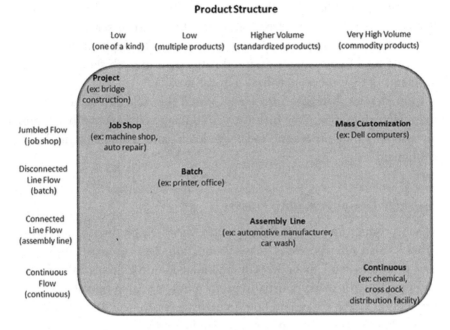

FIGURE 12.1
Product–process matrix.

thus, people, equipment, and supplies are moved to where they are being constructed or worked on.

Job Shop Process

Job shops typically make low-volume, customer-specific products. Machine shops, tool and die manufacturers, and opticians (i.e. prescription glasses) are primary examples of a job shop. As such, they require a relatively high level of skill and experience as they must create products based upon the customer's design or specifications.

Each unique job travels from one functional area to another, usually with its own piece of equipment, according to its own unique routing, requiring different operations, different inputs, and varying amounts of time.

Job shops can be extremely difficult to schedule efficiently.

Batch Process

Companies that run a batch process deliver similar items and services on a repeat basis, usually in larger volumes than a job shop. Batch processes have average to moderate volumes, but variety is still too high to justify dedicating many resources to an individual product or service. The flow tends to have no standard sequence of operations throughout the facility. There do tend to be more substantial paths than in a job shop, and some segments of the process may have a linear flow.

Examples of batching processes would be scheduling air travel, manufacturing apparel or furniture, producing components that supply an assembly line, processing mortgage loans, and manufacturing heavy equipment.

Assembly Line or Repetitive Process

When product demand is high enough, an assembly line or repetitive process, also referred to as mass production, may be used. Assembly line processes tend to be heavily automated, utilizing special-purpose equipment, with workers usually performing the same operations for a production run in a standard flow. In many cases, there is a conveyor-type system that links the various pieces of equipment used.

Examples of this are automotive manufacturing (the classic example) and assembly lines. In service industries, examples are car washes, registration in universities, and fast-food operations.

Continuous Flow Process

A continuous flow process, as the name implies, flows continuously rather than being divided into individual steps. Material is passed through successive operations (i.e. refining or processing) and eventually comes out the end as one or more products. This process is used to produce standardized outputs in large volumes. It usually entails a limited and standardized product range and is often used to manufacture commodities. Very expensive, complex equipment is used, and so these facilities tend to produce in large quantities to gain "economies of scale", spreading the considerable fixed costs over as much volume as possible so the cost per pound or unit is as low as possible. Labor requirements are on the low side and typically involve mainly monitoring and maintaining equipment.

Examples of this include chemical, petroleum, and beverage industries. This type of process is less common in service industries, but good emerging examples in supply chains are cross-dock distribution facilities, which move finished goods and products through a distribution facility in as little as 24–48 hours.

Mass Customization

Mass customization is a process that produces in high volume and delivers customer-specific products in small batches; it can provide a business with a competitive advantage and maximum value to the customer. It is a relatively "new frontier" for most goods and service businesses, and, as a result, there aren't that many examples of it.

In manufacturing, Dell Computers is a primary example used by many as it allows customers to, more or less, assemble their own personal computer (PC) online. Dell then assembles, tests, and ships the PC direct to the customer in as little as 24–48 hours. Some clothing companies will manufacture blue jeans to fit an individual customer.

In service industries such as financial planning and fitness, the service is customized specifically to meet individual needs and, therefore, is an example of mass customization.

AGGREGATE PLANNING AND MASTER PRODUCTION SCHEDULING PROCESS OVERVIEW (FIGURE 12.2)

An aggregate plan, also known as a sales and operations plan (S&OP), is a summarized statement of a company's production rates, workforce, and inventory levels based upon estimates of customer requirements and capacity limitations.

Many service organizations perform aggregate planning in the same way as goods organizations, except that there is more of a focus on labor costs and staffing as they are critical to the service industry (and "pure" service companies don't have inventory to manage, other than supplies).

A variety of methods can be used for aggregate planning, from simple spreadsheets to packaged software using algorithms such as the transportation method of linear programming, which is an optimization tool to minimize costs.

Graphical tools can also be used to supplement this process to allow the planner to compare different approaches to meeting demand (see "Supply (Capacity) Options" later in this chapter).

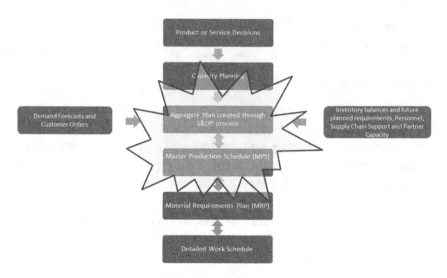

FIGURE 12.2

Typical planning and scheduling process.

As the name implies, the plan is usually stated in terms of an aggregate such as product family or class of products and displayed in monthly or quarterly time periods. It will determine resource capacity to meet demand in the short to medium term (3–12 months) and is usually accomplished by adjusting capacity (i.e. supply) or managing demand.

Once the aggregate plan is formalized, it is then disaggregated to create a master production schedule (MPS) for independent demand inventory (i.e. finished goods), which is also referred to by many as a production plan. The MPS is stated in SKU production requirements, usually in daily, weekly, or sometimes monthly time periods.

It should be noted that, for many organizations, the MPS or production plan is created first and then aggregated for the S&OP process (to be discussed in detail in the next section). No matter; in the end, the two should be kept in synch.

The MPS is then "exploded" using a bill of materials (BOM), which is basically a "recipe of ingredients" (i.e. dependent demand) that goes into the final product (i.e. independent demand). This activity is known as material requirements planning.

Once MRP has been run and material availability has been confirmed, a short-term or detailed work schedule is created. This schedule is "where the rubber meets the road", as this is a schedule of the actual work to be done, resulting in either meeting or not meeting customer requirements. The work schedule is usually in days or even hours and goes out up to a week or so. It has the specifics as to what product or service will be delivered, when, and who will deliver it.

AGGREGATE PLANNING

Aggregate planning, also referred to as sales and operations planning, is operational activity that generates an aggregate plan, usually for product or service families or classes for the production process, from approximately 2 to 18 months out. The idea is to ensure that supply meets demand over that period and to give an idea to management as to what material and other resource requirements are required and when, while keeping the organization's total cost of operations to a minimum.

S&OP Process

Best-practice companies have a structured S&OP process to ensure success for aggregate/S&OP planning. The "executive" S&OP process itself (Figure 12.3) actually sits on top of the number crunching and analysis being done at a lower level of the organization and involves a series of meetings prior to a final S&OP executive-level meeting; they are used to create, validate, and adjust detailed demand and supply plans. The meetings are:

- **Demand planning cross-functional meeting** (step 2) – generated forecasts are reviewed with a team that may include representatives from supply chain, operations, sales, marketing, and finance. As mentioned in Chapter 9, forecasts have been generated statistically and aggregated in a format that everyone can understand and confirm (e.g. sales might want to see forecasts and history by customer in sales dollars).
- **Supply planning cross-functional meeting** (step 3) – this occurs after confirmed forecasts have been "netted" against current on-hand inventory levels to create production/purchasing plans. Again, this data will usually be reviewed in the "aggregate" by product family in units, for example.

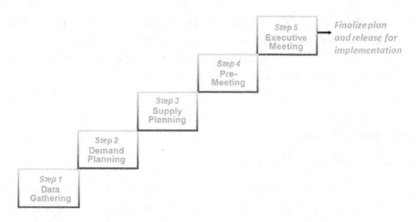

FIGURE 12.3
S&OP process.

- **Pre-S&OP meeting** (step 4) – data from the first demand and supply meetings are reviewed by department heads to ensure that consensus has been reached.

The discussions in this series of monthly management meetings highlight issues and look at possible resolutions before the outcome of the discussions is presented to the senior management team as a series of issues to be resolved. These issues form the basis of the executive S&OP meeting.

The actual aggregate plan requires inputs that include:

- Resources and facilities available to the organization.
- Demand forecast with appropriate time horizon and planning buckets.
- Cost of various alternatives and resources. This includes inventory holding cost, ordering cost, and cost of production with various production alternatives such as subcontracting, backordering, and overtime.
- Organizational policies regarding the usage of these alternatives.

Table 12.1 is an example of an aggregate plan for a company that manufactures bicycles.

As was mentioned earlier, some companies start with an aggregate plan and disaggregate to an MPS (i.e. SKU level), and others start at the MPS

TABLE 12.1

Aggregate Plan Example

January	February	March	April	May	June	July	August	September
50,000	30,000	55,000	60,000	80,000	150,000	150,000	125,000	80,000

and then aggregate to a class or family of products or services. In any case, the plans, at all levels including detailed work schedule, are tested for various constraints (manpower, machine, and material) and then adjusted accordingly.

It's Time to Bring the Outside-In to Your S&OP Process

As we know, S&OP is an integrated business management process through which the leadership team continually achieves focus, alignment, and synchronization among all functions of the organization to ensure that supply meets demand while meeting general business objectives of profitability, productivity, competitive customer lead times, etc.

The goal of S&OP is to understand how the company achieved its current performance and to direct its focus on future actions and anticipated results.

As the time horizon on an S&OP process may be anywhere from one to six plus months, it is critical to also include an element of risk management in this process on a regular basis in today's volatile external environment, as risk management (risk identification, assessment, treatment, and monitoring), through S&OP, is equally important as financial alignment since risk management permeates all functions and levels of an organization and might even extend to suppliers and/or customers. So it should naturally be part of S&OP.

Historically, this was more of an "inside-out" approach used in S&OP, guided by the belief that the inner strengths and capabilities of an organization will produce a sustainable future to meet anticipated demand and looking primarily at internal supply elements and then working outwards.

In today's volatile global environment, to achieve success, there is a need to have a more "outside-in" approach, using information from your extended supply chain to maximize customer value and overall supply chain surplus. This includes not only collaboration with key customers and suppliers, but also demand sensing, shaping, and enterprise trade-offs, including risk/reward analyses.

Besides matching demand with supply while meeting financial and operations goals, mature best-practice S&OP processes uncover risks and opportunities, which leads to scenario planning and helps the organization prepare for a range of future circumstances.

To help develop scenario planning capabilities in your S&OP process, you consider:

- Identifying risks and opportunities that might impact the demand or supply plan by validating key assumptions as well as a range of internal and external supply chain drivers.
- Developing a culture of identifying risks and opportunities and challenging the plan by engaging finance teams while using a common language (i.e. develop a strong link between S&OP and financial planning).
- Using risks and opportunities to drive decision-making by moving them through the S&OP process using an agreed-on way of handing over information to the following step. The final executive S&OP step requires teams to think about sharing not only the risk or opportunity but also the impact, the possible actions, and the expected results.

Risk management (to be discussed in detail in Chapter 17) can no longer be considered a purely long-term, strategic tool, but must now be integrated with more tactical tools such as S&OP to ensure the future success of your organization [Myerson, 2022].

S&OP in Retail

Also, while S&OP has been a best practice in manufacturing for 25 or so years, the retail industry has been slow to adapt it to their planning processes. The migration toward a broader more "outside-in" approach often referred to as "integrated business planning" (described below) may prove to be an impetus to pull retailers into using an S&OP process. In any case, when it is used in retail, the S&OP process is very similar to that used by manufacturers. The main differences are that the sponsors and titles of each step, as well as the details of each review, such as issues, data, and decisions, are different.

Integrated Business Planning

There is a movement or evolution toward what has been called an "integrated business planning" (IBP) or "advanced S&OP" model for some leading organizations; it moves from fundamental demand and supply balancing to a broader, more integrated, outside-in strategic deployment and management process, especially considering the fact that we are in a "whitewater rapids" phase of today's global economy.

On the operations side, manufacturing develops plans to balance demand and supply but doesn't always know if the plans will meet the budgets on which the company's revenue and profit goals are based. The sales department may agree to quotas that meet finance's revenue goals without a detailed understanding of what manufacturing can deliver. IBPxs attempts to bridge those gaps by making sure that revenue goals and budgets are validated against a bottom-up operating plan, and that the operating plan is reconciled against financial goals.

While the most common tool since the 1990s has been sales and operations planning, at least until recently (as previously discussed), it has been primarily an internal, or inside-out, method for a business to make sure that supply meets demand at the lowest possible cost. Its goal is to help a leadership team focus, align, and synchronize all functions of the organization.

Planning and Control

Furthermore, from a lean, agile supply chain perspective, a robust S&OP process acts as both a planning and control method at an executive management level. It externally benchmarks various metrics indicating the level of waste – such as forecast accuracy, inventory turns, and on-time and complete shipments – to set objectives, as well as match the company's strategic plan. The metrics also measure whether things are under or out of control.

While S&OP was quite an advancement over previous methods (or lack of a method), it is insufficient to deal with today's business challenges. That is why IBP, which uses an outside-in approach, is more appropriate in today's business world.

IBP extends the principles of S&OP throughout the supply chain, product and customer portfolios, customer demand, and strategic planning to deliver one integrated management process. With the use of scenario planning and what-if analysis, IBP can help decision-making regarding more profitable supplier collaboration, demand sensing and shaping, marketing, and product growth and development.

Obstacles to Implementation

It's not easy to make the change from traditional or more advanced S&OP-type processes (I say "type", because many companies, whether they realize it or not, don't have a fully developed S&OP process in place). Among the barriers are:

- Conflicting goals among business units and functions.
- Lack of or outdated technology that relies too much on spreadsheet tools and isn't integrated internally and/or externally, which can prevent effective collaboration. Fortunately, today, an abundance of great tools can not only integrate internal functions but also help you connect and gain access to accurate, timely data downstream and upstream in your supply chain.
- Cultural or political resistance to changing processes. As we know, change starts – or ends – at the top.

Get Motivated

There should be plenty of motivation here as you start to imagine how much more helpful a fully developed, outside-in methodology such as IBP can be in successfully creating and managing a lean, agile supply chain.

IBP and lean are mutually complementary to business vision and success. I say this because lean requires the elimination of waste and wasteful practices, which reduces costs and cuts lead times while synchronizing all partners and activities in the value chain. IBP is a process that, when used with enabling technologies, focuses directly on ensuring a continuous alignment between demand, inventory, supply, and manufacturing plans, and between tactical and strategic business plans.

Seems like a match made in heaven [Myerson, 2019].

View from the Control Tower

As mentioned, integrated business planning is a process that uses outside-in thinking by integrating demand forecasts, supply plans, inventory projections, and financial plans into one medium-term strategic model. That's a great starting point.

But the leading-edge way to manage your short- to mid-term global supply chain in real time (or close to it) is through a control tower that utilizes technology, organization, and processes that capture product movement visibility from the supplier all the way to the customer.

The control tower, which we will discuss a bit more in Chapter 15 ("Information Technology in Supply Planning") from more of a technical standpoint, creates an overview of total supply chain performance using KPI dashboards. It resolves problems with management functions to deliver visibility and provide capabilities such as collaboration with trading partners and functionality enabling supply chain planners to automate processes and controls.

Control Towers Help to Support a Lean Supply Chain

A lean philosophy and culture are compatible with a control tower system. While a control tower helps to plan and control a more reliable supply chain, a lean philosophy helps achieve that goal. The end-to-end supply chain visibility and transparency a control tower provides, combined with a lean culture of continuous improvement, can produce coordinated, sustainable execution processes allowing companies to successfully manage the complexities of today's supply chains and gain a competitive advantage.

It's one thing to envision having a lean, agile supply chain, but another thing to see one in action. Like sales and operations planning and IBP, control towers can be a critical component in achieving that goal [Myerson, 2019].

Demand and Supply Options

During the aggregate planning process, when trying to match supply with demand at the lowest cost and highest service, an organization has options to adjust both demand and supply capacity for the short, medium and long term.

Demand Options

These options refer to the ability to adjust customer demand in order to fit that demand to current available capacity. These options include:

- Influencing demand – this can be accomplished to some degree via advertising, pricing, promotions, and price cuts. Examples would be "early bird" meals in a restaurant or discounts offered if you buy before a certain date. These methods may not always have enough of an effect upon demand to free up capacity.

Also, as we have discussed, the use of heavy promotions and discounting can also have the negative "bullwhip" effect as a consequence; this is the reason why some companies have gone to "everyday low pricing".

- Backorders – these occur when a goods or service organization gets orders that it cannot fulfill. In many cases, customers are willing to wait. In others, it can result in lost sales. In some industries, such as grocery stores, backorders are not used. Instead, if an item is out of stock, it is cut from the order and reordered next time. This is, of course, dangerous if your product is substitutable as it might not be reordered next time.
- New or counter-seasonal demand – this can be used to balance demand by season. For example, a company that sells lawn mowers may begin production of snow blowers. Companies must be careful not to go beyond their expertise or base markets.

Supply (Capacity) Options

These options refer to the ability of an organization to adjust its available resource capacity to meet demand and include:

- Hiring and laying off employees – as demand hits peaks and valleys, flexibility in the workforce can be used to compensate for these fluctuations. While this can be beneficial to the company, it can also have risks and costs in terms of unemployment and new hire training costs.
- Overtime/idle time – most companies have the ability to run some overtime when things get busy. The opposite may be true when things slow down, by moving idle workers to other jobs, at least to some extent. Equipment and workers' efforts, to some degree, can also be sped up or slowed down. While this may extend capacity a bit in the short term, employees may burn out. In the case of slack demand, profitability may suffer as a result of having too many workers doing "make work".
- Part-time or temporary workers – this is especially common for contract manufacturers and in the service industry during the

holiday season. It isn't usually an option in more technical jobs other than some exceptions, such computer programming and nursing. Also, quality and productivity may suffer as a result of this approach.

- Subcontracting (or contract manufacturing) – very common in some industries such as cosmetics, as well as household and personal care products, especially when the demand for a new item is uncertain or a company doesn't yet have the capability to make the product. The downsides are that costs may be greater as the subcontractor has to make a profit too, quality may suffer a bit as you have less control, as well as the fact you may be working with a future competitor.
- Vary inventory levels – inventory may be produced before a peak season when excess capacity may be limited. However, it can also drive up holding costs, including for obsolete or damaged inventory. An example of this is the ice cream industry, where ice cream can be produced in the winter and put in a deep freeze until the busy season starts.

Aggregate Planning Strategies

There are three general aggregate planning strategies that are commonly used and use many of the demand and supply options discussed above; they are:

- Level strategy – use a constant workforce and produce similar quantities each time period. This method uses inventories and backorders to absorb demand peaks and valleys and therefore tends to increase inventory holding costs.
- Chase strategy – this method minimizes finished goods inventories by adjusting production and staffing to keep pace with demand fluctuations. It looks to match demand by varying either workforce level or output rate. This can, of course, negatively affect productivity as well as costs.
- Mixed (or hybrid) strategy – probably used the most, with a mix of both of the first two methods. In some cases, inventory is increased ahead of rising demand, and, in other cases, backorders are used to level output during extreme peak periods. There may be layoff or furlough of workers during extended slower periods, and companies

may subcontract production or hire temporary workers to cover short-term peak periods. As an alternative to layoffs, workers may be reassigned to other jobs such as preventive maintenance during slow periods.

An example of this may be where a company has two production facilities that manufacture the same products, one on the East Coast and one on the West Coast. If one plant has a distinct cost advantage, it may make sense to sometimes shift production to the lower-cost plant and expand its service area temporarily, such as during a slow period of demand. This will, of course, result in less production required at the higher-cost plant during those periods, possibly requiring layoffs. This decision isn't to be taken lightly and must consider the total "landed" cost of the product for each plant, including transportation and distribution to the customer.

Production, Sales, and Inventory Method of Planning

Before moving onto a description of the MPS process, it is important to understand a very basic, yet powerful, tool in planning, commonly known as the production, sales, and inventory (PSI) method of planning (see Figure 12.4 for an example).

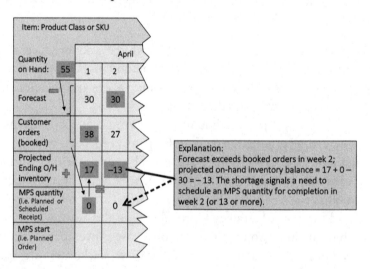

FIGURE 12.4
PSI planning method example.

It can be used at any level of aggregation or detail such as MPS, DRP, MRP, and short-term scheduling. Basically, it is a rolling projection of current and future needs.

It starts with a current on-hand inventory level and then, based upon current and future forecasts and actual demand, as well as current "scheduled" production work orders, purchase orders, and "planned" receipts (i.e. desired work and purchase orders based upon forecasts, inventory targets, lead times, lot size technique, etc.), creates a satisfactory future planned inventory level.

All of this is done within given constraints of machine, manpower, and material availability.

The level of aggregation or detail (product family, item at a factory vs. distribution center, etc.), unit of measure, and time planning buckets vary for each PSI.

MASTER PRODUCTION SCHEDULE

Once the S&OP process has been completed, the aggregate plan is "disaggregated" into an MPS for a production facility, which shows net production requirements for the next two to three months, usually in weekly or monthly time periods by SKU for independent demand items (see Table 12.1 from earlier in the chapter). This is known as "time phased planning".

However, in many cases, organizations have complex distribution networks such as consumer packaged goods companies (CPG). CPG's companies for example, may start planning at the MPS level (or even more detailed item-distribution center level, using a tool known as DRP described below) and summarize upwards to the aggregate plan. In either case, this aggregate/disaggregate iteration may occur multiple times until it is finalized.

The net requirements above and beyond existing known ones, which are referred to as "scheduled receipts", are called "planned orders" and "planned receipts"; the only difference being that planned orders are planned receipts that have been offset by the item's lead time.

It should be noted that the lead time for manufacturing, which is the time required to manufacture an item, is the estimated sum of order preparation time, queue time, setup time, run time, move time, inspection time, and put-away time. In the case of purchased items, the lead time is usually stated by the vendor and may or may not include inbound transit times.

Production Strategies

Manufacturers typically have one or a combination of the production strategies below:

- Make to stock (MTS) – production for finished goods is based upon a forecast using predetermined inventory targets. Customer orders are then filled from existing stock, and that stock is replenished through production orders. MTS enables customer orders to be filled immediately from available stock and allows the manufacturer to organize production in ways that minimize costly changeovers and other disruptions.
- Make to order (MTO) – goods are produced specifically to customer order and are usually standardized (but low-volume) or custom items produced to meet the customer's specific needs. MTO environments are slower to fulfill demand than MTS and assemble-to-order environments (described below), because time is required to make the products from scratch. There also is less risk involved with building a product when a firm customer order is in hand.
- Assemble to order (ATO) – products are assembled from components after the receipt of a customer order. The customer order initiates assembly of the customized product. This strategy can be useful when there are a large number of end products based on the selection of options, and accessories can be assembled from common components (this is one example of the concept of "postponement").
- Engineer to order (ETO) – this strategy uses customer specifications that require unique engineering design, significant customization, or new purchased materials. Each customer order results in a unique set of part numbers, bills of material (i.e. items required to make the product), and routings (i.e. steps to manufacture a product).

For the service industry, the MPS may only be an appointment book or log to make sure that capacity, in this case skilled labor or professional service, is in balance with anticipated demand.

Depending on the production strategy used, the production requirements in the MPS can be expressed based upon a forecast, customer orders, or modules that are required for the manufacture of other items (e.g. Table 12.2).

System Nervousness

Frequent changes to the MPS (or, subsequently, the material requirements plan, which we will be discussing shortly) can cause what is known as "system nervousness", where small changes, usually as a result of updating the MPS (and then the MRP) plan too often, cause major changes to the requirements plan.

To avoid this, many companies use a "time fence" whereby the planning horizon is broken down into two parts:

- Demand (or firm) time fence (DTF) – a designated period where the MPS is "frozen" (i.e. no changes to current schedule). The DTF starts with the present period, extending several weeks into the future. It can only be altered by senior management. Unfortunately, all too often from what I've seen, the frozen segment is changed owing to "firefighting" and customer emergencies.
- Planning time fence (PTF) – a designated period during which the master scheduler is allowed to make changes. The PTF starts after the DTF ends and extends several weeks or more into the future.

Distribution Requirements Planning (DRP) Software

As mentioned earlier in the chapter, there is a particular tool called distribution requirements planning that is more geared to businesses that

TABLE 12.2

Disaggregation of Aggregate Plan Example

Months:	January				February			
Aggregate Plan Quantity:	50,000				30,000			
Weeks:	1	2	3	4	5	6	7	8
MPS quantity:								
26" Boys Blue	10,000		10,000		5,000		5,000	
12" Boys Red		12,500		12,500	8,500		8,500	
12" Boys Yellow		5,000					3,000	

have to manage a network of finished goods distribution centers (typically in make-to-stock industries such as consumer packaged goods).

The mechanics of DRP are similar to MRP's (just further downstream in the supply chain) in that it develops replenishment plans by evaluating information such as order size, desired safety times/service levels, on-hand inventory, scheduled receipts, and both forecasted and actual demands. However, in the case of DRP, replenishment requirements are for independent demand inventory vs. dependent demand for MRP.

DRP compares future demand with available inventory (plus scheduled receipts such as purchase orders or intracompany transfers) to predict future shortages and schedules planned replenishment orders (factoring in lead times) based upon user-set criteria including safety stock or safety time targets.

DRP is "hierarchical" as the SKU net requirements can be summarized up the supply chain to the plant level to create the master production schedule, which can then be "exploded" with a bill of materials to generate requirements for raw materials and components (see Figure 12.5).

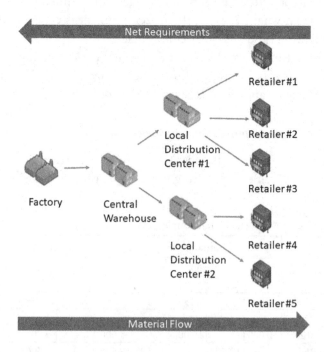

FIGURE 12.5
Distribution requirements planning (DRP).

DRP is ideal for organizations that have a high number of SKUs and a fairly large network of distribution centers and want to transition from a "push" to a "demand pull" (or hybrid) process, resulting in a more efficient, lean supply chain.

Rough-Cut Capacity Planning

Rough-cut capacity planning (RCCP) deserves a mention here as, while it may not be used by everyone (and is often done in spreadsheet form), it is a long-term capacity planning technique. RCCP validates the master production schedule. The goal is to ensure that companies don't purchase or release an excess of materials.

It is not uncommon for the MPS to overstate the need for more materials than production can process. Once the RCCP analysis takes place, changes may trickle down to the MPS or available capacity to better balance raw materials, capacity, and demand.

Following the S&OP and MPS processes, plans for dependent demand inventory are developed and refined in more detail, which is the topic of our next chapter.

13

Resource Planning – Dependent Demand Inventory and Purchasing

MATERIAL REQUIREMENTS PLANNING

Once the MPS has been solidified, it can then be "exploded" through a bill of materials file to determine raw material and component (i.e. dependent demand) requirements typically used to generate purchase orders or releases.

The most common tool for this is MRP, which is a production planning, scheduling, and inventory control process (and system) used to manage manufacturing processes and generate direct goods requirements (i.e. raw materials and production goods).

We should also consider here requirements planning for indirect goods, referred to as maintenance, repair, and operating goods, which is typically run outside an MRP process. MRO, for our purposes, includes machinery, tooling, parts used to create a product, as well as fluids, lubricants, office supplies, shop supplies, furniture, light fixtures, toolboxes, safety protection, and other consumables.

It should be noted that MRO items are often given a lower priority, but, without them, businesses would not be able to operate in an effective fashion. In fact, indirect procurement can range from 15 to 25 percent of a company's total revenue.

The information needed to run an MRP model includes the MPS, a bill of materials, inventory balances, lead times, lot sizes, and scheduled receipts (i.e. purchase orders and production work orders). These inputs need to be accurate and up to date. Otherwise, it's the old "garbage in, garbage out" situation, resulting in poor execution and, ultimately, customer dissatisfaction.

All of the inputs are fairly straightforward, but it would be helpful at this point to delve a little bit into the BOM.

Bill of Material

A bill of materials is like a recipe for a product (in fact, in the case of food, it is). A BOM file has a defined structure to it. In this structure, the independent demand item is called the "parent" item (e.g. 26" boys blue bike), and any dependent demand requirements (e.g. two wheels for each bike) are called "child" items, with a quantity (two per bike in our example) of each child item needed to make each parent item. This is often referred to as the "product structure" (see Figure 13.1).

The finished good or parent item is referred to as being on "level 0", and the child is on "level 1". There can be multiple levels in a BOM, in which case the child item on level 1 of the wheel in the bike example can then be the parent to the child items of the rim, tire, and spokes (i.e. level 2), and so on.

MRP Mechanics

The calculations involved in an MRP system are fairly routine. Think of it as a giant calculator that crunches the information supplied to create

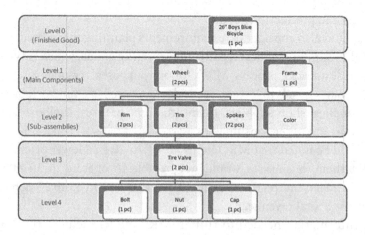

FIGURE 13.1
Bicycle bill of materials (BOM) and product structure.

net, future replenishment requirements based upon some user-defined parameters.

As mentioned previously, an MRP system is driven by the MPS (which may, in turn, potentially be driven by a DRP system). The mechanics of the MPS and MRP systems are basically the same, with the requirements from the MPS (independent demand) driving MRP requirements (dependent demand) via the BOM file.

In our bicycle example, Figure 13.2 illustrates the basic calculation where we have gross requirements (in MPS, "gross" would be the forecast "consumed" by open customer orders) for the production of 75 bikes in week 8. Typically, safety stock or safety time targets would be in place for independent demand items, but, for the sake of simplicity, there is none in the example. As we have 50 bikes in inventory, we will need to produce an additional 25 units by week 8. To do so, we will need to have 50 wheels and 25 frames available in week 6, after offsetting the components' lead time, for the bike production. Through the BOM "explosion", these requirements show up as gross requirements for the wheels and frames in MRP. The same "netting" calculations are then performed to create planned receipts and planned orders for the wheels and frames (and then level 2, level 3, etc. items).

Although it has been said that no safety stock or safety time is required for raw material or components since they are factored into finished goods

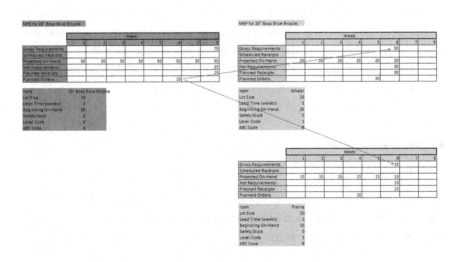

FIGURE 13.2
MPS and MRP mechanics.

requirements, the reality is that quality and other issues may arise, as well as vendor minimum order quantities, that may call for safety stock as the prudent thing to do.

The actual quantity required is typically rounded up based upon various lot sizing techniques. They range from "lot for lot" (i.e. exact requirements, no matter how small), which is appropriate for JIT operations, to economic order quantity (EOQ) calculations and beyond.

For slow-moving items, an "order time" may be used which basically states that the planned orders will be grouped together, so that one larger order vs. many frequent small orders will be placed. In the case of purchased material or parts, vendors may set order minimums (which can always be negotiated). While this may result in greater holding costs, in the case of slower-moving items, it may be the right thing to do.

It should be noted that, in the case of both DRP and MRP, there are "resource" versions (vs. "requirement") that look beyond material requirements and consider other resources impacted, such as labor, facilities, and equipment. Some are known as "closed-loop" systems which allow for the planners to schedule work based upon period capacity constraints using smoothing tools that allow the system (manually or automatically) to move requirements around to meet capacity based upon priority rules set by the planner, such as order splitting (running parts of a work order at two different times) and overlapping (part of a work order can move to a second operation while the rest is still on the first operation).

The planned orders for both independent and dependent demand are then used (either manually or sent electronically to either an ERP or accounting system) to create production work orders and purchase orders in what is known as short-term scheduling.

PURCHASING

Purchasing, part of the overall procurement process, as discussed in Chapter 7, is a basic function in most organizations and, for the purposes of this book, will be defined as the transactional function of buying products and services. In a business setting, this commonly involves the placement and processing of a purchase order through the receipt and payment of goods (steps 5–8 in the procurement process shown in Figure 13.3).

FIGURE 13.3
Steps in the procurement process.

We will now discuss the purchasing steps in the overall procurement process in terms of its basic mechanics.

Step 5 – Issue Purchase Orders

Issuing purchase orders involves the execution of the master schedule- and MRP-recommended purchasing requirements to ensure good use of resources, minimize WIP, and provide the desired level of customer service. This is usually supervised by someone known as a buyer/planner, who works hand in hand with the master scheduler. Buyer/planners are responsible for the control of production activity and the flow of work through the plant and can also be responsible for purchasing, materials requirements planning, supplier relationship management, product life cycle and service design, and more. They also coordinate the flow of goods from suppliers.

The purchase order is used to buy materials from a supplier. It specifically defines the price, specifications, and terms and conditions of the product or service and any additional obligations for either party. The purchase order must be delivered by fax, mail, personally, email, or other electronic means.

Types of purchase orders may include:

- Discrete order – used for a single transaction with a supplier, with no assumption that further transactions will occur.
- Pre-negotiated blanket order – a purchase order made with a supplier containing multiple delivery dates over a period of time, usually with predetermined pricing, which often has lower costs because of greater volumes (possibly through centralized purchasing and/or the consolidation of suppliers) on a longer-term contract. It is typically used when there is an ongoing need for consumable goods.
- Pre-negotiated, vendor-managed inventory (VMI) – the supplier maintains an inventory of items at the customer's plant, and the customer pays for the inventory when it is consumed (or, in some cases, when delivered). This usually used for standard, small-value items such as MRO supplies, e.g. fasteners and electrical parts.

- Bid and auction (e-procurement) – this involves the use of online catalogs, exchanges, and auctions to speed up purchasing, reduce costs, and integrate the supply chain. There are many e-commerce sites for industrial equipment and MRO inventory auctions which vary in format from catalog (e.g. www.grainger.com, www.chempoint.com) to auction (e.g. www.biditup.com). Websites can be for standard items or industry-specific.
- Corporate purchase card (pCard) – this is a company charge card that allows goods and services to be procured without using a traditional purchasing process; it is sometimes referred to as a procurement or "p" card. There is always some kind of control for each pCard, such as a single-purchase dollar limit, a monthly limit, and so on. A pCard holder's activity should be independently reviewed periodically.

To further enhance the speed and accuracy of transactions, many companies use what is known as electronic data interchange, which is the computer-to-computer exchange between business partners of business documents in a standard electronic format. In the past, electronic data interchange (EDI) transactions either went directly from business to business (in the case of large companies) or through third parties, known as value-added networks (VANs). Today, a large portion of EDI transactions flow through the internet.

Sometimes included in the category of EDI is the use of electronic funds transfer (EFT), which is the electronic transfer of money from one account to another, within a single financial institution or across multiple institutions, through computer systems. This also includes e-commerce payment systems, which facilitate the acceptance of electronic payment for online transactions, which have become increasingly popular from the widespread use of internet-based shopping and banking.

Step 6 – Follow Up to Assure Correct Delivery

ERP software modules assume that scheduled deliveries will be received on time. However, a scheduled delivery date must be monitored and managed to identify and avoid possible missed dates, in advance where possible. In some cases, delays may be inevitable, and, as a result, recovery plans must be developed and managed to minimize the negative effects of delays.

It is also critical to understand the supplier's production process, capacity, and constraints to collaboratively resolve problems in a timely and efficient manner.

On occasion, expediting is necessary, but should be on an exception basis. However, supplier performance should be monitored on an ongoing basis, and, if an individual supplier is consistently being expedited, then corrective action should be taken.

In many organizations, purchasing may work hand in hand with either the traffic or transportation department or that of the vendors (depending on shipping terms, which, among many things, determine when ownership transfer takes place and who arranges and pays for transportation).

Step 7 – Receive and Accept Goods

The key objective at receipt of goods is to ensure that proper physical condition, quantity, documentation, and quality parameters are met. To accomplish this requires cross-functional activity involving purchasing, receiving, quality control, and finance.

Receiving is technically a "non-value-added" activity from a customer perspective as it is designed to ensure that everything up to that point has been done properly. The goal is to ensure quality throughout and reduce or eliminate the need for inspection. In many cases, technology such as barcode scanners and handheld computers can automate the process. Some of the inspection processes can also be reduced or eliminated by various inspection and certification processes being performed by the vendor.

Step 8 – Approve Invoice for Payment

The final step in the procurement process is approving an invoice for payment (see Figure 13.4) according to the terms and conditions of the purchase order (PO).

The purchase requisition and purchase order forms are compared to make sure the order that was requested by a department was actually ordered by the purchasing department. Then, the data in the request and PO are matched with the data on the packing slip that was received and checked when the product arrived and was invoiced.

FIGURE 13.4
Document flow.

If all three of these documents agree, the invoice price, date, and payment terms are compared with the prior three documents. This should show that the amount billed by the vendor is the same amount that was ordered by the company. After all the forms have been reviewed and compared, the accounting department can approve the payment to the vendor and authorize the cashier to issue a payment check to the vendor.

Any discrepancies must be reconciled before payment is issued to the vendor. In some cases, small levels of discrepancies can be ignored (e.g. ±3 percent or ±$20).

Freight bills are the carrier's invoice for charges for a given shipment, and special attention should be paid to them as there tend to be large changes to fuel costs, low visibility of future freight costs, and a relatively high complexity of freight quotes. Therefore, freight invoices are susceptible to human and process errors and require auditing (pre- and post-payment) to ensure that the organization does not overpay for services it did not receive.

These audits can be performed internally or externally, both pre-payment and, in some cases, post-payment, and can lower a shipper's overall transportation costs by as much as 2 percent.

Discounts for early invoice payment should be taken whenever possible, although, in a sluggish economy, many customers try to extend payment as long as possible owing to cash flow issues.

This brings us to the point where "the rubber meets the road" (literally, in the case of our bicycle example) in terms of short-term scheduling and delivery, which will be covered in our next chapter.

14

Resource Planning – Short-Term Scheduling and Omni Channel Delivery

SHORT-TERM SCHEDULING

As mentioned before, the short-term schedule (Figure 14.1) is "where the rubber meets the road", as effective schedules are necessary to meet promised customer delivery dates with the highest-quality product or service at the lowest possible cost.

Operations scheduling is the allocation of resources in the short term (down to days, hours, and even minutes in some cases) to accomplish specific tasks.

Scheduling includes:

- Assigning jobs to work centers/machines.
- Job start and completion times.
- Allocation of manpower, material, and machine resources.
- Sequence of operations.
- Feedback and control function to manage operations.

Scheduling techniques vary based upon the facility layout and production process used.

Effective scheduling can support the supply chain to create a competitive advantage for an organization, as we discussed earlier in the book.

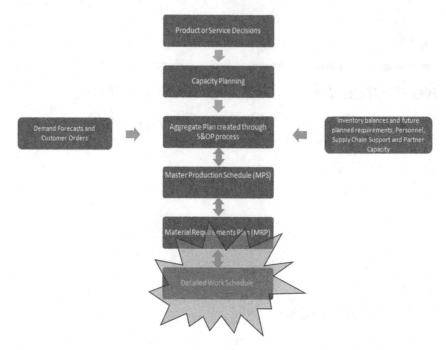

FIGURE 14.1
Typical planning and scheduling process.

Types of Scheduling

There are two general types of operations scheduling which help to determine the "load" or amount of work that is put on process centers. They are:

1. Forward scheduling – plans tasks from the date resources become available to determine the shipping date or the due date, used in businesses such as restaurants and machine shops.
2. Backward scheduling – plans tasks from the due date or required-by date to determine the start date and/or any changes in capacity required, used heavily in manufacturing and surgical hospitals.

In many cases, organizations may use a combination of both, depending on the product or service.

The load put on a work center can be "infinite" (e.g. unlimited capacity such as in the basic MRP model) or "finite", where capacity is considered.

Sequencing

Sequencing involves understanding and minimizing flow time, which is the sum of: (1) moving time between operations, (2) waiting time for machines or work orders, (3) process time (including setups), and (4) delays. As a result, sequencing is critical to good scheduling and the efficient utilization of resources.

The concept of sequencing uses both priority rules, to determine the order that jobs will be processed in, and the actual job time, which includes both the setup and running of the job, to schedule efficiently.

Priority Rules

While there are many priority rules, including the catch-all "emergency" (i.e. rush or priority customers), the basic rules are:

- First come, first served (FCFS) – jobs run in the order they are received. Perhaps the fairest, although not always the most efficient, way of scheduling.
- Earliest due date (EDD) – work on the jobs due the soonest.
- Shortest processing time (SPT) – shortest jobs are run earlier to make sure they are completed on time. Larger jobs will possibly be late as a result.
- Longest processing time (LPT) – start with the jobs that take the longest to get them done on time. This may work well for long jobs, but the others will suffer as a result.
- Critical ratio (CR) – jobs are processed according to the smallest ratio of time remaining until due date to processing time remaining.

The planner can create schedules based upon these methods (manually or automated) to both see the impact on job lateness and flow time and to determine what works best for the company and its customers. It may not always be possible to satisfy all customers, however.

SHORT-TERM SCHEDULING PROCESS

At this point, it is important to note the difference between the medium-term planning models described in Chapters 11–13 and the detailed scheduling models discussed in this chapter.

A medium-term planning model is designed to allocate the production of the different products to the various facilities in each time period (e.g. production or aggregate planning), while taking into account inventory holding and setup costs, transportation costs, and lateness. Aggregate planning looks at different product families, but usually doesn't differentiate between different products within a family. It may determine the lot size for a product family at a facility. MPS, on the other hand, does schedule at the finished good SKU level, but is usually in weekly planning buckets.

On the other hand, a short-term detailed scheduling model is usually confined to a single facility and takes more detailed information into account than a planning model. It is typically planning in daily (and possibly in shifts) or even hourly planning buckets and can include both interrelated independent and dependent (e.g. components or modules) scheduled production. There are usually a number of jobs, and each one has its own parameters. The jobs have to be scheduled so that one or more objectives are minimized (e.g. lateness, average completion time, etc.).

Medium-term planning and short-term scheduling models should also tie to long-term strategic models, facility location models, demand management models, and forecasting models. If there is a disconnect, service and profitability will be less than optimal.

Continuous vs. Discrete Industry Scheduling

Short-term scheduling in continuous manufacturing industries, such as chemical and food and beverage, and that in discrete manufacturing industries, such as automotive and consumer electronics, differ significantly.

Continuous manufacturing industries (Figure 14.2) typically have main processing operations with very high changeover and fixed costs. Scheduling tools in this area can be quite sophisticated and include cyclical scheduling procedures and mixed-integer programming approaches.

Continuous industries also may have finishing operations which convert the output from the main production facilities. They may involve cutting the material, bending, folding, and possibly painting or printing, and are usually a mix of make-to-order (MTO) and make-to-stock (MTS) production strategies. Sequencing of customer orders may be important (MTO), as well as forecasts and inventory targets (MTS).

Relatively Few Inputs

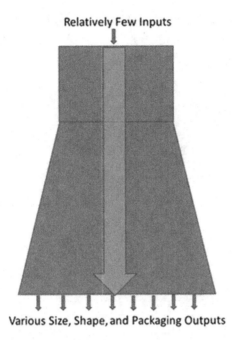

Various Size, Shape, and Packaging Outputs

FIGURE 14.2
Continuous manufacturing.

Discrete manufacturing (Figure 14.3) may involve three operations: converting, such as cutting and shaping of sheet metal, main production, and assembly operations.

The end product of converting is usually not a finished good and usually feeds a downstream operation. Main production operations require multiple different operations using different machine tools. The product and its parts may have to follow a certain route through the facility, going through various work centers. Each order has its own route through the system, quantity, processing times, and shipping date.

Assembly operations may be organized into work cells or assembly lines and usually require material handling systems, but do not typically require machine tools.

There are some basic differences between the parameters and operating characteristics of discrete vs. continuous facilities:

1. The planning horizon in continuous manufacturing facilities tends to be longer than the planning horizon in discrete manufacturing facilities.

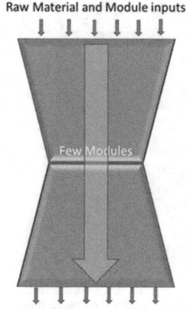

Raw Material and Module inputs

Few Modules

Modules Combined for a Variety of Outputs

FIGURE 14.3
Discrete manufacturing.

2. In discrete manufacturing facilities, plans and schedules may have to be changed or adjusted more often, and, as a result, planning and scheduling tend to be more reactive.
3. In discrete manufacturing, there may be a significant amount of mass customization and product differentiation. In continuous manufacturing, mass customization does not play a very important role. The number of SKUs in discrete manufacturing tends to be significantly larger than the number of SKUs in continuous manufacturing.

As a result, the planning and scheduling issues in discrete vs. continuous processes can be very different [Kreipl and Pinedo, 2004].

Finite Capacity Scheduling

Finite capacity scheduling (FCS; see Figure 14.4) is a short-term scheduling method that matches resource requirements to a finite supply of available

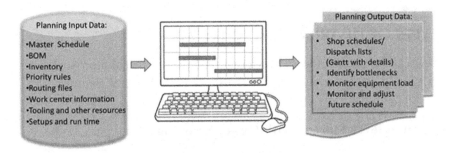

FIGURE 14.4
Finite capacity scheduling (FCS) system.

resources to develop a realistic production plan. The MPS and MRP schedules are usually imported into this tool, along with other information such as priority rules, setup times, etc., to create short-term daily and hourly schedules.

It not only uses rules-based methods, but also allows for the planner to make up-to-the-minute changes and adjustments as well as perform "what if" simulation analysis. It allows the planner to handle a variety of situations, including order, labor, and machine changes. The schedules in FCS are usually displayed in Gantt chart form (a kind of sideways bar chart which can show the planned, as well as current, status of schedules) and can be accomplished using a range of tools, from relatively simple spreadsheets to sophisticated optimization FCS software applications.

Service Scheduling

While service industries need to schedule production and assembly of product (e.g. restaurants), most are primarily interested in scheduling staff. To do so, they use tools such as appointment systems to control customer arrivals for service and consider patient scheduling or reservation systems to estimate demand for service and workforce scheduling systems often using seniority and skill sets to manage capacity for service.

These can be manual or automated software systems, depending on the size and complexity of the organization.

Once the product rolls off the production line, it either goes to storage at the production site for delivery or ships to a company-owned distribution center or a customer site (distribution center, store, or consumer).

TYPES OF DISTRIBUTION NETWORKS

There are a variety of ways that a manufacturer or distributor/wholesaler can distribute its products. We will discuss a number of these now.

Manufacturer Storage with Direct Shipping

In this type of distribution network design (Figure 14.5), product is shipped directly from the manufacturer to the end customer, bypassing the retailer or seller (who takes the order and initiates the delivery request). This is also referred to as "drop shipping", where product is delivered directly from the manufacturer to the customer. This tends to work for a large variety of low-demand, high-value items where customers are willing to wait for delivery and accept several partial shipments.

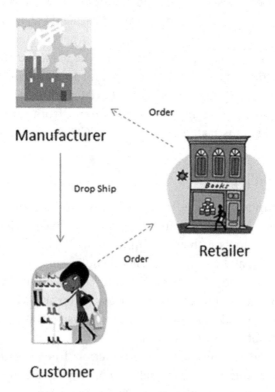

FIGURE 14.5
Manufacturer storage with direct shipping (drop shipping).

Impact on Costs

In general, this type of network has lower costs because of aggregation, which works best with low-demand, high-value items. Transportation costs are greater because of increased distance and individual item shipping. Facility costs are lower owing to this aggregation of demand, and there may be some saving on handling costs if the manufacturer can directly ship these small orders from the production line. However, this type of design requires a fairly large investment in information infrastructure as the manufacturer and retailer need to be tightly integrated.

Impact on Service

In terms of service, this type of distribution network design requires fairly long response times of one to two weeks because of increased distance and the two stages for order processing. The response time may vary by product, which may complicate receiving. Product variety and availability are relatively easy to provide owing to aggregation at the manufacturer. Home delivery may result in high customer satisfaction, but this can be negatively affected if orders from multiple manufacturers are sent as partial shipments. This type of network can help to get products to market fast, with the product available as soon as the first unit is produced. However, customer visibility and product returnability may be more difficult and expensive.

Manufacturer Storage with Direct Shipping and In-Transit Merge

In-transit merge by a carrier combines pieces of an order coming from different locations so that the customer gets a single delivery (Figure 14.6).

For example, when a customer orders a PC from Hewlett Packard (HP) along with a Samsung monitor, the package carrier picks up the PC from the Samsung factory and the monitor from the HP factory; it then merges the two together at a hub before making a single delivery to the customer.

This type of network works best for low-to-medium-demand, high-value items that a retailer is sourcing from a relatively low number of manufacturers.

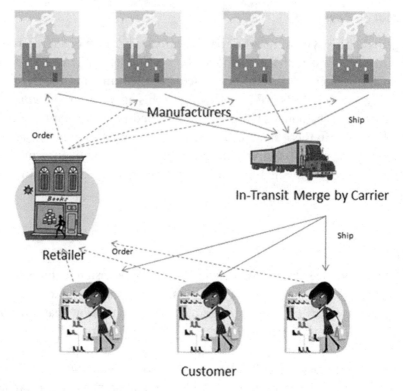

FIGURE 14.6
Manufacturer storage with direct shipping and in-transit merge.

Impact on Costs

The inventory costs associated with this type of distribution network are similar to drop shipping. However, handling and information investment costs may be higher than drop shipping, while transportation costs, as well as receiving costs at the customer, are somewhat lower than drop shipping. As a result of more coordination required to combine shipments, the information investment is somewhat higher than for drop shipping.

Impact on Service

The impacts on service such as response time, variety, availability, visibility, and returnability are all similar to drop shipping. However, the customer experience may be better than with drop shipping because a single order has to be received rather than multiple orders.

Distributor Storage with Carrier Delivery

When using the distributor storage with carrier delivery option (Figure 14.7), inventory is not held by manufacturers at the factories but instead is held by distributors/retailers in intermediate warehouses, and package carriers are used to transport products from the intermediate location to the final customer. This works well for medium-to-fast-moving items. It also makes sense when customers want delivery faster than is offered by manufacturer storage but do not need it immediately.

Impact on Costs

In this type of configuration, inventory and warehouse operations costs are higher than manufacturer storage with direct shipping and in-transit merge. Transportation costs are lower than manufacturer storage, with a simpler information infrastructure required compared with manufacturer storage.

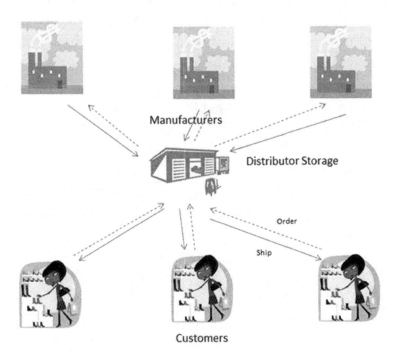

FIGURE 14.7
Distributor storage with carrier delivery.

Impact on Service

Distributor storage with carrier delivery typically has faster response times than manufacturer storage with drop shipping but offers less product variety and higher product availability costs. The customer experience, order visibility, and product returns are better than manufacturer storage with drop shipping.

Distributor Storage with Last-Mile Delivery

Last-mile delivery refers to the distributor/retailer delivering the product to the customer's home instead of using a package carrier (Figure 14.8).

In areas with high labor costs, distributor storage with last-mile delivery is very hard to justify on the basis of efficiency or improved margin and can only be justified if there is large enough demand that is willing to pay for this convenience.

It is always a good idea to group last-mile delivery with an existing distribution network to gain economies of scale and to improve asset utilization.

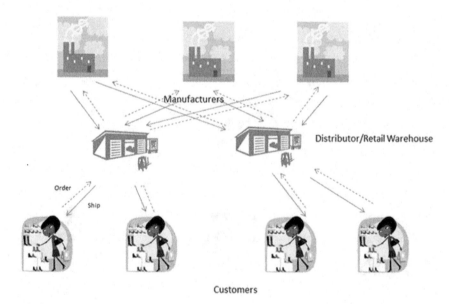

FIGURE 14.8
Distributor storage with last-mile delivery.

Impact on Costs

The inventory costs of distributor storage with last-mile delivery are higher than for distributor storage with package carrier delivery. Warehouse operations costs are greater than for manufacturer storage and distributor storage but lower than the costs of a retail chain. The transportation costs are greater than any other distribution network option. Information costs are similar to distributor storage with package carrier delivery.

Impact on Service

Service response times are very quick and, in some cases, can be same-day or next-day delivery, with a very good customer experience, particularly for bulky items. Product variety is less than distributor storage with package carrier delivery but greater than retail stores, with availability being more expensive to provide than any other option except retail stores. There is less of an issue of order traceability than for manufacturer storage or distributor storage with package carrier delivery, and returnability is easier to implement than with other options, except perhaps a retail network.

Manufacturer or Distributor Storage with Customer Pickup

Manufacturer or distributor storage with customer pickup (Figure 14.9) involves inventory being stored at the manufacturer or distributor warehouse and customers placing their orders online or on the phone and then having to travel to designated pickup points to collect their merchandise. Orders are shipped from the storage site to the pickup points as needed. Such a network is likely to be most effective if existing locations such as coffee shops, convenience stores, or grocery stores are used as pickup sites, because this type of network improves the economies from existing infrastructure.

Impact on Costs

Manufacturer or distributor storage with customer pickup is similar to the other distribution configurations in terms of inventory costs.

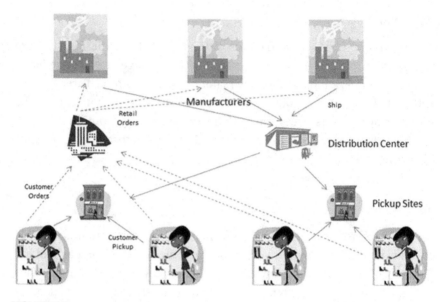

FIGURE 14.9
Manufacturer or distributor storage with customer pickup.

Transportation costs are on the low side as there isn't a great use of package carriers, especially if using an existing delivery network (plus customers pick up themselves). Warehouse operations costs can be high if new facilities have to be built, lower if existing facilities are in place (and handling costs at the pickup site can be fairly high). Information costs to provide infrastructure in this option can be very high as well.

Impact on Service

Response times are similar to package carrier delivery with manufacturer or distributor storage, with same-day delivery possible when items are already stored locally at pickup sites. Product variety and availability are similar to other manufacturer or distributor storage options. Order visibility is extremely important and can be greatly aided with the help of technology. Product returns are somewhat easier, as pickup locations can typically process returns. The customer experience may be lower than the other options owing to the lack of home delivery, but, in densely populated areas, the loss of convenience may be small.

Retailer Storage with Customer Pickup

Retailer storage with customer pickup is, of course, the most common form of distribution network where inventory is stored locally at retail stores. Inventory can be supplied to the stores from the retailer warehouse in the case of a chain, a distributor/wholesaler warehouse, or even directly from the manufacturer (factory or warehouse) for larger retailers. Customers walk into the retail store or place an order online or by phone and pick it up at the retail store. This option is best for faster-moving items or items for which customers want a quick response.

Impact on Costs

Retailer storage with customer pickup has the highest inventory and warehouse operations costs and lowest transportation costs of all the options. There may be an increase in handling costs at the pickup site for online and phone orders, which may also require some investment in infrastructure as well.

Impact on Service

Response times are the quickest of the options, as same-day pickup is possible for items stored locally at the retail location. Product variety, while great, is lower than the other options, and availability is more expensive to provide than all other options. The customer experience may be considered positive or negative based upon how shopping is viewed by the customer. Order visibility really only applies for online and phone orders, and returnability is easier than other options given that retail locations can handle returns.

DELIVERY IN TODAY'S OMNI CHANNEL RETAIL WORLD

There are many ways to get a product from a brick-and-mortar storefront, distribution center, or even a manufacturer to the customer's hands (whether that ultimate destination is at home, a store, or a locker, for example), not to mention the expanding modes of transportation delivery available, including private or public motor carrier, small package delivery van, store employees, air and land drones, and the customer themselves, of course. The challenge is to find the most effective and efficient transportation solution to keep customers happy without driving up the landed product costs. Selecting the right shipping method for the right customer situation is essential to omni channel logistics.

General shifts in consumer behavior point to a need for faster shipping to a wider range of destinations. But these movements don't exist in isolation. They are happening at the same time as the freight sector is experiencing a capacity and driver shortage, and manufacturers face mounting pressure to create more customized product lines and implement service-oriented shipping models.

In an attempt to accommodate the need for faster shipping, changing regulation, and infrastructure limitations, transportation and logistics providers have begun to research and offer alternative delivery solutions including: click-and-collect locations (also known as buy online, pick up in-store, or BOPIS), drones, robots, local regional delivery services, Uber delivery, and more (Figure 14.10).

These changing demand patterns can also have a negative effect on transportation costs. So, when planning your omni channel strategy, increased transportation cost is a big contributor to escalating fulfillment costs for omni channel operations. In a PwC survey (2016), 67 percent of CEOs said their fulfillment costs were increasing, and the cost to ship direct to customers (67 percent) and that to ship to stores for customer

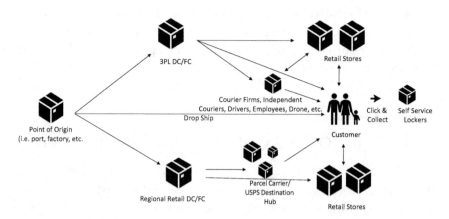

FIGURE 14.10
Last-mile delivery options.

pickup (59 percent) were the second and third biggest contributors to these rising costs (just behind the cost of returns at 71 percent).

Consumers' demand for "buy anywhere, pick up anywhere, deliver anywhere" shopping experiences won't let transportation be an afterthought, as the *Wall Street Journal* has reported that fulfillment costs are on the rise across the retail industry. As revenues rise, fulfillment costs also go up, as retailers have seen a 300 percent increase in the cost-to-serve for omni channel customers. It has been estimated that 18 cents out of every dollar generated online go to the costs of fulfillment. In the Retail Industry Leader Association's annual survey (as reported in *Supply Chain Quarterly*), controlling supply chain costs was identified as a top strategic priority for 2017, with omni channel costs a significant part of the picture. Just 50 percent of respondents recover some of the costs of omni channel fulfillment, 40 percent don't recover any of the costs, and 10 percent aren't measuring them.

Today's best-in-class omni channel leaders often have the ability to:

- Segment the supply chain based on customer profile data and manage these shipping and supply chain processes as a single connected entity to accelerate operations and eliminate inefficiencies.
- Maintain online visibility into fulfillment costs.
- Track actual costs as shipments/orders progress.
- Gain cost-to-serve modeling capabilities down to the product, customer, or location level.
- Optimize carrier sourcing to use the best possible shipping specialist for each product and delivery type, potentially implementing multimodal capabilities to improve processes around omni channel experiences.

Positioning the right inventory and assortments close to customer delivery points is critical for achieving customer satisfaction and profitability.

At the same time, it appears that, at least for now, CEOs are focusing more on growing revenues than on profitability as, in the PwC survey (2016) of retailers, it found that the number one initiative (57 percent) was spending capital on creating new customer experiences, closely followed (56 percent) by using stores as fulfillment centers for faster deliveries of online purchases; when retailers were asked to rank strategic growth enablers, reducing/reformatting physical store footprints to focus on expanding their e-commerce business was the top choice, at 53 percent [PWC, 2017].

MANAGING LAST-MILE COSTS AND EFFICIENCY IS CRITICAL

Last-mile delivery is a critical part of an organization's transportation network, as it can make up 28 percent of a shipment's total cost. This is especially true with the emergence of e-commerce and omni channel retail.

To be clear, last-mile delivery refers to the final step of the fulfillment process, from a distribution center, store, or other facility, such as a manufacturer when drop shipping, to the end user, where the actual "last mile" can range from a few blocks to up to 100 miles. Last-mile delivery has typically involved the use of parcel or small package carriers (but has expanded to store employees and even drones) to deliver products to consumers. As a result, the last mile can have a significant impact on both growth and profitability.

For example, Amazon's e-commerce business lost $7.2 billion from shipping in 2016, which was basically the difference between its shipping costs and what it charged for it (it made up for that loss through Amazon Web Services, or AWS, with a 2016 corporate profit of $2.4 billion).

However, it is reducing its transportation expenses on a per package and per order basis every quarter of every year. In fact, by 2018, AWS and Amazon (e-commerce) North America had operating incomes (net sales, less operating expenses) of $7.3 billion each. It should be noted that it took $141.4 billion in sales for Amazon North America to accomplish this, while AWS only needed $25.65 billion.

At Amazon, items are typically warehoused within 90 miles of each customer, so it lowers shipping prices as it's moving items the shortest distance to the customer. Beyond that, it is now creating a network of "Amazon Logistics" partners, to expand its delivery service partner (DSP) program in which the company helps small business owners start their own companies to deliver Amazon packages and reduce last-mile costs even more from local facilities.

Another example can be found at Walmart, which offers free two-day shipping for some $35+ orders with no membership fees (in addition to a free pickup in store option for many items, as well as store fulfillment and shipping, which it is testing at various stores). For items priced below that, it charges $5.99 for shipping and handling (i.e. handling = fulfillment). Shipping costs alone are $2.50 minimum, rising to $3.50–5.00, depending on the shipping distance and the cube size, a fee that covers both fulfillment and shipping.

With free shipping, there's not necessarily a correlation between what is charged for shipping and the actual cost. The retailer makes the decision to offer it based on a business strategy, which might be merging the costs into the product price, increasing the sales dollars to qualify, or some other tactic.

For example, Alpha Industries, a military-inspired fashion retailer, uses a shipping pricing model which is promotionally based, offering a discount coupled with free shipping around certain holidays.

In any case, it is important that the retailer understands the true economics of its business to decide at what point free shipping pays off (including knowing the total landed cost of items), while making money as an entity and returning shareholder value.

As e-commerce includes residential deliveries as well as B2B deliveries, carriers are seeing a steady increase in last-mile delivery (for example, 40 percent of all FedEx's US deliveries now go to residences). So, retailers and carriers need to work together when designing a last-mile strategy for omni channel retail.

Some Ideas to Reduce Last-Mile Transportation Costs

As "free shipping" isn't really free, there are some ways retailers can reduce transportation costs:

- Offer a range of shipping options – for Alpha, that means offering customers several shipping options, including ground, two-day, and overnight shipping, and usually charging for it. However, it has negotiated competitive rates with UPS and continues negotiating new rates as the e-commerce business grows.
- Drop off at access point – shippers may charge less for recipients to pick up their packages at a central point (in essence, the customer becomes the "last-mile delivery"), such as the retailer's store, as it's less expensive to deliver more packages to one location. That can

have a positive impact on the retailer, who may get additional sales from the customer at pickup.

- Limit the travel distance – some companies choose to use regional fulfillment centers or even stores to lower shipping costs, and, as mentioned previously, some larger chains are experimenting with using their brick-and-mortar stores as fulfillment centers, rather than warehouses, so the packages travel shorter distances (for example, it is estimated that 90 percent of all Americans live within 15 miles of a Walmart).

- Change the box size – many small-to-medium-size retailers buy cardboard boxes in small quantities, and so they tend to buy the size in the middle to save on costs, which may be bigger than they need, wasting valuable cube when it comes to transportation costs. They can work with carriers to design and buy more appropriate packaging sizes, to decrease transportation costs [Kaplan, 2017].

HOW OMNI CHANNEL FULFILLMENT IS AFFECTING TRANSPORTATION SOURCING AND EXECUTION

Traditional carrier transportation models are not designed to handle the challenges of omni channel service, especially in the area of "ship from store" and "pick up at store" fulfillment models which require multi-stop planning for last-mile deliveries and advanced scheduling capabilities, along with end-to-end visibility into order location and status for the customer.

As a distinct subset of omni channel commerce, last-mile deliveries pose a different set of challenges that must be understood and met. These include more sophisticated planning for multi-stop routing, tight delivery windows, and more frequent non-dock deliveries to residences and businesses.

Internally, it is often not a clear picture of who owns transportation in this omni channel environment. In some cases, the person who owns the parcel side and the last-mile delivery reports to the e-commerce team, not the transportation team that is responsible for the rest of the company's transportation operations.

Omni channel fulfillment also affects transportation sourcing and execution in that you need to understand that, as you're talking about a different model, you can't just use your baseline data set and requirements in the bidding process and expect to be successful.

You have to understand that you're talking about different models with "ship to store" and "ship from store" as they are different concepts than many companies have dealt with before when developing a transportation sourcing strategy.

For example, in the case of a large brick-and-mortar store chain with 4,000 stores, moving to omni channel required it to use a combination of static and dynamic routes that used less-than-truckload or multi-stop truckload weekly shipments to stores, coupled with parcel deliveries in between to replenish fast-selling critical products driven by point-of-sale data.

However, instead of using traditional metrics such as cost per hundredweight or cost per pound to determine if it should use a parcel network to deliver 25 cartons to a store, it instead looked at the sell-through rate and the gross margin that it is making by getting products back in stock faster. By doing that, it found that the amount of gross margin it made far outweighed the fact that it was going to spend more in transportation. In the end, the additional gross margin surpassed the transportation cost by 10:1.

In order to create an omni channel transportation strategy, you must use a combination of traditional approaches plus strategies that also integrate omni channel [Gonzalez, 2015].

WHERE IS LAST-MILE DELIVERY HEADED?

Today, retailers need to have great distribution, an online presence, and the ability to perform same-day delivery. In the United States, the delivery network is fragmented and often somewhat disorganized, and so direct-to-consumer deliveries, same-day delivery of automotive parts, legal documents, pharmaceutical and medical products, as well as other goods have been handled by messenger and courier services. Now, with the tremendous increase in the need for direct-to-consumer deliveries from online stores, distribution patterns and delivery networks have evolved in multiple directions. From Amazon and Walmart to Uber drivers, last-mile delivery seems to have changed forever.

Not too long ago, a trend toward independent transportation and logistics providers started. Couriers with fleets of employees began to examine new ways to provide a last-mile delivery service in more cost-effective ways.

In addition, retailers such as Walmart and Target have also looked to supplement this by using employees to deliver packages ordered online from brick-and-mortar locations.

Amazon, with its Flex program, uses on-demand contract drivers to help with this especially labor-intensive and expensive hand delivery; it also has started its Amazon Delivery Service Partner (ADSP) program, where it is seeking hundreds of entrepreneurs across the country to launch and operate their own Amazon package delivery business.

Below are some examples of how the supply chain industry is trying to solve the last-mile delivery challenge:

- Hyperlocal delivery services. Uber is a pioneer in this field.
- Retailers (and manufacturers) drop shipping goods to consumers.
- Acquiring logistics providers, such as the Target purchase of Shipt and Grand Junction.
- Acquisition of e-commerce companies by retailers, such as the Walmart acquisition of Jet and Bonobos.

Speed of delivery is also a major challenge owing to numerous factors, including traffic congestion, lack of transportation and logistics providers, and other issues, with younger consumers having the strongest desire for immediate delivery (which can also increase their loyalty to a retail brand). However, cost is still an issue, as Amazon Prime has gotten many used to fast (within two days), free delivery.

It has gotten complicated, with consumers regularly leaving instructions to deliver parcels to neighbors, put parcels out of sight, or customize the final-mile delivery in other ways.

Technology and the Last Mile

Innovation in technology has provided a glimmer of hope, with some of the latest trends below helping last-mile logistics providers to meet consumer demands:

1. Crowdsourced mobile apps for last-mile delivery – local, non-professional delivery service providers transport packages to customers' doors, often the same day; this has shown a lot of potential

for speeding up deliveries in urban areas as the high density of deliveries can be matched with potential couriers within the given area.

Current crowdsourced last-mile delivery options include Postmates, Instacart, Deliv, and Hitch.

2. Cargo drones – Amazon, Google, Uber, and Airbus currently have R&D programs in this mode of delivery using plane-sized autonomous air delivery vehicles. In fact, cargo drones are used today in areas with challenging environments such as Africa and Canada, primarily to transport medication to remote areas.

   Cargo drones may be important in the future of e-commerce fulfillment and last-mile delivery as, in urban areas, more parcels result in more vehicles, traffic congestion, and emissions, and they may even replace some delivery trucks and vans someday. However, there is quite a resistance currently to drones flying overhead in residential areas, which would have to change for them to be successful in urban areas.

3. Autonomous vehicles and delivery robots – land drones or unmanned ground vehicles (UGVs), which operate while in contact with the ground and without an onboard human presence, may have a better chance of success as a delivery alternative in urban areas, at least in the shorter term. So, it's no surprise that, from pizza and restaurant food to e-commerce parcels, autonomous guided vehicles (AGVs) are projected to gain momentum in coming years.

AGVs with parcel lockers have the potential to replace existing forms of regular parcel delivery, with up to a 40 percent reduction in delivery costs.

It seems very "Jetsons-like" that the world would use drones and robots to deliver packages, but, because of the boom in online shopping, the supply chain industry is turning to autonomous vehicles, crowdsourced delivery apps, independent delivery drivers, and other innovations for parcel delivery. Consumers expect fast, cost-effective delivery options, and last-mile technology may be at least part of the solution [Datex Corp, 2019].

This leads us to the discussion of information technology in supply planning, the topic of our next chapter.

15

Information Technology in Supply Planning

DOI: 10.4324/9781003281078-18

VIEWPOINTS OF SUPPLY CHAIN INFORMATION SYSTEMS

Since there are so many applications in today's global supply chain, it is best to look at information needs from strategic, tactical, routine, and execution viewpoints. The viewpoints are:

- Strategic – develop long-term decisions that help to meet the organization's mission and focus on strategic plans for meeting it such as new products or markets, as well as facility capacity decisions.
- Tactical – develop plans that coordinate the actions of key supply chain areas, customers, and suppliers across the tactical time horizon. Systems focus on tactical decisions, such as inventory or workforce levels. They plan, but do not carry out, the actual physical flows.
- Routine – support rules-based decision-making, usually in short time frames where accuracy and timeliness are important to the user.
- Execution – typically more transaction-oriented, systems record and retrieve transaction processing data and execute control of physical and financial information flow. These systems usually have very short time frames, are highly automated, and use standardized business practices [Bozarth et al., 2008].

Supply Chain Macro Processes

Another way to look at the supply chain in terms of its functional technology needs, at least at a high level, is by breaking it into what are called "macro processes". They are:

1. Supplier management (SM) – ensures that supplies are at the best cost and terms; can range from a strategic buy, tactical negotiated purchase, or a heavily engineered item.
2. Internal supply chain management (ISCM) – includes a number of activities with respect to receiving, conversion, and movement of finished goods.
3. Distribution channel management (DCM) – manages the links in a distribution network that has multitier arrangements; will depend upon the industry and types of products shipped and can also include service providers such as transportation, distribution, and third-party logistics (3PL) companies.
4. Customer relationship management (CRM) – manages the practices, strategies, and technologies that companies use to manage and analyze customer interactions and data throughout the customer life cycle, with the goal of improving business relationships with customers, assisting in customer retention, and driving sales growth.
5. Transactional management (TM) – manages the basic transactional data such as order and inventory information to run the day-to-day aspects of a business.

These processes (also shown in Figure 15.1) provide access to and reporting of supply chain transaction data. Advanced systems use analytics based

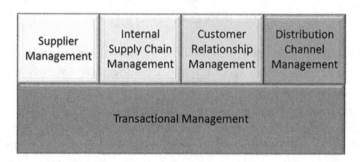

FIGURE 15.1
Supply chain macro processes.

upon transaction data to improve supply chain performance, and enterprise resource planning (ERP) systems form the foundation of a supply chain IT system.

ERP systems today, either through internal development or acquisition, have grown to include many of the functional advanced planning and execution applications found within SM, ISCM, CRM, and DCM (although they can still be licensed from other software companies and integrated to the ERP system).

Supply Chain Information Technologies

On a more practical level, supply chain management systems can be also viewed in terms of planning (SCP) and execution (SCE) technologies tied to processes across the supply chain.

Specifically, they are:

- SCP – applies algorithms to predict future requirements of various kinds and help to balance supply and demand; can include systems for demand management, supply management, and sales and operational planning to ensure supply matches demand.
- SCE – monitors physical movement and status of goods, as well as the management of materials and financial information for all participants in the supply chain; can include systems such as warehouse management systems (WMS), transportation management systems (TMS), and, of course, ERP systems.

There are also information technologies for:

- Supply chain event management – systems used for managing events that occur within and between organizations or supply chain partners. The goal is to keep all users in the supply chain, from materials suppliers and buyers to warehouse managers and product carriers, informed about activity across the supply chain. They typically perform event monitoring, notification, simulation, control, and measurement processes.
- Business intelligence (BI)/supply chain analytics – applications, infrastructure, tools, and best practices to help turn data into actionable information through analysis to improve and optimize decisions and performance. These systems can include reports, real-time dashboards, and benchmarking.

One relatively new but very important subset of the BI-type systems contains "control towers", which are both strategic *and* tactical in nature.

Control Towers

A supply chain control tower is defined as a connected, personalized dashboard of data, key business metrics, and events across the supply chain. A supply chain control tower, which is very visual and operates in real time, enables organizations to understand, prioritize, and resolve critical issues more fully in real time.

Control towers, many of which use AI, provide actionable visibility to orchestrate your end-to-end supply chain network, identify and understand the impact of external events to predict disruptions (i.e. helping to enable more of an "outside-in" approach to planning), and take actions based on recommendations to mitigate the upstream and downstream effects. They allow you to respond faster to changes, enable efficient collaboration, and drive operational automation.

Currently, software vendors offer two general types of operational control tower systems:

1. Transportation control towers are mainly focused on inbound and outbound transportation. They are usually offered as a module in a TMS.
2. Supply chain control towers typically focus on the multi-enterprise supply chain, ensuring visibility and control across internal as well as external supply chain processes and milestones. These control towers enable end-to-end visibility and control across your entire supply chain network and include real-time collaboration with suppliers and partners.

Moving beyond Decision Support

Until recently, supply chain control towers have been largely about providing visibility to your immediate trading partners. But, with the development of multiparty, consumer-driven networks, advanced control towers now provide real-time visibility, collaboration, analytics, and artificial intelligence capabilities to move beyond decision support to decision-making and autonomous control.

Leading technology vendors allow users to set parameters for supply chain elements, such as inventory levels and replenishment plans, and then leave the tool to make adjustments when issues arise.

Additionally, vendors are providing capabilities that help enterprises work with multiple tiers of trading partners, manufacturers, transportation and logistics providers, and customers to better coordinate their operations. If designed and managed properly, a supply chain control tower can increase inventory turns and significantly reduce safety stocks, stock-outs, and expediting costs.

Some advantages that control towers offer include:

- End-to-end visibility – they remove data silos and establish real-time visibility across your global supply chain through a standardized data platform. They also turn data into actionable insights with personalized dashboards that provide a 360-degree view of KPIs and significant supply chain events.
- Management by exception – they detect, display, and prioritize work tasks in real time, allowing you to sense and react to issues quickly while managing risks and disruptions in your supply chain proactively.
- Intelligent workflows – they provide actionable workflows that can be customized to meet unique requirements and process steps required to automate actions within source transactional systems. They allow you to make informed decisions with a supply chain virtual assistant that provides responses to issues based on your supply chain data, using a natural language search.
- Smarter integration – they use integration patterns to connect all your existing supply chain systems and services. They allow you to collaborate with your supply chain stakeholders and take immediate action to resolve issues. They deploy, integrate, and scale easily to meet your business needs [IBM, 2021].

Linking Technologies

As information links all parts of the supply chain, other hardware and software tools are used for this purpose, including:

- Internet – allows companies to communicate with suppliers, customers, shippers, and other businesses around the world, instantaneously.

In recent years, the IoT has supplemented the internet using physical objects that are embedded with sensors, processing ability, software, and other technologies that connect and exchange data with other devices and systems over the internet or other communications networks.

- E-business – the gradual replacement of physical business processes with electronic ones. It comes in two general forms, the largest being business-to-business (B2B), and the other, business-to-consumer (B2C).
- Electronic data interchange (EDI) – the computer-to-computer exchange of standardized business documents. Today, EDI may also use the internet.
- Barcode and point-of-sale data – creates an instantaneous computer record of a sale and/or inventory position and movement.
- Radio frequency identification (RFID) – technology that can send product data from an item (containing an RFID chip) to a reader via radio waves.

Next, we will look at a variety of software systems that are used to help manage and control supply.

ENTERPRISE RESOURCE PLANNING SYSTEMS

ERP systems have grown to incorporate a huge diversity of functionality (and today are not just transactional and not just supply chain functionality, per Figure 15.2). Here, we will discuss them more from a perspective of enabling production and related internal supply chain and logistics operations processes.

While some may not consider ERP systems as supply chain management tools, a great deal of the functionality is supply chain and logistics related (see Figure 15.2), especially when you consider potential "add-on" modules such as forecasting, warehouse management systems, etc.

Much of the functionality is on the supply side (although sales management and order management certainly are demand-side applications typically found in ERP systems), hence their inclusion in this chapter.

FIGURE 15.2
Typical modules in a basic enterprise resource planning (ERP) system.

ERP systems were originally an extension of an MRP system used to integrate all internal processes as well as customers and suppliers. They allow for the automation and integration of many business processes, including finance, accounting, human resources, sales and order entry, raw materials, inventory, purchasing, production scheduling, shipping, resource and production planning, and customer relationship management. An ERP system shares common databases and business practices producing information in real time and coordinates business processes ranging from supplier evaluation to customer invoicing.

E-businesses must also keep track of and process a tremendous amount of information and, as such, have realized that much of the information they need to run an e-business, such as stock levels at various warehouses, cost of parts, and projected shipping dates, can already be found in their ERP system databases. As a result, a significant part of the online efforts of many e-businesses involves adding web access to an existing ERP system.

ERP systems have the potential to reduce transaction costs and increase the speed and accuracy of information, but they can also be expensive and time consuming to install.

ERP Technology

Enterprise system software is a multibillion-dollar industry that helps to support a variety of business functions and has been the largest category of capital expenditure in US businesses over the past decade or so. While early ERP systems focused on large enterprises, smaller enterprises increasingly use ERP systems to run their businesses in industries such as manufacturing, wholesalers/distributors, healthcare, government, retail stores, hotels, and financial services.

There are literally hundreds of ERP software vendors that range from the very large ones with expensive offerings (SAP and Oracle; up to millions of dollars) to mid-sized, mid-priced, relatively small vendors with offerings costing as little as $100,000 and up. They can vary in terms of functionality and platforms (e.g. client-server and cloud-based on-demand software as a service, or SAAS) and serve general or only specific industries.

It is beyond the scope of this book and this chapter to get too much into the detail of this technology beyond what we have already covered in terms of basic functionality and impact on the lean supply chain. However, the actual selection and implementation of these very critical systems can mean success or failure for an organization, as speed and accuracy are not only important from a lean perspective but can offer a company a distinct competitive advantage in today's global economy.

Additionally, when poorly managed, the selection and implementation can be very costly and wasteful to a company as not only is the software license itself expensive, but the "total cost of ownership" can be three to five times the cost of the software license and can include items such as training, consulting, technical and maintenance, hardware upgrades, and customization costs.

In this regard, it is worthwhile to point out that an article in *CIO* magazine offered "9 Tips for Selecting and Implementing an ERP System" [Schiff, 2014]:

1. Get upper management support – lack of upper management support and involvement can lead to resources at lower levels not being as dedicated and engaged in the implementation project.
2. Make a clear and extensive list of requirements before you start looking at vendors – any good project must start by defining its scope. This includes identifying specific business processes and their functional and system requirements. It is critical that you work with

end users, IT, and senior management from the start so you can find an industry-specific ERP system, with tools and features designed to solve your business requirements. This up-front effort will pay off in the long run.

3. Don't forget mobile users – accessing ERP systems from desktops only is no longer an option, so look for an ERP solution that allows users to also connect securely via smartphones and tablets.

4. Carefully evaluate your options before selecting your ERP system – make sure you have clear requirements and priorities as well as participation and input from key stakeholders during the evaluation stage to ensure better acceptance and user adoption.

   Reporting and metrics in the selected system are also important, so make sure the existing reports in the system have available the metrics you will need to drive your business, hiring, and resourcing.

   Integration is important as it must work with your existing legacy and/or critical office systems.

   If possible, try to find a vendor that specializes in your industry or, at the very least, has clients in your industry who can supply references.

5. Get references – so that you can ask the customers what went right, what went wrong, and what they might have done differently.

   You can also network with industry associations that you might belong to and ask colleagues for ERP recommendations.

6. Think before you customize – think about the amount of customization required for the ERP system as, the more customization required, the higher the cost, not only initially, but also when upgrading to new releases.

   Also, understand your tolerance for longer implementation cycles as, while a turnkey solution may have less flexibility, it will also likely have more stability and lower initial and ongoing cost.

   Many companies' basic business processes are very similar, such as paying invoices, collecting revenue, and procuring supplies (even though they may not think so!). So, there may be an opportunity to take advantage of standard best-practice processes that have been tested by many other companies.

   If a business function believes it has a case for a customization, make it justify it, as the cost of the customization not only covers writing and testing the code but also providing long-term support for the custom code, which may require special handling when you upgrade your software.

7. Factor in change management – most ERP projects entail huge changes in organizations and impact the culture of your company. So, you need to develop control and communication plans and workshops to help with implementation and adoption of the systems.

Appoint an internal ERP product champion – don't just use a vendor-appointed project manager.

8. It is important to put your best, most experienced people on the job as a lot is at stake.

9. Provide the necessary time and resources for training on the ERP system – you should identify department-specific needs up front and allow for sufficient time to develop and deliver training programs and, where possible, use employees within departments who can be given the opportunity for more in-depth instruction (i.e. "train the trainer") to become expert resources for their fellow employees. This can help to reduce the "us vs. them" dynamic which can often occur.

INVENTORY (AND PRODUCTION) PLANNING AND CONTROL TECHNOLOGY

As opposed to forecasting software, inventory planning and control software (at least for the perpetual tracking of inventory) is usually included in an accounting, ERP, or WMS software system as a basic function, although it can be licensed as a stand-alone system as well.

The basic inventory control systems track inventory balances, orders, receipts, shrinkage, allocation, and shipment of products. They will produce reports such as current inventory balance, out of stock products, and inventory transactions.

Many inventory control systems can also track purchase orders and other inventory value information that is helpful for accounting.

A large number of inventory systems have barcode or RFID functionality to scan items that are received, picked, or transferred and can be used to automate other functions such as cycle counting. The types of equipment required for this include barcode scanners, RF tags and readers, hand-held mobile computers, and barcode labelers and printers.

There is a breed of inventory planning and control (aka "management") software designed specifically for warehouse operations, called a warehouse management system, that helps to manage all inventory within the four walls of a warehouse; it will be discussed shortly.

There are also a variety of what are called inventory planning (or inventory management) software systems, often part of ERP and/or WMS software. Included in this category are production, purchasing, and distribution applications such as OMS, CRM, TMS, DRP, MPS, MRP, and short-term scheduling systems, which we will also briefly describe in the remainder of this chapter.

Sales and Operations Planning

Many people do not even think of S&OP (more of a short-to-medium-term focus) as a software application. As a result, even today, it is very common for organizations of all sizes to run their S&OP processes primarily using data downloaded, summarized, and analyzed in spreadsheets. This is neither timely nor accurate, and it can be hard to drill down to details for the "what if" type of analysis that is a necessary part of S&OP.

With advanced system support and Supply Chain 4.0 (using networked technologies and digital tools to accelerate, enhance, and optimize the supply chain to deliver both stronger business results and greater supply chain resilience), a majority of planning tasks, including S&OP, can be automated, ensuring better quality than tasks conducted manually. Once this is accomplished in the coming years, the S&OP process will move to a weekly rhythm, and the decision process will be built on scenarios that can be updated in real time. The accuracy, granularity, visibility, and speed have implications for the other elements, such as service, supply chain costs, and inventory. Systems will be able to detect the exception where a planner needs to jump in to make a decision.

One best-in-class example that exists today is SAP's integrated business planning. It is a real-time cloud-based solution that combines sales and operations planning (S&OP), forecasting and demand, response and supply, demand-driven replenishment, and inventory planning. SAP's integrated business planning (IBP) is automated, coordinates supply chain planning processes, uses advanced machine learning algorithms and planning capabilities, and is integrated with SAP's supply chain control tower and other solutions.

So, while S&OP-type systems/modules may not be too common yet, their time will come soon enough.

Warehouse Management Systems

As was previously mentioned, WMS are software applications used to manage the receipt, movement, and storage of materials within the "four walls" of a facility and process the related transactions necessary for receiving, put-away, picking, packing, and shipping. Early WMS only provided simple storage location functionality. Today's best-in-class systems, such as those offered by Manhattan Associates and High Jump Software, go beyond basic picking, packing, and shipping and use advanced algorithms to mathematically organize and optimize warehouse operations and may include tracking and routing technologies such as RFID and voice recognition.

While many ERP vendors include WMS modules, companies more typically license WMS from vendors that specialize in that type of system and then integrate them with their ERP or accounting systems. They can be run as installed systems or cloud-based on-demand SAAS systems.

As mentioned above, many sophisticated warehouse management systems are capable of using automatic identification and data capture technology, such as barcode scanners, mobile computers, and potentially RFID, to efficiently manage and monitor the flow of products, as speed and accuracy are paramount in a warehouse. Once data have been collected, they are synchronized, either via batch or real-time wireless transmission, with a central database which provides a variety of reports about the status of material in the warehouse.

In warehouses where there are multiple picking locations requiring fast and accurate picking, a "pick to light" or light-directed system can be used to enhance the capabilities of the employees. A pick to light system has lights above the racks or bins the employees will be picking from. The operator then scans a barcode that is on a tote or picking container representing the customer order. Based on the order, the system will require the operator to pick an item from a specific bin. A light above the bin will illuminate, showing the quantity to pick. The operator selects the item or items for the order and then presses the lighted indicator to confirm the pick. If no further lights are illuminated, the order is complete.

Voice-directed picking systems are gaining popularity. In this type of picking system, workers wear a headset connected to a small wearable computer which tells the worker where to go and what to do using verbal commands. The operators then confirm their tasks by saying predefined commands and reading confirmation codes printed on locations or products throughout the warehouse. These systems are used instead of paper or mobile computer systems requiring workers to read instructions and scan barcodes or enter information manually to confirm their tasks, thus freeing the operators' hands and eyes.

Order Management Systems

An order management system is a computer software system used in many industries for order entry and processing. In most cases, it is part of a larger ERP, WMS, or accounting system (Figure 15.3).

OMS applications manage processes including order entry, customer credit validation, pricing, promotions, inventory allocation, invoice generation, sales commissions, and sales history.

A distributed order management (DOM) system is different from an OMS in that it manages the assignment of orders across a network of multiple production, distribution, and/or retail locations to ensure that logistics costs and/or customer service levels are optimized.

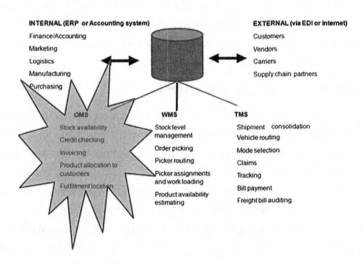

FIGURE 15.3
Order management system (OMS) and other supply chain execution systems.

An OMS is usually deployed as part of an enterprise application such an ERP system as its sales engine is integrated with the organization's inventory, procurement, and financial systems.

Customer Relationship Management Systems

The term "customer relationship management" refers to processes, strategies, and technologies that companies use to manage and analyze customer interactions and data throughout the customer life cycle. Its goal is to improve business relationships with customers while assisting in customer retention and increasing sales revenue.

A CRM "system" is a software application that manages a company's interactions with current and future customers and involves using technology to organize, automate, and synchronize sales, marketing, customer service, and technical support. This includes the management of business contacts, clients, contract wins, and sales leads within the sales function, sometimes referred to as sales force automation (SFA) software. The four largest vendors of CRM systems are salesforce.com, Microsoft, SAP, and Oracle. There are also many other smaller CRM vendors that are popular with small-to-mid-market businesses.

Perhaps the biggest benefit to most businesses when moving to a CRM system comes from having all their business data stored in and accessed from a single location, whereas, before CRM systems, customer data were spread out in office productivity suite documents, email systems, mobile phone data, and even note cards and Rolodex™ entries, in various departments.

Transportation Management Systems

Transportation systems which are used to connect your supply chain must be managed and controlled properly, with complete visibility and great communication between partners. Transportation and logistics (primarily warehouse operations) costs can account for as much as 7–14 percent of sales, depending on the industry. Transportation costs alone comprise the vast majority of this expense for most companies. Best-in-class companies have transportation- and logistics-related costs in a range of 4–7 percent, depending on industry sector. So, it is not hard to see how important transportation is to a successful business, both operationally and financially.

As a result, not surprisingly, TMS have existed, in one form or another, to manage this process for quite a long while. Historically, they have been a "add-on" to an existing ERP or legacy (i.e. "home-grown") order processing or warehouse management system.

Like most software today, they can be installed as resident software or web-based and accessed on demand.

A TMS offers benefits to an organization such as automated auditing and billing, optimized operations, and improved visibility (see Figure 15.4).

It typically includes functionality to plan, schedule, and control an organization's transportation system with functionality for:

- Planning and decision-making – helps to define the most efficient transport schemes according to parameters such as transportation cost, lead time, stops, etc. Also includes inbound and outbound transportation mode, transportation provider selection, and vehicle load and route optimization.
- Transportation execution – allows for the execution of a transportation plan such as carrier rate acceptance, carrier dispatching, EDI, etc.
- Transport follow-up – tracks physical or administrative transportation operations, such as traceability of transport event, receipt, customs clearance, invoicing, and booking documents, and sends transport alerts (delay, accident, etc.).
- Measurement – offers cost control and key performance indicator (KPI) reporting as they relate to transportation.

Ultimately, a supply chain system is made up of connecting links and nodes, where the transportation system provides the links, and the facilities provide the nodes. As the saying goes, "a chain is as strong as its weakest

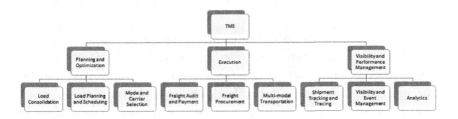

FIGURE 15.4
Transportation management system (TMS) components.

link", and so efficient, timely management of the links is especially critical in today's global supply chain.

A yard management system (YMS), which may be a module of a TMS (or WMS) or a stand-alone application, integrates warehouse operations with inbound and outbound transportation and maximizes yard and warehouse efficiency by managing the flow of all inbound and outbound goods.

The YMS enables a business to plan, execute, track, and audit loads based on critical characteristics such as shipment type, load configuration, labor requirements, and dock and warehouse capacity.

The YMS is used to arrange dock appointments for receiving orders and for arranging and scheduling outbound transportation equipment and also helps to manage materials and transportation equipment in the warehouse or factory yard.

Distribution Requirements Planning (DRP)

Similar to many advanced planning and scheduling (APS) systems (discussed later in this chapter), DRP traditionally was an "add-on" type of system as many of its inputs (inventory balances, existing purchase and production work orders, forecasts, etc.) and outputs (deployment/transfer requirements, new purchase and work orders, etc.) come from ERP or accounting systems.

Today, many ERP vendors have added DRP as a module as the demand for it has significantly increased.

DRP software is a continuation of the MRP logic used for outbound movement of finished goods from facilities. The deployment requirements, after being summarized by item, are used to generate the item master production schedule, which then drives the MRP system through the bill of material file to create raw material and component requirements (Figure 15.5).

The software itself is fairly similar from vendor to vendor, using the aforementioned logic. However, it can vary in terms of user interface and ability to collaborate and share internally and externally. Additionally, like most software today, it can be installed at a company on its IT infrastructure (and possibly be web-enabled or web-based as well) or, in some cases, be offered as SAAS (software as a service or on demand) cloud software.

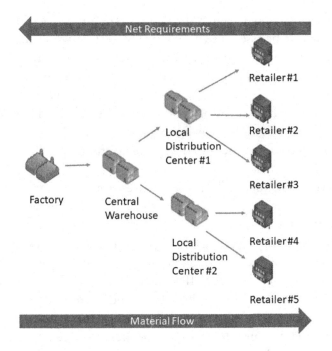

FIGURE 15.5
Distribution requirements planning in a network.

MRP and DRP were pioneering technologies for the computerization of supply chain planning. In the late 1980s to mid-1990s, the APS software vendors marketed aggressively against the ERP vendors. The ERP vendors, for their part, tried to downplay the importance of "best-in-breed" external solutions – that is, until they began acquiring APS applications including DRP themselves (some ERP vendors developed the capabilities on their own rather than through acquisition). Eventually, many mid-to-large companies implemented MRP and DRP. In the case of DRP, it had become more prevalent in make-to-stock (MTS) companies with extended distribution networks, such as are found in the consumer products industry, for example.

Master Production Scheduling (MPS)

An MPS takes a business plan and other inputs from financial plans, customer demand, engineering, and supplier performance to create a comprehensive product manufacturing schedule, by facility, for independent demand inventory (i.e. end items or finished goods). The MPS covers what is to be assembled or made, at what time, with what materials, and the cash required during each week of a relatively short-range planning horizon. MPS is a key driver of material requirements planning (MRP) which determines raw material and component requirements, known as "dependent demand" inventory and covered in Chapter 13, as well as a short-term manufacturing schedule (Chapter 14).

The MPS must be in sync with the aggregate production plan (covered in Chapter 12), which attempts to create a supply plan that satisfies demand at the lowest cost, and, as the process moves from planning to execution, each step must be tested for feasibility in terms of manpower, machine, and material constraints.

Rough cut capacity planning (RCCP) involves a quick check on a few key resources to implement the MPS in order to ensure that it is feasible from the capacity point of view. The MPS and RCCP are developed interactively. This determines the impact of the MPS on the key or aggregate resources such as man or machine hours. Rough cut capacity plans can be "finite", or constrained, because they have to operate within certain constraints, or can be "infinite", or unconstrained, leaving adjustment decisions to the expertise and knowledge of the planners themselves.

Inputs for a master production schedule can include forecasted demand, production costs, inventory, customer needs, lot size, production lead time, and capacity. Inputs can be automatically generated by an ERP system.

A typical output for a finalized MPS is a production plan, in a format often referred to as a production, sales, and inventory (PSI) report (see Figure 15.6) and can include quantities to be produced, staffing levels, quantity available to promise, and projected available balance. It is usually generated

ABC Company
PSI Report

February 23,2011

Plant/Market Zone : EAST
Item : 016
Description : WINDOW CLEANER 1002
Safety Time : 9
Safety Stock: 1611

Period	Past Due	23Feb11	28Feb11	07Mar11	14Mar11	21Mar11	28Mar11	04Apr11	11Apr11	18Apr11	25Apr11	02May11	09May11	Total
Periods of Supply	6.2	1.83	1.53	2.05	2.0	1.95	1.67	2.0	2.1	2.07	2.53	2.06	2.82	
Beginning Inventory	620	528	1037	1677	1638	1599	1268	986	1033	1020	1247	1534	1508	16479
Forecast	0	503	823	819	819	819	754	493	493	493	493	746	746	8001
Customer Orders	100	300	1200	0	0	0	0	0	0	0	0	0	0	1600
Dependent Demand	0	0	0	0	0	0	0	0	0	0	0	0	0	0
Scheduled Receipts	0	1700	200	0	0	0	0	0	0	0	0	0	0	1900
Planned Orders	0	120	840	780	780	480	480	540	480	720	780	720	780	7500

Plant/Market Zone : ALL
Item : 016
Description : WINDOW CLEANER 1002
Safety Time : 9
Safety Stock: 1611

Period	Past Due	23Feb11	28Feb11	07Mar11	14Mar11	21Mar11	28Mar11	04Apr11	11Apr11	18Apr11	25Apr11	02May11	09May11	Total
Beginning Inventory	620	528	1037	1677	1638	1599	1268	986	1033	1020	1247	1534	1508	16479
Forecast	0	503	823	819	819	819	754	493	493	493	493	746	746	8001
Customer Orders	100	300	1200	0	0	0	0	0	0	0	0	0	0	1600
Dependent Demand	0	0	0	0	0	0	0	0	0	0	0	0	0	0
Scheduled Receipts	0	1700	200	0	0	0	0	0	0	0	0	0	0	1900
Planned Orders	0	120	840	780	780	480	480	540	480	720	780	720	780	7500

FIGURE 15.6

Production, sales, and inventory (PSI) report example.

at the item level for a particular sourcing facility (internal or outsourced) or market zone and is shown in weekly or monthly time planning buckets.

The technology used to generate a master production schedule can range from fairly complex spreadsheets to modules within ERP or supply chain planning systems. Integrated solutions offer the benefit of being connected to the aggregate, material requirements planning and short-term scheduling systems, creating more efficient and effective results.

Material Requirements Planning

While some small-to-medium-size enterprises (SMEs) may use a spreadsheet, as shown in Figure 15.7, or an affordable stand-alone MRP system, most enterprise resource planning systems from companies such as SAP, Oracle, etc. have MRP (and usually RCCP and CRP) functionality.

The reason for this is that ERP systems, developed in the 1990s, were extensions of the MRP system that tie in customers and suppliers, allow automation and integration of many business processes, share common databases and business practices, produce information in real time, and coordinate business from supplier evaluation to customer invoicing.

ERP modules typically can include functionality for basic MRP, finance, human resources, supply chain management, customer relationship management, and even sustainability.

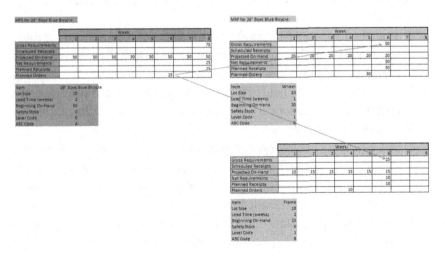

FIGURE 15.7
MPS and MRP spreadsheet screen examples.

Since the 1990s, ERP systems have expanded their functionality, through internal development and/or acquisition, to include other applications such as supply chain (forecasting, warehouse management systems, etc.) and S&OP and down to the plant floor with tighter integration with manufacturing execution systems (MES). Originally, they were geared toward large manufacturing companies, but they are now available for companies of all industries and sizes.

While the basic functionality of MRP technology hasn't changed that much over the years, the technology itself has changed and continues to change with the times.

Kowalke [2015] pointed out five ways that MRP technology is changing:

1. Better resilience – With longer supply chains and the need to adapt more quickly at the same time, MRP is increasingly stressing automation and automatic reconfiguration in the face of potential disruptions.

2. Increased data sharing – Every engineer knows that the more complex a system, the more points for potential failure. With supply chains stretching in more directions, effectively managing material resources without surprises is requiring firms to better coordinate and share data among each other.

   Beer manufacturer, Heineken … [brought] supplier data in house … and integrate[ed] it with its MRP systems as if the suppliers were directly part of the business …

3. Smarter analysis – The good news is that there's more data for intelligent MRP, but the bad news is that it can be a challenge to corral all that data and make sense of it.

   Enter the emerging field of big data analytics, which is helping firms pull together the raw data coming from consumers, manufacturing facilities and suppliers …

4. Self-reporting inventory – Tapping into another major trend, MRP is starting to leverage the Internet of things (IoT), which delivers automation and self-reporting to materials resource planning for added efficiency and better resiliency …

5. Easier implementation – No trends story would be complete without examining the impact of the cloud. In the case of MRP, the cloud doesn't add functionality as much as it enables fast MRP systems deployment and reduced costs.

Short-Term Scheduling Technology

In general, when it comes to short-term scheduling, organizations use a range of tools from spreadsheets (some can be fairly sophisticated) through modules in ERP systems to separate optimization systems. Below are some examples of these systems.

Advanced Planning and Scheduling Systems

Historically, manufacturers have relied heavily on the planning functionality in their ERP legacy systems. These systems are based upon early 1980s concepts such as infinite capacity, time buckets, and backwards scheduling. The software that drives MRP applications was primarily designed to address the needs of make-to-stock manufacturers and entailed the use of excess buffers of inventory and time in all levels of the manufacturing process.

On the other hand, lean systems are manually intensive and, over time, they tend to become disconnected from a company's legacy planning systems. It is also harder to implement them in companies that have many SKUs, limited capacity, and unpredictable demand, at least one reason for the high failure rate of lean initiatives in the United States.

Bridges for this disconnect are what are known as advanced planning and scheduling systems, which can accurately manage time, react to changes at the operation level, and still create a schedule that quickly and accurately synchronizes multiple constraints.

An APS system is a manufacturing management process by which raw materials and production capacity are optimally allocated to meet demand. APS is especially well suited to environments where simpler planning methods cannot adequately address complex trade-offs between competing priorities. Production scheduling is very difficult owing to the interaction of limited capacity and the number of items/products to be manufactured.

Finite Capacity Scheduling Systems

A specific tool of APS used to deal with this complexity from a short-term scheduling perspective is known as a finite capacity scheduling (FCS) system (Figure 15.8). Finite capacity scheduling is an approach used to understand how much work can be produced in a certain time

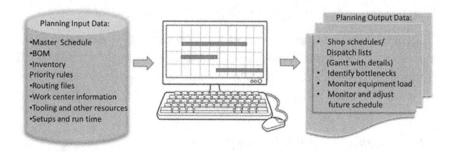

Planning Input Data:

- Master Schedule
- BOM
- Inventory
  Priority rules
- Routing files
- Work center information
- Tooling and other resources
- Setups and run time

Planning Output Data:

- Shop schedules/
  Dispatch lists
  (Gantt with details)
- Identify bottlenecks
- Monitor equipment load
- Monitor and adjust
  future schedule

FIGURE 15.8
Finite capacity scheduling system inputs and outputs.

period, with limitations on different resources taken into consideration. The goal is to make sure that work proceeds at an even and efficient pace throughout the plant. Software applications for determining the best way to schedule work are called decision support tools. Finite scheduling tools are different than infinite capacity scheduling tools. Infinite scheduling tools, which are simpler, do not account for limitations on the system that occur in real time.

Different types of finite capacity scheduling tools are:

- Electronic scheduling board (ESB) – this provides a graphical view of all jobs currently in production. When the digital board receives data from the factory floor, it can calculate performance times automatically, even if the administrator makes changes, and can issue a warning if there is a bottleneck.
- Order-based scheduling (OBS) – the scheduler (person or software application) prioritizes which work will be completed first by selecting only the orders that meet the plant's preset work in progress (WIP) criteria.
- Constraint-based schedulers (CBS) – bottlenecks in the production line determine the schedule for the rest of the components in the system.
- Discrete event simulation (DES) – this models random events and predicts the domino effect one event would have on the rest of the system.
- Genetic algorithms – these are similar to the scientific theory of natural selection: new schedules (children) are developed using

characteristics, such as sequences of work, from previous (parent) schedules.

Advanced Planning and Scheduling Systems Technology

Many of the larger ERP software vendors offer APS modules. There are also best-of-breed solutions offered by vendors such as Asprova and Preactor.

Detailed scheduling software is an important tool for many companies, where it can have a major impact on the productivity of a process.

The difference between planning software and scheduling software is that planning systems are "bucketed" (monthly, weekly, daily) and don't preserve operation sequences within the time bucket. Scheduling systems are "bucket-less"; they preserve sequencing and can generate dispatch lists or shop schedules. The assignment of an operation to a resource is a critical component of an FCS system for achieving operational efficiency and optimized performance. Detailed scheduling uses a shorter time horizon and a much more detailed process route than a planning system.

The inputs to an FCS system are manufacturing work orders; there is a process route associated with each order that defines the operation steps to make the product. The user then can load the orders onto individual resources using scheduling rules and interact with the schedule using the Gantt charts and plots that are generated. A typical output would be a dispatch list for each resource.

By now, the reader should have a good idea as to the best practices in demand and supply chain planning, along with the current types of technology used in these processes.

However, as this is just a "snapshot" of existing processes and the information technology used in demand and supply chain planning, it's time to see how things are rapidly changing and try to get a feel for where they will end up over the next decade or so.

Section IV

The Road Ahead

16

The Impact of Omni Channel, the Pandemic, and Other Natural and Manmade Events on the Supply Chain

The growing need for a seamless, accurate, timely, and personalized omni channel response is coming at us at an ever-increasing rate.

Consumer demands coupled along with trends such as shorter product life cycles, free shipping, and competition around delivery times mean retailers can't operate within channel silos anymore. They need to anticipate and stay ahead of market disruptions such as COVID-19 and be agile and flexible to rapidly adapt to consumer expectations. The retailers who try to use legacy systems and processes to meet these new consumer demands may lose market share and struggle to stay profitable.

To remain competitive, at the minimum they must:

- Meet customers in the channel of their choice.
- Recognize and acknowledge who individual customers are, the products and services they have purchased, and their prior interaction history, regardless of channel.
- Operate as a single brand and channel, orchestrating customer experiences across all touch points.
- Show customers they are valued through personalized offers, treatment, and rewards.

What are some concerns of retailers when it comes to successfully adapting to today's volatile environment?

DOI: 10.4324/9781003281078-20

OMNI CHANNEL RETAIL AREAS OF ATTENTION

"Omni Channel Retail, a Deloitte Point of View" [2015] identified three areas of heightened attention during the shift toward omni channel retail:

1. Return on marketing spend – as we know, omni channel marketing is about delivering a more interactive, personalized brand experience that goes beyond siloed behavior, where the consumer is reached through all possible touch points or channels. Both e-tailers and traditional retailers need to create a marketing strategy specific to their business and products, with the marketing going through the appropriate channels for each customer group.
2. Ever-changing payment solution landscape – while multiple payment solutions have existed in the e-commerce market for some time, it is only recently that they have become a consideration to drive sales across the various channels. Online customers expect multiple payment options, requiring retailers to offer the right mix of payment options.
3. Increased supply chain complexity – the supply chain supports e-commerce operations as its organization and execution will determine the customer experience. A supply chain with optimized and aligned warehousing and distribution operations can help you to deliver on your promises as well as the management of returns, with its inherent high costs.

OMNI CHANNEL SUPPLY CHAIN ENABLERS

Delving a little more into the supply chain area, which requires great attention (as that is the primary focus of this book), Deloitte found that customer-driven delivery and return strategies were critical enablers of an omni channel strategy.

Specifically, the enablers mentioned included:

- Drop shipping – this is where a customer order triggers a shipment from a third-party logistics provider (3PL) or direct from the manufacturer; it can be an effective way for e-tailers to reduce inventory holding costs and warehouse space, freeing up capital for other investments.

- Drop shipping may not be applicable in all industry segments. For example, in fashion, customers might order multiple products from different brands but would expect one delivery, not multiple shipments from different vendors. On the other hand, in the furniture industry, drop shipping works quite well as it can lower margins, as the 3PL or manufacturer builds inventory holding costs into the price.

- Click-and-collect – this is where the customer purchases items online and has the option to pick up at a brick-and-mortar (or other designated) location of the customer's choosing. While it may seem easy, it is a challenging strategy to actually implement. However, click-and-collect does give customers flexibility and control over their purchase because they are able to choose a convenient location to pick up their item.

- Curbside pickup (often "contactless") – a variation on click-and-collect, it is gaining popularity during the COVID-19 pandemic and allows the customer to place their order online or by phone (typically requires payment upfront via credit card, PayPal, etc.) and to pick up curbside at the retail location later. While this began at restaurants and grocery stores, it has rapidly gained popularity in other types of retail. Only time will tell if this is a lasting option after the pandemic is behind us.

- Reserve-and-collect – this is similar to click-and-collect, except that checkout occurs after the customer views the item(s) in person. The customer reserves an item online and picks it up and pays for it later at a brick-and-mortar store, requiring retailers to have very organized inventory supported by a good order management system.

- Delivery lockers – lockers are placed in convenient locations such as train stations and grocery stores. The customer opens the locker with a code given to them in connection with a purchase online. Customers can also return items to the lockers, but this can become an issue during periods of peak sales.

- Same-day delivery – customers are increasingly requiring fast delivery, and so being able to provide same-day delivery can give your company a competitive advantage. From a fulfillment strategy standpoint, this means the item ordered is in stock in a brick-and-mortar store or a warehouse that is located close to a major city and is delivered the same day to the customer. This type of delivery can be extremely challenging outside of larger cities and only works in some industries.

Many (Un)Happy Returns: Return Strategy as an Enabler

The high costs associated with returns (up to 40 percent in some industries) continue to challenge the e-commerce industry. Customers expect generous returns policies, especially when buying in an omni channel environment where they usually don't physically see and touch the product before buying it.

Customers also expect longer free return periods for products bought online as well as to be able to return an item wherever they like.

A generous returns policy can drive sales (e.g. Zappos and Warby Parker), but it is also a major cost driver. Omni channel retailers that can figure out how to combine a generous policy that drives additional sales with optimizing the costs of returns management will be the leaders of tomorrow. If properly handled, returns can greatly contribute to increased revenues; if not handled well, they can reduce profits through higher transportation, handling, and warehouse costs.

TECHNOLOGY AS AN ENABLER

Dynamically changing supply chain and fulfillment strategies have increased the importance of an enterprise-wide system for inventory that breaks down barriers and integrates channels with each other to create the better visibility needed for an omni channel experience.

Omni Channel Order Management Systems and Their Benefits

A truly integrated OMS is critical in omni channel retail since the customer interacts and moves between physical and digital channels.

OMS is becoming increasingly important as it is at the center of e-commerce operations, integrating the order and delivery channels by not only processing orders, but also providing intelligence and visibility surrounding inventory, delivery options, and customer information.

It is important to have a good OMS to offer the various delivery options today's customer is demanding as it has to share information about the order throughout the entire order cycle, from the point of order to the final delivery, and provide the organization with real-time information regardless of delivery channel or point of order.

Below are some of the benefits of an integrated OMS in an omni channel environment:

- Distributed order management – an OMS provides assistance with order routing, returns management, order splitting, tax calculations, payment processing, partial shipments, and order exception management, all critical components for e-tailers.
- Single view of inventory – having a single view of inventory is critical to success in omni channel retail and its supply chain, as it can provide real-time information about available inventory across all channels in the organization. An OMS can also combine an "outside-in" view of inventory information with an "inside-out" view, seamlessly integrating internal store and distribution inventory with drop-shipping vendors, in-transit inventory, and third-party delivery facilities.
- Store fulfillment – the rising trend of store fulfillment is important for e-tailers that also have physical stores, as it provides information on surrounding shipping from stores, store pickup, and click-and-collect.
- Customer service – of course, OMS is an effective way to increase customer service as it provides information about order details, order capture, and refunds/credits among other things.

NEXT STEPS IN YOUR SUPPLY CHAIN'S OMNI CHANNEL JOURNEY

The question then becomes, "how can your organization take the next step" in its omni channel evolution?

To do this, you need to know where you are and where you want to be. Table 16.1 is a great starting point. I am a firm believer in "evolution not revolution", and so I wouldn't recommend skipping any steps.

TABLE 16.1

Supply Chain Omni Channel Evolution

Entry level Functionality does not exist	Developing Basic functionality exists	Performing Advanced functionality exists	Leading Industry leader
No clear vision exists for e-commerce supply chain and order fulfillment	A supply chain strategy with a clear vision exists for the e-commerce operations	The supply chain strategy is well designed and executed with the use of systems (WMS, OMS, etc.)	A tailored supply chain with a mix of fulfillment strategies
Limited shipping options offered to customers	Several shipping options, treated as separate/isolated channels, are available to the customers	Optimized returns management	Real-time tracking of order and shipment is made available to the customer
Shipments are made on an ad-hoc basis	Shipments are planned and consolidated where possible, with accurate estimated vs. actual delivery date	Multiple shipping and delivery options exist (e.g. click-and-collect, same day delivery, etc.) with integration between the various channels	Order fulfillment and shipments are enabled by technologies
No strategy for optimizing returns management	Policies are developed for returns management to reduce cost	Shipment and return KPIs are tracked and benchmarked against industry peers	Seamless integration between all channels

Source: "Omni Channel Retail: A Deloitte Point of View", Deloitte (2015).

OMNI CHANNEL SUPPLY CHAIN CHALLENGES

Omni channel retail means consumers want the same experience across all retail channels. However, while many customers want to view in-store inventory online and to be able to buy online and pick up in store (or have shipped, preferably for free, to their homes), only around a third of retailers can perform those basic omni channel functions. On top of that, retailers must enable customers to choose how to return goods (i.e. ship back or return to stores).

Omni channel retailing involves seamlessly integrating the customer experience across all interaction channels – in store, on the web, and on mobile devices.

The buying process is less predictable and more dynamic, through increasing internet and mobile use, with more "touch points". Consumers have also become more powerful, partially owing to social media.

While we can more easily see this in the business-to-consumer (B2C) (retail) sector, the business-to-consumer (B2B) (manufacturer and wholesaler/ distributor) sector also has to deal with more complex transactions and processes, with a variety of partners, customers, and suppliers having to be integrated.

WHY IS OMNI CHANNEL IMPORTANT?

The changing needs and desires of today's consumers (especially millennials) have put added stress on the retail supply chain.

Omni channel, when executed properly, can help to meet these demands; consumers love omni channel retail since it is easy to customize delivery choice, they have more chances to check an item before purchase, they feel safe to purchase items, and it's a way to access the store's products conveniently.

Furthermore, consumers want quick and correct delivery. While two days was considered fast a few years ago, many today can hardly wait two hours.

An added advantage of omni channel is that it has the potential to increase sales as it can add new customers and new sales channels.

So, while there are great challenges and opportunities with omni channel retail, they have a great variety of impacts on the supply chain that need to be dealt with.

THE IMPACT OF OMNI CHANNEL COMMERCE ON THE RETAIL SUPPLY CHAIN

Today's customers expect a consistent buying experience across all retail channels. This has significant impacts on the retail supply chain in a variety of areas.

Processing Customer Orders

A traditional retail supply chain is hierarchical, with complete customer demand fulfilled at the store. Shifting that volume of sales to a B2C channel requires filling a truck with boxes holding only one to five items – many thousands of boxes a day. The major impact is increasing the number of deliveries exponentially while decreasing the number of line items in the system.

Furthermore, the volatility of online ordering requires companies to broaden the portfolio of items they keep in stock to maximize customer demand, and so retailers must broaden their portfolio of stock-keeping units and reduce the number of delivery lines shipped per delivery.

For example, in the recent past, a shoe retailer running a shop needed to have approximately 100 types of shoes to meet demand. Today, with Zappos and shoes.com offering over 20,000 types, to stay competitive, the same shoe retailer needs to be able to offer and ship almost every brand and type of shoe (and they need also to carry the most popular shoe sizes).

So, when adding an e-commerce component, the brick-and-mortar shoe store has exponentially more orders and SKUs to manage (see Figure 16.1).

Delivery from Store or Distribution Center?

Implementing an omni channel process usually requires creating or enhancing a "standard" e-commerce strategy as, at some point, the company needs to halt the distribution process and ship goods directly to the customer (usually at the distribution center, or DC).

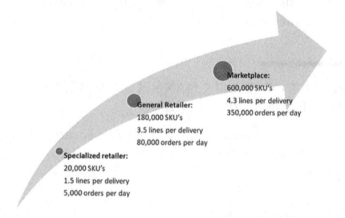

FIGURE 16.1

Fundamental effects of e-commerce engagement on a traditional retailer's supply chain.
Source: Kourimsky and van der Berk (2014).

As stores can be supplied from several distribution centers, a customer order might need to be fulfilled from several distribution centers.

Delivery from a store to the customer may be easier than from a DC, depending on transportation cost, picking efficiency, trained manpower, etc. So, supply chain organizations must choose between the two models (or use some combination of both).

Inventory Optimization and Sales and Operations Planning

One of the critical challenges of implementing an omni channel process is that the safety stock levels and stock deployment must be redetermined throughout the supply chain. Sales forecasts will have to adapt, and service levels will need to be re-evaluated.

Adapting sales forecasts to include both store and e-commerce demand requires visibility along the entire supply chain. Additional data can come from collaboration with other channels, such as distributors, or from social media measuring tools, for example.

Given today's market dynamics and global competition, companies following an omni channel strategy will also need to explore new ways to optimize inventory which can be supported by effective sales and operations planning (i.e. making sure that aggregate supply matches demand) assisted by demand-sensing tools that combine next-generation forecasting methods with "big data" technologies.

Impacts on Distribution/Fulfillment Centers and IT

Most companies will want to adapt their distribution center to deliver B2C orders, at the very least owing to transportation, workforce, and process issues, with new areas set up for packing stations (vs., as opposed to traditionally, shipping out cases and sometimes full pallets of individual SKUs) and consolidation.

Distribution centers may even need to be relocated to cover a wider variety of goods, in some cases.

The foundation of providing an omni channel experience starts with a company's core technology. The ability to deliver an omni channel experience rests on having a single commerce platform that unifies front-end and back-end systems and provides a central hub for order management, customer, item, and inventory data. The back-end systems of the platform will then funnel data to all sales channels, ensuring that accurate information across all customer touchpoints is delivered in real time, creating efficiencies and opportunities to improve the customer experience.

Real-time visibility into inventory levels across all channels means you will never miss out on sales opportunities because of inadequately stocked merchandise and inefficient modes of tracking product levels. Centralized order management delivers on the promise of fulfilling, buying, and returning anywhere. And unifying siloed sources of customer data into a single repository to get one complete view of the customer across all channels and touchpoints will deliver consistent customer service and support personalized marketing, merchandising, and targeted promotions across all channels.

Specifically, there will be a large impact on warehouse IT processes, as modifying traditional warehouse processes to handle the increased volume of smaller-sized "pick-and-pack" web-based orders is just one of the many impacts that the warehouse management system will face (Figure 16.2).

Making the received goods available for immediate sale is a key challenge for e-commerce retailers.

At Amazon, for example, incoming goods are immediately put into the closest available bin. They unload and put away the goods as fast as possible (vs. up to three days at some DCs), even putting cosmetics, shoes, and books in the same storage bin. This helps to reduce stock levels in the distribution centers and free up cash.

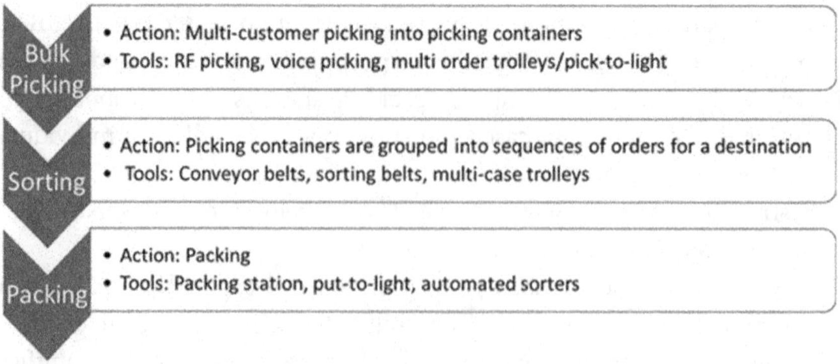

Bulk Picking
- Action: Multi-customer picking into picking containers
- Tools: RF picking, voice picking, multi order trolleys/pick-to-light

Sorting
- Action: Picking containers are grouped into sequences of orders for a destination
- Tools: Conveyor belts, sorting belts, multi-case trolleys

Packing
- Action: Packing
- Tools: Packing station, put-to-light, automated sorters

FIGURE 16.2
Best practice for B2C picking. Source: Kourimsky and van der Berk (2014).

Impact of a Multi-step Picking Process

Distribution centers will not only have to look at the physical layout and receiving process, but will also have to adapt their shipping operations significantly.

Internet orders are much smaller and more numerous than B2B processes, and so the distribution center will typically have to set up a multi-step picking process. Picking will usually be "consolidated", where a warehouse operator will pick for several sales orders at a time. These items will be conveyed to a packing station where the consolidated picks will be sorted and packed into a box for the end customer and, finally, loaded onto the correct carrier vehicle [Kourimsky and van der Berk, 2014].

THE IMPACT OF OMNI CHANNEL COMMERCE ON MANUFACTURERS

While a lot of the focus on omni channel has been on retail, it's easy to lose sight of the impact on manufacturing.

Even before omni channel became a "hot" topic, manufacturers were focusing on having timely and accurate visibility to retail demand and consumption on the production line, distribution center, and store in order to fulfill orders on time and at the lowest cost possible. So, omni channel is just an extension to that effort, and, as a result, at least to some extent, the B2B and B2C sides of e-commerce are merging.

An omni channel solution is practically impossible without e-commerce, and vice versa in the case of manufacturers. Customers want to be able to have options and maintain accountability with the manufacturer at practically any stage in the shipping and order process.

The traditional way of manufacturers selling to retail only is rapidly being supplanted by the idea of working in an integrated and collaborative omni channel environment, to include e-commerce, in order to survive and thrive.

Key Challenges

The consumer today is everywhere and has a large impact on the entire supply chain, all the way down to the manufacturing level. As a result, consumers now expect an endless assortment of goods that reaches all the way up to the manufacturer.

Organizations must bring on additional items or variations of existing items (such as more sizes or colors) and make those items available anywhere, at any time, according to customers' increasing demand for personalization and customization. So the impact on the manufacturer can be huge.

Furthermore, the distinction between brands and retailers doesn't concern most consumers. Smart manufacturers can take advantage of this opportunity to get closer to the consumer. However, they will need the required fulfillment and supply chain capabilities, which is the case as some larger brands, such as LG and L'Oréal, are creating frictionless direct-to-consumer fulfillment options. Currently, manufacturers' sales direct to consumers are under 10 percent of revenue, but, with less resistance from retailers, there is opportunity to grow this channel.

Manufacturers must react to more frequent, smaller orders of more items. Some manufacturers are now even being asked to drop ship programs, which requires the manufacturer to act as a direct-to-consumer company.

This results in a reduction in the number of single SKU pallets, complicating the pick-and-pack process, with increased flexibility and planning needed, as well as more labor for preparing goods for shipment.

Manufacturers must become more flexible and agile in fulfilling orders to ensure on-time and accurate customer deliveries. They also must gain visibility beyond the factory into distribution centers and across the entire supply chain to track raw materials, works in progress, and finished goods, while also managing new pick-and-pack operations and shipping processes. Transportation routing must be efficiently planned, trailers must be efficiently loaded with contents that don't necessarily align and stack like pallets, and the increasing number of trailer appointments owing to smaller orders with mixed items must be managed to minimize congestion in the yard.

Ultimately, to stay competitive in the emerging omni channel world, manufacturers must adapt their processes as well as their systems to the new lean, agile world of omni channel retail.

PANDEMICS, CLIMATE CHANGE, AND OTHER SUPPLY CHAIN DISRUPTIONS: THE ROAD MAP OUT OF THIS MESS

As I have mentioned earlier, the pandemic accelerated the move to omni channel, allowing consumers more options for having their needs met.

However, it also appears that the COVID-19 pandemic has revealed the shortcomings of a supply chain that is perhaps too lean, so that, when labor, materials, and equipment shortages occur as a result, inventory shortages and price increases tend to occur.

To be "lean", however, doesn't mean maintaining extremely low inventory levels with no coordination or backup plan. It also appears some have forgotten the "agile" part, meaning they need flexible alternatives at the ready.

In any case, it appears that many companies and their supply chains were caught off guard by the COVID-19 crisis, despite recent disasters such as the earthquake and tsunami in Japan, volcanic eruptions in Iceland, and Hurricanes Maria and Harvey.

In order to minimize risk in their supply chains, companies need to first identify the sources and types of potential risk and estimate their probability and impact. Supply chain risks come from an array of potential sources, including global pandemics.

Risk Mitigation Strategies

To combat this type of scenario, companies should look to supply chain risk mitigation strategies (covered in more detail in the next chapter) that include boosting capacity, engaging redundant suppliers, increasing responsiveness and flexibility, aggregating demand, and increasing source capabilities. Where appropriate, companies can also consider adding inventory by decentralizing the stock of predictable, lower-value products and centralizing the stock of less predictable, higher-value products (such as personal protective equipment and ventilators in our current case).

Where to Start

According to a 2013 Deloitte survey, while many company executives realized supply chain risk was an important factor in their decision-making, many didn't feel their programs were effective. I don't think things have changed much since then.

A good place to start in the risk mitigation process is mapping your supply chain. Make sure you know the answers to questions such as:

- What are the physical locations of your suppliers' manufacturing facilities and those of their suppliers?

- Which parts are manufactured at each location?
- What is the history and frequency of disruptions that occur at each facility and geographic region, owing to either natural forces (hurricanes, floods, earthquakes) or other factors (labor strikes, power outages, quality issues)?

Many sophisticated software tools are available to help map your supply chain. Smaller companies that can't afford the investment can analyze their bill of materials and focus on key components.

Work from the Top Down

This analysis typically starts with the top products by revenue, working down through their component suppliers and their suppliers, all the way to raw materials suppliers. The goal is to go down as many tiers as possible.

The map should also include information about which activities a primary site performs, alternate sites the supplier has that could perform the same activities, and the lead time for the supplier to begin shipping from the backup site.

Companies that invested in mapping their supply networks before the pandemic were better prepared, with clearer visibility into the structure of their supply chains. The mapping gives them a vast resource of information at their fingertips within minutes of a potential disruption.

Mapping helps you determine which suppliers, sites, parts, and products are at risk, giving your company a better chance to secure constrained inventory and capacity at alternate sites [Myerson, 2020].

No doubt the pandemic has accelerated the transition to omni channel retail. Some organizations are just starting their omni channel journey; others are already well on their way with varying degrees of success.

No matter where you are on this journey and what your role is in it, with today's volatile, ever-evolving global supply chain, it's important to consider the risks involved and how to manage them in some detail, as we will document in the next chapter.

17

Global Supply Chain Risk Management: Identification and Mitigation

Companies can help avoid at least some of the pitfalls of supply chain risk – including COVID-19 – by developing risk mitigation strategies.

We can also apply the lessons learned from the COVID-19 pandemic to help develop risk management strategies and tactics for the future. Now is a good time to prepare.

In general, to mitigate supply chain risk, your company needs to have the following five capabilities:

1. Digitally integrated supply chains – just 15 percent of retailers worldwide have what a recent Warwick Manufacturing Group survey calls "digitally ready supply chains". Many companies still rely on legacy processes, such as spreadsheets, for demand and supply planning processes.

   Retailers recognize, however, that they need to better understand automation, artificial intelligence, and other technologies, with a view toward having prescriptive or autonomous supply chains in place by 2025.

2. Efficient vs. responsive supply chains – in today's global and dynamic economy, it is important for companies to consider when it is appropriate to operate a supply chain that is more heavily weighted toward being lean (efficient), one that is more agile (responsive), or one that is both, which is known as a hybrid supply chain strategy – for example, a mass-customized product.

   Executing a hybrid strategy requires great teamwork, using a digital supply chain to gain the real-time visibility needed to take quick action through flexibility and adaptability.

DOI: 10.4324/9781003281078-21

3. Redundancy where there is high risk – develop relationships with alternate vendors and suppliers so you can pivot efficiently when delays occur with primary – and even secondary and beyond – vendors and suppliers.

   Consider reshoring and near-sourcing, at least as backup strategies. This is especially critical when operating a global supply chain.

4. Improved visibility, downstream and upstream – you need not only to have visibility, but also to be able to use it – for example, a digital supply chain combined with good internal and external communications. Not fully understanding downstream demand shifts and a lack of effective stress tests have left supply chains unprepared, often resulting in the bullwhip effect.

   A good first step here is supply chain mapping which involves gathering information about your key customers, suppliers, their own suppliers, and the people who work in your supply chain to create a global map of your supply chain network.

   Active engagement with upstream suppliers is also critical for quick and flexible reactions. Employ delivery performance data, capacity data, and control tower solutions to better assess the risk profile for your suppliers' products and services.

5. Sophisticated and integrated "outside-in" demand and supply chain planning – this is where the rubber meets the road, as it's hard to be lean and agile without good planning.

   If you have the capabilities previously mentioned, you can achieve a high level of demand and supply chain planning to maximize service and minimize cost. To accomplish this, you need a great combination of people, process, and technology.

There will be constant challenges ahead for your supply chain. You have the choice between planning ahead or reacting to challenges when they inevitably arrive [Myerson, 2020].

MANAGING AND MITIGATING RISK

While the move to omni channel retail can be difficult to accomplish but is both required and made harder by today's volatile environment, it is also fraught with risks. If you are not prepared to deal with them in advance, it can have huge negative impacts on your business, as we've seen during the COVID-19 pandemic.

Riding Out the (Whitewater) Rapids

These days, it seems that we are moving from crisis to crisis – tariffs, a plummeting stock market, cyber-attacks, recalls, and the COVID-19 pandemic – at an ever-increasing pace. Although we can't avoid these crises, we can minimize their impact with a lean, agile supply chain.

While that's easy to say, it's hard to do. Some key components to focus on include:

Supply chain visibility, both downstream and upstream – better information sharing and collaboration with business partners and customers, along with a strong use of analytics, can help anticipate and minimize the impact of disruptions.

Supply chain network optimization – reduce network complexities and improve responsiveness to customer needs by optimizing asset locations across the supply chain. Develop an ongoing capability to evaluate business and environmental changes that affect the supply chain to increase flexibility while reducing costs and improving customer service.

Identify and mitigate risk – global supply chains face increased risks from demand and supply variability, limited capacity, and quality issues. Identify the sources and types of potential risk and estimate their probability and impact. Then create and implement risk mitigation plans to minimize their impact.

Strategic sourcing – formalizes the way organizations gather and use information to leverage consolidated purchasing power and find the best sources of supply in the marketplace. Sourcing strategies include outsourcing, insourcing, near-sourcing, few or many suppliers, and vertical integration.

Instead of a Crystal Ball ...

While it's difficult to predict future risks, you can find help in a variety of ways:

- Big data and predictive analytics – can potentially provide insights that help anticipate or respond to events or disruptions.

- Cloud technology and the IoT – are expected to remove physical boundaries and create a centralized system, thereby increasing supply chain efficiency and productivity.
- Next-gen analytics and AI – provide real-time, accurate information and insights that enable enterprises to rapidly adapt to shifts in the business landscape. AI-based technology helps supply chain professionals to strategize by providing insights and recommendations based on the study of market trends and automated forecasts.
- Collaborative forecasting – collects and reconciles information from diverse sources inside and outside the company, using various tools and methods to come up with a single unified statement of demand.

So, how do we manage our supply chain during these turbulent times? Consider these metaphors that describe how managers navigate change.

The "calm waters" metaphor is a description of traditional practices and theories that likens the organization to a large ship making a predictable trip across a calm sea and experiencing an occasional storm.

The "Whitewater rapids" metaphor describes the organization as a small raft navigating a raging river.

As discussed in the first chapter, we are currently in a "Whitewater rapids" phase in terms of today's global economy, at least for the foreseeable future. So, it's best to strap on your life jacket and find ways to ride out these rapids, as supply chain risks have grown exponentially as we have moved to a global economy over the past 30 years [Myerson, 2019].

To plan ahead, it is sometimes best to see how we got here in the first place.

GLOBAL SUPPLY CHAIN OPERATIONS AND INCREASED NEED FOR RISK MANAGEMENT

In the late 1980s, a considerable number of companies began to integrate global sources into their core business, establishing global systems of supplier relationships and expansion of their supply chains across national boundaries and into other continents around the globe.

This has grown to the point where, as of 2021, US imports had grown from $56 billion in 1970 to over $3 trillion in goods.

The globalization of supply chain management in organizations had the goals of increasing their competitive advantage, adding value to the customer, and reducing costs through global sourcing.

In addition to sourcing globally, many companies sell globally and/or compete with other companies that do.

Ultimately, global supply chain management is about sourcing, manufacturing, transporting, and distributing products outside of your native country. It ensures that customers get products and services that they need and want faster, better, and more cost-effectively, either locally or from around the world.

Thus, we can define global supply chains as worldwide networks of suppliers, manufacturers, warehouses, distribution centers, and retailers through which raw materials are acquired, transformed, and delivered to customers.

GROWTH OF GLOBALIZATION

In recent years, we have seen a change in how firms organize their production into global supply chains where companies are increasingly outsourcing some of their activities to third parties and are locating parts of their supply chain outside their home country (known as "offshoring").

They are also increasingly partnering with other firms through strategic alliances and joint ventures, enabling not only large but also smaller firms and suppliers to become global.

These types of global business strategies have allowed firms to specialize on "core" competencies to sustain their competitive advantage.

This is not limited to outsourcing manufacturing and supply chain operations but also includes business process outsourcing (BPO) and IT services that are supplied from a large number of locations as well as other knowledge-intensive activities such as R&D.

Factors Influencing Globalization

There are some key factors influencing the growth of globalization. They include:

Improvements in transportation – larger container ships mean that the cost of transporting goods between countries has decreased.

Economies of scale are found as the cost per item can reduce when operating on a larger scale. Transportation improvements also mean that both goods and people can travel more quickly.

Freedom of trade – there are a number of organizations such as the World Trade Organization (WTO) that promote free trade between countries, helping to remove barriers between them.

Improvements in communications – the internet and mobile technology have allowed greater communication between people in different countries.

Labor availability and skills – less-developed nations in Asia and elsewhere have lower labor costs and also, in some cases, high skill levels. Labor-intensive industries such as clothing can take advantage of cheaper labor costs and reduced legal restrictions in these less-developed countries.

Transnational corporations – globalization has resulted in many businesses setting up or buying operations in other countries. When a foreign company invests in a country, by building a factory or a shop, this is sometimes called inward investment. Companies that operate in several countries are often referred to as multinational corporations (MNCs) or transnational corporations (TNCs). The US fast-food chain McDonald's is a large MNC, having nearly 30,000 restaurants in 119 countries.

Many multinational corporations not only invest in other economically developed countries but also invest in less-developed countries (e.g. Ford Motor Company makes a large numbers of cars in the UK as well as India).

Reasons for a Company to Globalize

The reasons a company may choose to globalize vary but are usually influenced by global, technological, cost, political, and economic concerns. Some reasons to globalize within each of these influences include:

- Global market forces:
  - Foreign competition in local markets.
  - Growth in foreign demand.
  - Global presence as a defensive tool.

- Companies forced to develop and enhance leading-edge technologies and products.
- Technological forces:
  - Knowledge diffusion across national boundaries, hence need for technology sharing to be competitive.
  - Global location of R&D facilities.
  - Close to production (as product cycles get shorter).
  - Close to expertise (e.g. Indian programmers).
- Global cost factors:
  - Availability of skilled or unskilled labor at lower cost.
  - Integrated supplier infrastructure (as suppliers become more involved in design).
  - Capital-intensive facilities utilize incentives such as tax breaks, price breaks, etc. which can influence the "make versus buy" decision.
- Political and economic factors:
  - Trade protection mechanisms such as tariffs, quotas, voluntary export restrictions, local content requirements, environmental regulations, government procurement policies (discount for local).
  - Customs duties which differ by commodity and the level of assembly.
  - Exchange rate fluctuations and operating flexibility.

GLOBAL SUPPLY CHAIN STRATEGY DEVELOPMENT

Today, in most industries, it is necessary to develop a global view of your organization's operations to survive and thrive. However, many companies find it difficult making the transition from domestic to international operations, despite the fact that there have been significant improvements in transportation and technology over the past 25 years.

To be successful in the global economy, a company must have a supply chain strategy. This should include significant investments in ERP and other supply chain technology to prepare it to optimize global operations by linking systems across its businesses globally, helping it to better manage its global supply chains.

Earlier in this book, we discussed organizational strategies and how the supply chain must support them. It is no different when discussing a global supply chain. In general, an organization should have its global supply chain set up to maximize customer service at the lowest possible cost.

Kauffman and Crimi, in their paper "A Best-Practice Approach for Development of Global Supply Chains" [Kauffman and Crimi, 2005], suggest that developing a global supply chain not only requires the same information as when developing one domestically, but also requires additional information on international logistics, law, customs, culture, ethics, language, politics, government, and currency. Cross-functional teams should be utilized that are supplied with detailed information, including the "what, when, and where" of the global supply chain as well as quantity demand forecasts. Supplier evaluations must include the ability for them to handle international operations and subsequent requirements.

To actually implement a global supply chain for your business, after identifying your supply chain partners, the team should document and test the required processes and procedures before implementing. All participants must be trained in the processes and procedures, with metrics established to manage and control the global operations. The team must establish a project plan with responsibilities and milestones for the implementation.

An actual step-by-step approach for developing global supply chains (as per Kauffman and Carmi) is as follows:

1. Form a cross-functional global supply chain development team.
   - Include all affected parties, internal and external.
   - The team composition may change as development and implementation proceeds.
2. Identify needs and opportunities for supply chain globalization.
   - Determine the requirements your supply chain must meet.
     - Commodities, materials, services required … dollar value of materials and services … importance of commodities, materials, and services …
     - Performance metrics for qualification and evaluation of suppliers.
   - Determine the current status of your supply chain "as is".
     - Existing suppliers of materials and services.
     - Customers …
     - Commodity markets …
     - Current performance, problem areas.

- Competitiveness ...
- "Fit" of your current supply chain with your operational requirements.

The main components of this particular framework ... should include all operational dimensions of supply chains which must be identified, considered, and included in any determination of requirements and assessment of current status of supply chains.

3. Determine commodity/service priorities for globalization consideration based on needs and opportunities.
4. Identify potential markets and suppliers and compare to "as is" markets, suppliers, and supply chain arrangements, operations, and results.
5. Evaluate/qualify markets and suppliers, identify supplier pool (determine best ones based on likely total cost of ownership (TCO), and best potential to meet or exceed expectations and requirements).
6. Determine selection process for suppliers, e.g. request for proposal (RFP), negotiation, etc.
7. Select suppliers or confirm current suppliers.
8. Formalize agreements with suppliers.
9. Implement agreements.
10. Monitor, evaluate, review and revise as needed.

[Kauffman et al., 2005]

Whatever your company's global strategy, it must be supported by a strong transportation network, which is briefly described below.

INTERNATIONAL TRANSPORTATION METHODS

The primary methods of international transportation are ocean and air between countries and motor and rail within overseas countries.

Ocean

Ocean transport is perhaps the most common and important global shipment method and accounts for approximately two-thirds of all international movements. Some of the advantages of this mode of international transportation are low rates and the ability to transport a wide variety of products and shipment sizes.

It breaks up into three major categories of: (1) liner service, which has regular routes and operates to a schedule and as a "common carrier"; (2) charter vessels, which are for hire to carry bulk (dry or liquid) or break bulk (cargoes with individually handled pieces) to any suitable port in the world; and (3) private carriers.

Air

International air freight transportation is primarily used for premium or expedited shipments owing to its fast transit times. However, this mode is subject to high transportation rates.

Motor

When in a foreign country, as domestically, motor transport is one of the most popular forms of transportation as its standardization reduces complexity. For example, motor transport is the primary form of transportation when shipping goods between the United States and Mexico or Canada and is very common in Europe. It also plays a major role in intermodal shipments, especially at ports when unloading container ships.

Rail

International railroad use is also highly similar to domestic throughout the world (both in-country and between countries in some cases). For example, there are four major interconnecting rail networks on the Eurasian land mass, along with other smaller national networks.

Intermodal container shipments by rail are also increasing around the world.

Global Intermediaries

In addition to the global intermediaries such as freight forwarders and customs brokers, there may be the need for storage and packaging expertise:

Storage Facilities

What are known as "transit sheds" can provide temporary storage while goods await the next portion of the journey in a foreign land. In some cases, the carrier may provide storage on-dock, free of charge, until the vessel's next departure date. Public warehouses are available for extended storage periods.

Bonded warehouses operate under customs agencies' supervision and can be used to store, repack, sort, or clean imported merchandise entered for warehousing, without paying import duties while the goods are in storage.

Packaging

Export shipments moving by ocean transportation typically require stricter packaging than domestic shipments, as the freight handling involves many firms, and the firms are located in different countries. As a result, the shipper may find settling liability claims for damage to export goods difficult.

GLOBAL SUPPLY CHAIN RISKS AND CHALLENGES

The global supply chain is fraught with risks and challenges.

As operations become more complex, logistics becomes more challenging, lead times lengthen, costs increase, and customer service can suffer. With a global footprint, different products are directed to more diverse customers via different distribution channels, requiring different supply chains.

There are many other, additional issues to address such as the identification of sources capable of producing the materials in the quality and quantity required, the protection of a firm's intellectual property, understanding import/export compliance issues, communication with suppliers and transportation companies, differences in time zones, language and technology, and product security while in transit.

Questions to Consider when Going Global

All of this raises some initial questions that companies need to consider as their operations globalize, as was pointed out in a PwC–MIT forum on supply chain innovation [www.pwc.com, 2013].

The questions and findings from the forum were as follows:

1. *What are the drivers of supply chain complexity for a company with global operations?*

   Supply chains are exposed to both domestic and international risks. The more complex the supply chain, the less predictable the likelihood and the impact of disruption. Over recent years, the size of the supply chain network has increased, dependencies between entities and between functions have shifted, the speed of change has accelerated, and the level of transparency has decreased.

   Overall, developing a product and getting it to the market require more complex supply chains needing a higher degree of coordination.

2. *What are the sources of supply chain risk?*

   Risks to global supply chains vary from controllable to uncontrollable ones and include:
   - Raw material price fluctuation.
   - Currency fluctuations.
   - Market changes.
   - Energy/fuel prices volatility.
   - Environmental catastrophes.
   - Raw material scarcity.
   - Rising labor costs.
   - Geopolitical instability.

3. *What parameters are supply chain operations most sensitive to?*

   Respondents replied that their supply chain operations were most sensitive to reliance on skill set and expertise (31 percent), price of commodities (29 percent), and energy and oil (28 percent). For example, when US diesel prices rose significantly in 2012, shippers rapidly adjusted budgets in order to offset the increased costs higher fuel prices produce.

4. *How do companies mitigate against disruptions?*

   A great majority of respondents (82 percent) said they had business continuity plans ready. Nissan, for example, had a well-thought-out and exercised business continuity plan ready to kick into action to facilitate a quick recovery. Respondents' other major strategies included:
   - Implement dual sourcing strategy.
   - Use both regional and global strategy.
   - Pursue (first- and second-tier) supplier collaboration.

- Pursue demand collaboration with customers.

Key Global Supply Chain Challenges

The COVID-19 pandemic has posed significant challenges for supply chains globally as multiple national lockdowns slowed or even temporarily stopped the flow of raw materials and finished goods, disrupting manufacturing, distribution, and retail as a result.

However, the pandemic didn't necessarily create new challenges for supply chains. To a great degree, it has accelerated and magnified challenges that already existed in the supply chain such as driver shortages, lack of flexibility and agility, the move to omni channel retail, etc.

For example, as early as 2010, a survey for Supply Chain Digest [www .scdigest.com; 2010] mentioned key global supply chain challenges that still exist today such as:

Supply chain volatility and uncertainty have permanently increased – Market transparency and greater price sensitivity have led to lower customer loyalty. Product commoditization reduces true differentiation in both the consumer and business-to-business (B2B) environments ...

Securing growth requires truly global customer and supplier networks – Future market growth depends on international customers and customized products. Increased supply chain globalization and complexity need to be managed effectively ...

Market dynamics demand regional, cost-optimized supply chain configurations – Customer requirements and competitors necessitate regionally tailored supply chains and product offerings. End-to-end supply chain cost optimization will be critical ...

Risk management involves the end-to-end supply chain – Risk and opportunity management should span the entire supply chain – from demand planning to expansion of manufacturing capacity – and should include the supply chains of key partners ...

Existing supply chain organizations are not truly integrated and empowered – The supply chain organization needs to be treated as a single integrated organization. In order to be effective, significant improvements require support across all supply chain functions.

So to a great extent the pandemic has just exacerbated existing challenges, but to some degree they were ignored or given a low priority.

The best practice to navigate a business in today's volatile environment is through a comprehensive risk management process.

RISK MANAGEMENT

Risk management is the identification, evaluation, and prioritization of risks followed by coordinated and economical application of resources to minimize, monitor, and control the probability or impact of unfortunate events or to maximize the realization of opportunities.

An organization's supply chain is greatly impacted by globalization and its inherent logistical complexity. This has resulted in being subject to risk beyond just the demand and supply variability, limited capacity, and quality issues that domestic companies have traditionally faced, with other trends now included such as greater customer expectations, global competition, longer and more complex supply chains, increased product variety with shorter life cycles, and security, political, and currency risks.

As a result, it is important for global supply chain managers to be aware of the relevant risk factors and build in suitable mitigation strategies.

Potential Risk Identification and Impact

Before planning for risks in your supply chain, you must first identify potential risks as well as their impact.

To accomplish this, many companies use a "vulnerability map" or risk matrix to visualize unforeseen and unwanted events, as shown in Figure 17.1 [Sheffield and Rice, Jr., 2005].

This type of analysis has two dimensions: disruption probability and consequences. Obviously, risks with a high disruption probability and severe consequences should be given a great deal of attention.

One problem with this method is that it relies heavily on risk perception, which can vary depending on recent events, a person's experience and knowledge, their appetite for risk, and their position in the organization, among other things.

Sources of Risk

Before determining a risk management strategy for your organization, it is important to consider the possible sources of risk. There are five sources of

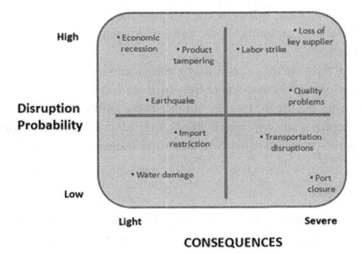

FIGURE 17.1
Vulnerability map.

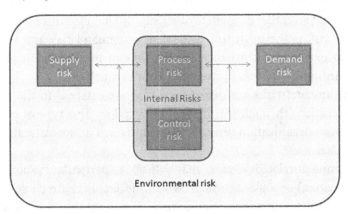

FIGURE 17.2
Sources of risk in the supply chain.

risk in a supply chain, some of which are internal (process and control risk), others external to your organization (demand, supply and environmental risk), as shown in Figure 17.2 [Christopher and Peck, 2004].

Internal Risks

Process risk refers to the value-adding and managerial activities undertaken by the firm and to disruptions to these processes. These processes are usually dependent on internally owned or managed assets and on the existing infrastructure, and so the reliability of supporting transportation, communications, and infrastructure should be carefully considered.

Control risks are the rules, systems, and procedures that determine how organizations exert control over the processes and are therefore the risks arising from the use (or misuse) of these rules. For the supply chain, they include order quantities, batch sizes, safety stock policies, etc. and any policies and procedures that cover asset and transportation management.

External Risks

Demand and supply risks are external to the organization but are internal to the networks through which materials, products, and information flow between companies. The organization should consider potential disruptions to the flow of product and information from within and between all parties in the extended supply chain network and at least understand and monitor the potential risks that may affect other supply chain partners.

Supply risk is the upstream equivalent of demand risk and relates to potential or actual disturbances to the flow of product or information from within the network, upstream of your organization.

Environmental risks are disruptions that are external to the network of organizations through which the products flow. This type of event can impact your organization directly, those upstream or downstream, or the marketplace itself.

Environment-related events may affect a particular product (e.g. contamination) or a place through which the supply chain passes (e.g. an accident, direct action, extreme weather, or natural disasters). They may also be the result of sociopolitical, economic, or technological events far removed from your firm's own supply chains, with the effects often reaching other industry networks. In some cases, the type or timing of these events may be predictable (e.g. regulatory changes); many will not be, but their potential impact can still be evaluated [Christopher and Peck, 2005].

Supply Chain Structure and Vulnerabilities

Supply chain disruptions are the actual occurrence of risks, including the categories mentioned above, and are unplanned and unanticipated events that disrupt the normal flow of goods and materials within a supply chain.

There is usually some triggering event followed by the situation (with its consequences) that occurs afterwards.

Disruptions that a company has to deal with come primarily – although not always, as previously mentioned – from customers, suppliers, and/or the supply chain. The consequences can be immense for your company and can include higher costs, poor performance, lost sales, lower profits, bankruptcy, and damage to your organization.

The actual characteristics of the supply chain structure you have may determine the drivers of your supply chain's vulnerability.

These characteristics may include:

- Complexity of the supply chain (e.g. global vs. domestic sourcing).
- Density of the supply chain (i.e. using these high-density regions leads to higher vulnerability of supply chains).
- Single or sole sourcing vs. multiple vendors for the same item.
- Lean and JIT production philosophies requiring precise timing.
- Centralization of warehouse/manufacturing locations resulting in lengthy lead times due to distance issues.
- Dependency on major suppliers/customers (i.e. the "all your eggs in one basket" syndrome).
- Dependency on IT infrastructure, electricity, etc.

Flexible, secure supply chains with a diversified supplier base are less vulnerable to disruptions than those that are not.

Therefore, to a great degree, potential disruptions are the result of "conscious" decisions regarding how you design the supply chain. Risk management is about using innovative planning to reduce potential disruptions by preparing responses for negative events.

Supply Chain Risks and Tactics for Mitigation

Depending on the type of supply chain risk, what follows are some common supply chain risks and examples of tactics for risk mitigation [Heizer and Render, 2013]:

Supplier Failure to Deliver Use multiple suppliers, with contracts containing penalties. When possible, keep subcontractors on retainer.
Example: McDonald's planned its supply chain many years before opening stores in Russia. All plants are monitored closely to ensure strong links.

Supplier Quality Failure Ensure that you have adequate supplier selection, training, certification, and monitoring processes.

Example: Darden restaurants (i.e. Olive Garden restaurants) uses third-party audits and other controls on supplier processes and logistics to reduce risk.

Logistics Delays or Damage Have multiple or backup transportation modes and warehouses. Make sure that you have secure packaging and execute contracts with penalties for non-conformance.

Example: Walmart always plans for alternative origins and delivery routes bypassing problem areas when delivering from its distribution centers to its stores with its private fleet.

Forecast Volatility Inaccurate forecasts can stem from long lead times, seasonality, product variety, short life cycles, small customer base, information distortion, and demand disruptions caused by external factors such as the pandemic.

Create forecasts that are good enough to enable scenario planning for minimum and maximum demand. Also, seek out alternative data sets by using, for example, a blend of simpler models and digging deeper for non-obvious, less structured data.

Example: One global food firm took the latter approach a few months after COVID-19 hit to sense demand in unmeasured channels such as restaurants, taverns, and hotels. It developed a tool that simulates different scenarios depending on vaccine availability, lockdown policies, economic stimulus, and other factors in each country.

Distribution Have a detailed selection and management process when using public warehouses. Make sure that your contracts have penalties for non-conformance.

Example: Toyota trains its dealers in improving customer service, logistics, and repair facilities.

Information Loss or Distortion Always back up databases within secure information systems. Use established industry standards and train supply chain partners in the understanding and use of information.

Example: Boeing utilizes a state-of-the-art international communication system that transmits engineering, scheduling, and logistics data to Boeing facilities and suppliers worldwide.

Political Companies can purchase political risk insurance. This is also the situation where you may decide to go the route of franchising and licensing your business.

Example: Hard Rock Cafe restaurants try to reduce political risk by franchising and licensing in countries where they deem that the political and cultural barriers are great.

Economic Hedging, the act of entering into a financial contract in order to protect against unexpected, expected, or anticipated changes in currency exchange rates, can be used to address exchange rate risk.

Example: Honda and Nissan have moved some of their manufacturing processes out of Japan since the exchange rate for the yen has made Japanese-made automobiles more expensive.

Natural Catastrophes In many cases, natural disasters can be planned for by taking out various forms of insurance (e.g. flood insurance). Companies may also consider alternate sourcing, for example.

Example: Toyota, after the 2011 earthquake and tsunami, has established at least two suppliers, in different geographical regions, for each component.

Theft, Vandalism, and Terrorism Again, in some cases, there is insurance available for these types of risk. Companies also enforce patent protection and use security measures such as RFID and GPS.

Example: Domestic Port Radiation Initiative: The US government has established radiation monitors at all major US ports that scan imported containers for radiation.

This book in its entirety has given readers a comprehensive, flexible, and easily understood description of demand and supply chain planning that will work not only in today's volatile environment but well into the future.

To be successful, though, I think it is as important to focus on the journey and not just the "destination", the topic of our final chapter.

18

Harmonized Demand and Supply Chain Planning – It's the Journey, Not Just the Destination

At this point, you should have a pretty good understanding of the components, implementation, operation, and control of an integrated demand and supply chain planning process.

How you get there will vary based upon your industry and company situation. However, it isn't something you can accomplish overnight.

Most companies range from a scattered, "back of the envelope" approach to supply chain planning, to having some components that are not necessarily integrated, to best-in-class companies that have it completely integrated and orchestrated (usually with the help of some great IT systems).

Table 18.1 shows the range of maturity levels that an organization's demand and supply chain planning process may currently be in.

Depending on which phase you are in, it will take a journey to reach the truly "enlightened" phase of being capable of "orchestrating" your future supply chain planning processes.

I think that a methodology used in various lean implementations relates well to this complex (and in some ways similar) journey. So, let's briefly take a look at it now to gain some insights that can be used in the evolution of a supply chain planning process.

DOI: 10.4324/9781003281078-22

TABLE 18.1

Demand and Supply Chain Planning Maturity Model

i	ii	iii	iv
REACTING	**ANTICIPATING**	**COLLABORATING**	**ORCHESTRATING**
MRP	VMI	Demand Visibility	Demand Shaping

WE ARE ALL IN THIS TOGETHER: TEAMWORK IN A LEAN WORKPLACE

In general, continuous improvement processes or methodologies are basically ongoing cyclical efforts meant to constantly improve a company's services, products, or processes using a method.

While they all involve a variety of methods or philosophies, such as kaizen (meaning continuous improvement), PDCA/PDSA (plan, do, check/study, act), etc., perhaps the most important component is the change required in culture and processes involving everyone.

It takes a real change management effort to successfully implement a lean program – especially when it involves changing workers' habits. Someone who has been doing a job for a long time may be reluctant to adopt new procedures. That's why a culture of teamwork is vital in creating a lean workplace.

Team Building

Two keys to success in any team-based activity are support from upper management and the participation of everyone in the organization. To build a successful team effort, a company should meet the following conditions:

- Executive leaders must communicate that they expect teamwork and collaboration.
- Organization members should talk about and identify the value of a teamwork culture.
- Management should encourage employees to emphasize teamwork.
- Proper training and tools must be made readily available.
- The company should reward and recognize teamwork.

A key feature of a team-based culture is the concept of employee empowerment. Empowered employees bring their knowledge and involvement to daily operations and can support teams through tasks such as training.

Management's Role

In addition to supporting teamwork in the organization, the company's management must have a vision for lean supply chain and logistics management. These goals can provide the foundation for operations excellence, continuous improvement, and supply chain efficiency.

Management should develop some guiding principles for the lean implementation effort related to employee involvement, quality, standardization, short lead times, and continuous improvement – and should communicate those principles to everyone involved.

When creating and running a lean team in a warehouse, for example, it is important for team leaders to own their processes; for supervisors and managers to remove roadblocks; and for hourly team members to earn bonuses tied to metrics and improved processes.

Keeping It Going

To keep everyone informed about the lean implementation's progress, discuss performance and improvement in weekly departmental meetings. Scheduling a monthly kaizen event to concentrate on improving the operation will let everyone know how important a lean culture is to management.

Lean tools can also be helpful in the warehouse environment, such as problem-solving using root-cause analysis and fishbone diagrams, and error-proofing with standardized work that includes visual instructions on how to perform tasks such as using strapping machines and loading/unloading trucks.

An estimated 50–70 percent of lean initiatives fail, often because management does not both lead and support the cultural change. When company leaders do support a lean culture, however, the long-term advantages can be extremely beneficial to the organization [Myerson, 2013].

I think you can see then that making major changes to a company's processes and culture is really a journey.

From my experience, in addition to not having the appropriate culture requiring executive leadership to support any kind of massive change, at least in the case of US companies, they are used to going for "home runs" (to use a baseball analogy), which don't come along very often, instead of the "steady as she goes" approach of looking for singles and doubles along the way required for continuous improvement.

PEOPLE, PROCESS, AND TECHNOLOGY: SYNCHRONIZED FOR THE EVOLVING SUPPLY CHAIN PLANNING STRATEGY

A lean and agile supply chain strategy (for operations *and* planning) can transform business operating models to deliver superior customer experiences, enable digital transformation, improve quality and visibility, and create additional value.

However, while organizations try to adapt to a digital world, the results may fall short without a strategy that considers your people, processes, and technology (PPT), the importance of which was discussed in Chapter 2.

Principles of a Supply Chain Strategy

Enabling a supply chain that is ready for the future requires new ways of thinking. Having new capabilities can increase the pace of innovation and allow organizations to react quickly to changing market conditions, trends, and customer expectations.

To help accomplish this in a productive way, it will be important to free up time for employees to focus on higher-value work. Helping in this endeavor, it now appears that many routine tasks can be automated by current technology.

Today's supply chain operating model is more and more based on insights from real-time demand. As a result, leading organizations are increasing investments in emerging technologies that support real-time demand, planning, and fulfillment execution capabilities.

Driving this are principles that include the following:

- Organizations have to manage global volatility and build a lean, agile, and resilient supply chain – one that can react to any shock, such as the recent global pandemic, as our world becomes more interconnected.

- The acceleration of omni channel networks requires more speed, complexity, and efficiency.
- Fast and decisive action is critical to supply chain management in any market condition and requires total visibility across the supply chain.

These principles should help determine the right roadmap toward achieving the future state an organization envisions.

Developing and Implementing a Future-State Vision

Building a strategic supply chain begins with assessing your organization's current state by identifying current pain points and limitations (using external and internal analysis, culminating in a SWOT analysis, as mentioned in Chapter 2, is a useful methodology in this task).

You should then build a future-state vision of your organization, targeting future capabilities and key areas for investment.

From a technology standpoint, you should identify where data management and standardization solve pain points and align findings with the technology necessary to converge data silos. From this, you should be able to create a technology roadmap outlining the application of technology and data standardization, defining the processes to support innovation, and resolving any major pain points.

Implementing emerging technology isn't enough to compete in the future of tomorrow. It also requires that organizations adopt a PPT framework into their technology roadmap, since, as supply chains evolve, so do the people and processes that work in and around them.

The success of realizing a future-state vision depends on identifying actionable insights, enabling a realistic technology roadmap, and integrating PPT to build a future-ready supply chain.

Leveraging the PPT Framework

People, processes, and technology coordination is necessary for organizational transformation and management and to gain a competitive advantage. Organizations need to develop a "holistic" PPT methodology to balance and maintain good relationships among them and to drive action.

This framework especially applies to organizations strategically using business intelligence (BI) through technology-enabled supply chain improvements.

To change supply chain performance, technology needs to be synchronized *with* people and processes, rather than *against* them.

To summarize, building a future-ready supply chain begins with four steps:

1. Assess your organization's current state.
2. Build your future-state vision.
3. Create your pragmatic technology roadmap.
4. Adopt a PPT framework.

While all organizations are adopting digital technologies, leading-edge supply chains recognize technology is only one component of a far more holistic effort [Nicholas, 2020].

DEMAND AND SUPPLY CHAIN PLANNING CAPABILITIES NEEDED FOR THE FUTURE

As has been discussed throughout this book, supply chain planners need to prepare for continued variability and volatility in supply, demand, production, and sales and operations (S&OP) as a result of the pandemic, geopolitical events, and economic, environmental, and other disruptive factors.

To meet these ongoing challenges, organizations need to look at developing the following capabilities:

The Need for Resiliency

The resiliency of your supply chain is critical, as raw material backlogs, labor shortages, factory shutdowns, and capacity limits continue to force companies to adjust plans. A Capgemini Research Institute survey reported that 62 percent of respondents felt that supply chain resilience was a key priority for their supply chain organization, post COVID-19. In fact, 57 percent were planning to increase investment in building supply chain resilience.

Increasing resiliency in a supply chain can include such capabilities as increasing agility, diversification, and scenario planning, as described below:

- Agility – reflects how quickly a company can react when disruption occurs or in the face of volatile demand, such as increasing and decreasing production or setting up new channels of distribution.
- Diversification – applies to the sourcing of products and suppliers used to acquire goods or raw materials.
- Scenario planning – incorporates things such as demand planning and the ability to prepare for seen and unforeseen events using "what-if" analysis.

Of course, to maximize resiliency, it helps to have visibility up and down your supply chain.

Visibility into the Supply Chain

Supply chain visibility has always been important and has been even more so recently owing to the numerous disruptions (pandemic, supply chain disruptions, etc.) in 2020–22. A survey in *Forbes* magazine showed that 92 percent of supply chain professionals said visibility into their supply chain is important to success. However, only 27 percent have achieved visibility in their supply chain, illustrating that there is a lot of room for improvement.

In addition to enabling scenario planning (and other resiliency methods, as just discussed), which prepares for and prevents negative impacts from issues such as the pandemic, supply chain visibility gives businesses a view of the entire extended supply chain. A connected, unified, end-to-end supply chain planning approach allows different teams from across your organization to have visibility into data, plans, and decisions throughout your extended supply chain.

Supply chain visibility can also improve your company's overall customer experience by preventing and communicating issues related to stock shortages and order backlogs (an area where I see a lot of room for improvement).

Capacity and Cost vs. Timeliness

While many supply chain planners in the 21st century have prioritized timeliness by choosing suppliers that could deliver products the fastest, recent events have shifted circumstances to the point where suppliers around the globe and domestically have more business than they do labor. These capacity issues are leading planners to take whatever they can get in some cases. So, while organizations used to evaluate and make decisions primarily on suppliers' on-time performance (assuming they meet quality criteria), the focus in the last few years has been on keeping supply chains moving, albeit at as reasonable a rate as possible.

As the "whitewater rapids" environment seems to be with us to stay, at least for the foreseeable future, supply chain planners will continue to look for alternate suppliers, as multiple suppliers can help companies prevent the effects of single sourcing. While this typically increases costs and adds variability owing to multiple suppliers, it's simply no longer feasible to continuously shop suppliers to find the best rate.

Improving Forecast Accuracy

Accurate forecasting is fundamental to supply chain management and imperative for effective sales and operations planning. Improving demand forecast accuracy by employing different models and drawing data from a variety of sources, as described in this book, is a reality when you've established the right supply chain strategy, processes, and tools. By utilizing multiple models and data from sources across your organization, and pulling and sharing those data quickly, planners can add more value to the business.

Ongoing AI and Cloud Technology Adoption

As companies evolve their supply chain strategies, it is likely that the next generation of supply chains will be based on advanced technologies, such as AI, machine learning, IoT, cloud-based solutions, etc.

Companies will continue to implement technological ways of supporting end-to-end supply chain management, executions, predictive analytics, and data analysis. AI, machine learning, and cloud platforms are expected to help identify patterns, select best-fit forecasting methods, and better assist planners in correcting supply chain issues in real time (or close to it). This will allow supply chain planners to focus on priority issues and to mitigate disruptions, rather than spending time going through large data sets.

Many supply chains are large in scale and often lack visibility on a detailed level. Advanced analytical technologies can help improve the supply chain planning process and can help build a tighter relationship with your suppliers, partners, and customers. In such unpredictable times, utilizing the proper supply chain technology gives a competitive edge in being able to plan an operation successfully to improve both the top and bottom lines [CCH Tagetik, 2022].

The reader should now have a good understanding of the demand and supply chain planning process and the various challenges all businesses face today and will continue to face long into the future.

These are complex times, often requiring complex solutions using sound business sense. I believe that by developing a harmonized, integrated, "outside-in" demand and supply chain planning process as described in this book, which utilizes highly trained employees and the latest technologies, organizations will be up for the challenge.

Appendix A – Case Studies: Demand and Supply Chain Planning (Combining People, Process, and Technology)

In today's fast-moving, volatile world, I think it is critically important to view and consider cases which are at the intersection of people, process, and technology using a lean and agile supply chain philosophy for continuous improvement in the supply chain.

So, below are some examples like that from various areas of the demand and supply chain activities described in this book.

DEMAND-SIDE CASES

Case 1 – Caribou Coffee

Challenge

Logility, a leading supplier of collaborative solutions to optimize the supply chain, has helped many of its clients not only to implement its forecasting software but also to gain significant improvements. One such example was Caribou Coffee, with its headquarters and coffee-roasting facility in Minneapolis and locations across the United States, as well as over a dozen international markets.

Prior to selecting and implementing a forecasting system, like many companies, Caribou managed its supply chain with spreadsheets. This limited its ability to generate accurate and timely estimates of demand to efficiently drive replenishment activities. It needed more accurate visibility to optimize inventory levels, while maintaining customer service as product sales expanded.

Approach

The use of Logility's forecasting software enabled Caribou to automate the process of reliably predicting market demand, driving efficient sourcing and production as well as optimal inventory levels throughout the supply chain. By deploying Logility Voyager Solutions, Caribou Coffee's supply chain team went from month to weekly demand planning and forecasting. As it has grown, it has managed to triple its number of SKUs and launch a range of new products, while at the same time growing both domestic and international markets.

Results

Through a more automated forecasting process, Caribou Coffee's supply chain team was able to transition demand planning and forecasting from a monthly to weekly process; at the same time, it improved its reaction time, inventory turns, and customer service levels, all the while maintaining customer service levels at above 99 percent. It was also able to decrease write-offs due to aged inventory and improve inventory turns by 35 percent [www.logility.com, 2015].

Case 2 – Butterball

Challenge

Butterball produces a billion pounds of turkey products every year at five facilities in North Carolina, Arkansas, and Missouri and ships these products to the 98 percent of American grocers that carry part of the Butterball line, as well as retailers in more than 30 other countries.

As Butterball's products are highly seasonal, heavily promoted, and date-sensitive, it faced a number of significant supply chain challenges. To deliver a high level of customer satisfaction, maintain freshness, and minimize obsolete inventory, it needed to have highly accurate forecasts.

As a result, it turned to JDA Software (www.jda.com) for help to improve and manage its complex short- and long-term forecasting processes.

Approach

Butterball's approach had been focused more on the short term with heavy use of manual data manipulation, which tended to cause wasted time for the planners. JDA demand software allowed it to focus more on exception monitoring, longer-range planning, and demand shaping.

It has also allowed it to focus more on product perishability and meeting retailers' different service-level expectations and product freshness requirements. Planners can now modify Butterball's forward plans to minimize excess product and maximize customer satisfaction and now have the ability to separate normal demand from promotional demand streams.

Results

Benefits to Butterball include a 28 percent reduction in obsolescent inventory, a 2 percent improvement in short-term forecasting, and a 50 percent reduction in long-term forecast bias.

Butterball has leveraged this technology to create a VMI (vendor managed inventory) replenishment model with a key customer. Its increased level of retailer collaboration is providing the building blocks to further expand Butterball's demand network [www.jda.com, 2015].

Case 3 – Kimberly-Clark

Challenge

Kimberly-Clark makes personal care products including Kleenex facial tissues, Huggies diapers, and Scott's paper towels, with worldwide sales of $20 billion in 2011.

In 2006, company executives decided to change Kimberly-Clark's supply chain strategy from focusing primarily on supporting manufacturing to meeting the specific needs of its retail and grocery customers.

To do so, Kimberly-Clark realized it would need to include point-of-sale (POS) information about actual consumer purchases to improve the resupply process with retailers.

In 2009, the company used some minimal downstream retail data in its demand-planning software, but for the most part relied on historical shipment data for its replenishment forecasts, knowing that forecasts based on historical sales are subject to errors, owing to the bullwhip effect, resulting in excess safety stock and unsold inventory.

Approach

It conducted a pilot program with the software vendor Terra Technology which incorporated POS data into its North American operation. The pilot was successful, and, in 2010, the company licensed and implemented Terra Technology's multi-enterprise demand-sensing solution.

Kimberly-Clark has three retail customers which generate one-third of its consumer products business in North America. They provide point-of-sale data, which are fed daily into the software, recalibrating the shipment forecast for each of those retailers. The software evaluates any new data inputs from the retailers along with open orders and the legacy demand-planning forecast to generate a new shipment forecast for the next four weeks. Kimberly-Clark also uses that forecast to guide internal deployment decisions and tactical planning.

The software processes data from the retailers, such as point-of-sale information, inventory in the distribution channel, shipments from warehouses, and the retailers' own forecast and reconciles those data to create a daily operational forecast. It also identifies patterns in the historical data to determine how much influence each input has on the forecast. One example might be that POS is found to be the best predictor of a shipment forecast on a three-week horizon, but actual orders and legacy demand forecasts could be the best predictor for the current week.

Results

By incorporating demand signals from key retail customers into its shipment forecasting process, Kimberly-Clark has realized substantial improvements such as being able to develop a more granular metric for forecast errors. Ultimately, it found a reduction in forecast errors of as much as 35 percent for a one-week planning horizon and 20 percent for a two-week horizon.

Furthermore, forecast accuracy improvements, which resulted in reductions in safety stock, have helped Kimberly-Clark reduce its overall inventory, reducing finished-goods inventory by 19 percent over the previous year and a half [Cooke, 2013].

SUPPLY-SIDE CASES

Sales and Operations Planning

Case 1 – Infineon Technologies AG Takes Planning to the Next Level with JDA S&OP

Challenge

Infineon Technologies AG provides semiconductor and system solutions, focusing on energy efficiency, mobility, and security. It has customers worldwide, including auto manufacturers, industrial electronics companies, chip card and security businesses, and information and communications technology companies. Its industry is known for having volatile demand and long product lead times and requires significant capital investments and increasing product and supply network complexity.

So, it is critical that it can identify and respond to demand changes, while balancing global production capacity across its more than 20 facilities.

Approach

Infineon made the decision to re-engineer its planning processes and tools so it could respond quickly to market changes, across all planning levels and areas of the company. It determined that it needed new technology to accomplish this goal. It took two years and was jointly managed by its information technology and business departments.

At the time, it was using home-grown sales and operations planning tools, which didn't work because of limitations in scalability and integration. So, it chose JDA Software for this project as they had worked together in the planning area in the past.

The JDA consultants tried to understand its processes first and then tried to match them with the appropriate JDA solutions. Through this partnership, JDA was able to develop an interactive rough-cut capacity planning functionality within JDA S&OP, enabling Infineon to synchronize demand, supply, capacity, and load planning into one multidimensional view.

Results

Sales forecasts, pricing, and production capacity are now reviewed and adjusted in real time in one simulation model which gives Infineon an overview of its operational and financial plans. It can then react quickly to changes in the market. It can also shape demand to meet production constraints or identify a need for additional capacity (e.g. at a subcontractor site).

As a result of implementing the S&OP solution, Infineon has:

- Reduced its planning effort by more than 30 percent.
- Cut the lead time for its rolling forecast from four weeks to two weeks.
- Decreased planning errors by up to 90 percent.
- Reduced its "churn" (i.e. making minor adjustments to the plan) by a factor of 10.
- Improved forecast accuracy as well.

Most importantly, Infineon now has a new collaborative planning approach, enabling the business to be more agile and responsive so that demand, supply, capacity, and load are always synchronized and calculated together [www.jda.com, 2014].

Case 2 – Accelerated S&OP Collaboration at Lance

Challenge

Lance produces and distributes snack foods including cookies, crackers, nuts, and potato chips, largely under the Lance, Cape Cod, and Tom's brand names.

Its products are distributed via direct-store delivery with over 1,400 sales routes, independent distributors, and direct shipments to retail customer locations.

Its challenge was to increase visibility, improve forecast accuracy, and increase shelf-freshness for consumers.

Approach

To reach these goals, Lance implemented Logility Voyager Sales and Operations Planning software which transports information from sales, production, finance, marketing, transportation, and procurement into one central database. It allows sales and operations planning to work from a "one number" system, saving time and reaching better clarity. With this S&OP solution in place, it was determined that it could cut hours and days from its planning process, streamline the planning cycle, and complete analysis in a fraction of the time.

The goal was to allow Lance to have greater visibility into its business and be able to identify its most profitable customers and channels, optimize its product mix, improve procurement strategies, and maximize margins. Logility's S&OP best practices allow it to compare multiple "what-if" scenarios, evaluate critical decisions, and prepare contingency strategies to mitigate risk.

Results

After implementation, Lance had improved forecast accuracy, reduced inventory days-on-hand, decreased finished-goods storage, and improved S&OP collaboration.

Specifically, Lance:

- Improved forecast accuracy from 50 percent to 70 percent.
- Reduced inventory days-on-hand by 20 percent, from five days to four.
- Decreased finished good storage by two warehouses.
- Accelerated S&OP collaboration.
- Improved acquisition integration effectiveness [www.logility.com, 2015].

Case 3 – Continental Mills Increases Productivity with S&OP Process

Challenge

Continental Mills is a food manufacture of products such as pancake mixes, bake mixes, drink mixes, and breading and batters, in operation since 1932. It has three manufacturing facilities located throughout the United States. Its current supply chain system and processes have been struggling to cope successfully with the increasing complexity of its business, including many new SKUs and customers.

Its S&OP process was supported from the top down, with senior managers participating on a monthly basis. Up to that point, its supply chain team had calendar discipline, but with a very labor-intensive process.

The team had many challenges such as having many versions of spreadsheets emailed back and forth, some with corrupted data. They had no idea how much time and effort they put into chasing numbers and version control, only finding that out after they didn't have to do it anymore.

The company also has separate divisions that look outwardly in different ways, with each division having forecasts at different levels of detail.

Approach

As a result, it looked for a new solution to manage that growth, selecting Logility's Voyager Solutions.

One benefit of the Logility solution is that it provides Continental Mills with a flexible solution that allows all four divisions to manage their business in their own way, with different levels of detail, but still gives them a comprehensive corporate view through a single hierarchical structure.

Continental Mills used the Voyager Demand Planning system to convert its businesses from its hard-to-maintain forecasting process using spreadsheets to a statistical forecast, which reduced the time and effort previously dedicated to administration and "crunching" numbers.

It also can now do a much better job of driving the forecast and analyzing its options with a separate view for each one of the businesses. It has saved an estimated 40–50 hours of spreadsheet manipulation from the monthly S&OP process.

The S&OP software has allowed Continental Mills to streamline the production planning process and improve capacity planning for all its manufacturing facilities.

Results

Even with a record sales year, Continental Mills:

- Improved inventory turns by 20 percent.
- Increased resource efficiency in the forecasting process.
- Reduced forecast error in one division by close to 50 percent.
- Achieved a record service level of 99.48 percent.
- Improved data accuracy and visibility throughout the business [www.logility.com, 2015].

Case 4 – Radisys Improves S&OP Process, Supporting Tools Rapidly after Outsourcing Strategy Leads to Real Challenges

Challenge

Radisys makes embedded systems and related technology, located in Hillsboro, Oregon, in the United States. It had the beginnings of an S&OP

process with limited technology support and was managing to get along, until it outsourced its manufacturing operations in 2009, which resulted in a lack of visibility where even simple decisions became difficult for the company.

While the contract manufacturer had supply information and Radisys had demand information, they were stored in different places.

Radisys also had an outdated, home-grown demand planning software system with many limitations and problems. The demand planning tool could only generate a monthly forecast, while the contract manufacturer was operating on a weekly schedule and needed to commit to customers daily.

So, while this new outsource strategy was supposed to result in lower costs, it had created more problems and became a company-wide issue.

Approach

Radisys really needed to have supply and demand in one system, including contract manufacturers.

As a solution, it settled on licensing Steelwedge software for demand planning and S&OP and icon-scm for demand management and order prioritization.

Steelwedge is a cloud-based integrated business planning platform, with an interface and platform that are easy to configure and use.

icon-scm helps an organization to understand the impact of any decision on its company, customers, and suppliers. It has supply chain planning and supply chain collaboration planning solutions that maximize visibility and minimize response time.

Results

Implementing these tools allowed Radisys to manage more by exception which freed up staff for more value-added tasks, with 80 percent of their time now spent on analytics rather than on basic tasks as was previously the case.

Benefits of this new strategy include:

- Improvement in forecasting, demand and supply management, and the S&OP process.
- Cost advantages from the initial outsourcing strategy finally realized.
- A single plan that works across demand, supply, and the contract manufacturer.

- Integration of the supply chain plan with the company's financial plan, resulting in more of an "integrated business planning" environment beyond basic S&OP.
- Forecast cycle time reduced from 2.5 weeks to 1.5 weeks.

Radisys can now react quickly to market opportunities and demand, which is extremely important in the technology world [*Supply Chain Digest, 2013*].

Master Production Scheduling:

Case 1 – Energy Bar Company

Challenge

A fledgling energy bar company wanted to create a flexible production plan driven by various demand projections over a 12-month period. It wanted to use a low-cost strategy to schedule hiring of additional work force, ongoing raw material purchases, capital equipment purchases, and production facility decisions for current and forecasted demand. It initially did calculations on a spreadsheet, manually adjusting production and purchasing variables. It quickly realized that changes in demand caused issues in other areas not easily accounted for on the spreadsheet, causing this form of production planning to be a trial-and-error exercise.

Approach

ORM Technologies (www.orm-tech.com), which has an optimization and operations research engineering software system, utilized its production planning software module with the energy bar client to include all known production, cost, and staffing constraints to produce a 12-month plan based on current and forecasted product demand.

This technology allowed its energy bar client to:

- Quickly create production plans that maximize profit with dozens of different demand profiles.
- Select the optimal timing to hire additional workforce, purchase raw material, and make facility decisions to meet current and forecasted demand.
- Perform what-if analysis with current and forecasted product demand as well as facility, staff, production, raw material, and packaging costs and capacities.

Results

The system output provided the company with the information needed to make staffing and facility decisions, as well as capital equipment and recurring raw material purchases; it also allowed the company to save much-needed capital by delaying a move to a new facility by several months and optimizing the staffing plan. The client can now run what-if analysis whenever it likes to determine the production, cost, inventory, and staffing effects of changes in demand so that it can plan ahead rather than operate in a reactive mode [www.orm-tech.com, 2015].

Case 2 – Global Raw Materials Supplier

Challenge

A global manufacturer was running a production and materials planning process that has to be highly integrated with demand (customer orders) so as to minimize waste on the manufacturing floor while allocating demand across all global plants so as to optimize output. It used a "production planning" data mart to provide synchronization and a consolidated production view across each of the manufacturing facilities.

This data mart urgently needed to be updated, both in terms of the technology and the logic driving the process.

Approach

Corporate Technologies (CTI), a systems integrator and solutions provider (www.cptech.com), was brought in to reverse engineer the business logic and implement a new "production planning" data mart to reduce the cost of ownership while improving the maintainability of the system.

The strategic plan for all business units was to use an integrated SAP architecture, applying SAP Business Objects Data Services as the data integration technology across the manufacturing systems.

This involved the analysis of hundreds of different data flows from thousands of different data sources. Business rule logic was re-engineered in SAP Business Objects Data Services and tested for business integrity.

Results

Ultimately the updated technology and logic significantly reduced IT maintenance costs and improved data inputs to the manufacturing planning process [www.cptech.com, 2015].

Case 3 – Techlogix Helps Nestlé Innovate in Milk Production Planning

Challenge

Nestlé Pakistan operates the largest milk collection operation in Pakistan, working with approximately 190,000 farmers in the provinces of Punjab and Sindh. It produces a variety of dairy products including milk, powdered milk, cream, tea whiteners, and yogurt.

Even though demand for milk products is fairly constant year round, not surprisingly, milk production varies very significantly from season to season. As the content of milk (fat, etc.) from farmers varies, Nestlé has the added problem of managing its production capacity in the most efficient way with both supply constraints and demand variations.

Although Nestlé had invested in an ERP system, it was unable to automate the complex milk production planning process, and the manual planning that was being used had its own set of limitations.

To manage content variation, Nestlé prepares a production plan every month using a number of estimates and assumptions. Its typical production plan is generated on a spreadsheet by a production planner, following a set of objectives with a large number of rules and constraints. The objectives of its usual production plan include:

- Minimizing milk waste.
- Reaching planned production quantities for each SKU.
- Producing material ahead for future months when fresh milk supply may be inadequate.
- Efficient utilization of imported material.
- Creating requests in advance of anticipated material shortage.
- Utilizing available plant capacity for bulk production and line capacity for packaging.

The rules and constraints used in planning include:

- Maintaining production ratios between products when increasing or decreasing production.
- Following plant and packaging line capacities and maintenance schedules.
- Tracking raw material availability and stock expiration dates.
- Selecting the most appropriate bill of material (from a large of number of potential recipes), which depends on raw material and fresh milk availability.

Its current SAP ERP system did not fully capture the complexity of the milk production planning problem and, thus, the reliance on manual planning, which has multiple flaws:

- Suboptimal plans – the production planning process produced suboptimal plans, largely as a result of trying to solve a complicated multi-constraint optimization problem primarily using instinct, approximations, and heuristics from past experience. This could be seen in line capacity remaining idle, the use of less desirable BOMs, etc.
- Time consuming and repetitive – the entire planning process, which included the generation of multiple plans, took a considerable amount of time. This process had to be repeated each month and took a significant portion of the month to complete.
- Error prone – the production planner had to consider a wide range of conditions, rules, and constraints when creating the monthly production plan. As a result, human errors were fairly common.
- Expert dependent – the production plan at Nestlé is dependent on a very small number of experts, and training new resources is difficult and takes considerable time.

As a result, Nestlé decided to develop an automated solution in order to simulate multiple what-if scenarios using rules and constraints to prepare a final production plan that met all set parameters.

Approach

Techlogix (www.techlogix.com), an IT services, consulting, and business solutions company, was engaged to create a customized planning system. It proposed a multiphase approach starting with a feasibility study and part high-level solution design, followed by a detailed design, build, and delivery of the solution, with a final phase of maintenance and ongoing support.

Techlogix designed and delivered a web application to be used as a simulation engine to produce a production plan along with a variety of reports. The reports helped the planner look at different aspects of the production plan.

The production planning algorithm has two distinct aspects: planning and scheduling. The planning algorithm uses fresh milk quantity, raw material stock quantity, and other inputs to determine the optimal production of bulk material.

This quantity is the input to the scheduling algorithm, which attempts to schedule production on plants within specified capacities. If required production capacity is not available, the planning algorithm adjusts production and attempts a reschedule to find the best fit.

Reports are generated that allow a production planner to view production in terms of bulk produced, SKUs produced, plant and line capacities used, etc.

The goal during testing was to manage multiple production lines based on the system output. Five months of parallel runs were conducted where the system output was both compared with the manual plan and checked against all constraints.

Toward the end of testing, the system was able to consistently generate plans that met all criteria and significantly improved upon the manual plan.

Results

The automated production planning process now only takes a few hours vs. days of effort previously, with more time now for maneuverability. The new production planning output is more precise and accurate than before, which helps to reduce costs and eliminate waste [www.techlogix .com, 2015].

Case 4 – Durabuilt Windows and Doors Balances Lean and ERP for Production Scheduling

Challenge

Durabuilt is a manufacturer of windows and doors and operates a 180,000-square-foot plant with 450 employees. It has been using Cantor, an ERP system, since 2008 and has had the challenge of integrating lean practices at its plant for the past three years with Cantor ERP, which was a real balancing act as it needed both to survive and prosper.

Approach

In the past, Durabuilt's workflow on the production floor ran through ERP and would produce 50 or 100 boxes before going to the next order. As a result, large quantities of boxes waited for hours to be used. Before ERP, they sent paper documents to purchasing to order materials and then to receiving to wait for the materials to come in.

Results

Durabuilt's IT staff had to adapt the ERP system to support the lean management principles used at the facility.

As part of the lean initiative, the plant had modified its assembly line to single-piece flow and needed to configure the ERP to support that process. Now, instead of having batches of parts sitting around in boxes waiting for hours to be used, the parts are brought to the line as needed.

Management strongly believes that if it didn't have an ERP system, its lean initiatives wouldn't work.

For example, it no longer has a transfer of paperwork for purchasing, as orders for materials go straight to their suppliers.

It's now a faster process, and the company is not missing anything owing to human error, with material lead time built right into the system and providing an accurate delivery date to the customer up front.

In the new process, orders are entered into the ERP system by salespeople and then go to the scheduling department. Schedulers then create and adjust the production schedule in ERP and fine-tune it daily, factoring in variables such as capacity of individual manufacturing lines vs. complexity and time-sensitivity of customer orders. Schedulers then put consideration into the transport schedule for Durabuilt's fleet of trucks that deliver windows and doors to customers [Bartholomew, 2012].

Material Requirements Planning

Case 1 – Gables Engineering Moves to a "Real" MRP System

Challenge

Gables Engineering is an avionics manufacturer in business that builds custom cockpit controls, including the design and building of the switches, housings, and LCD display modules, for the airline and airframe industry.

Gables had a pseudo-MRP system based on reorder points which used current customer demand, as well as historical demand, to determine what it needed to buy. It was basically moving forwards by looking backwards (which assumes the past will repeat itself, which, as we know, isn't always the case). The company wanted a product using the Oracle database, which had a Windows front end, that would seamlessly interface with other third-party systems.

Approach

Gables formed a team to look at its business processes to see if it needed a new enterprise application system. A request for quotation (RFQ) was sent to a number of software vendors.

Gables selected an IFS ERP/e-business that includes a true MRP module with a better understanding of actual demand. Previously at Gables, demand was determined by customer orders as well as by a factor for historical demand, causing it to buy and build unnecessary parts, loading shops with unnecessary work and inflated purchased inventories.

Results

Once Gables implemented the new IFS system, it was able to calculate demand using actual customer orders and forecasts, enabling it to order and build parts by looking at forecasts, not at history. This reduced work in process and overall inventory by 50 percent and 30 percent, respectively. It used to take two days to get a spare part shipped out, from time of order to time of shipment; now, same-day shipping is possible.

The software also tracks the history of changes made to a product down to serial number, and the parts removed from inventory to manufacture it are maintained for now. During a customer audit, Gables was able to show the traceability of a component using the audited part's subassembly, which it could never have done previously.

Gables has also reduced kitting time to less than one month before assembly, kitting almost 99 percent of the entire product right before assembling it. It also now has notebooks allowing stock room personnel to review pick lists online and pick and update inventory instantly [www .top10erp.com, 2008–16].

Case 2 – Raytheon Streamlines and Automates Its Material Requirement Planning Processes with Exostar's Supply Chain Platform

Challenge

Raytheon is a technology and innovation leader specializing in defense, homeland security, and other government markets around the world; it provides electronics, mission systems integration, and other capabilities as well as a broad range of mission support services.

Raytheon divisions relied on a variety of MRP processes and "home-grown" and packaged software systems for the delivery of products and services to customers, but, as a result, had the following issues:

Siloed processes and systems – each of Raytheon's six business units had implemented its own MRP solutions.

Manually intensive interactions – as the MRP systems couldn't be accessed directly by suppliers, all scheduling communications required an excess of manual intervention, resulting in increased cost, time, and risk.

Approach

Raytheon decided to transition to a collaborative MRP (cMRP) supply chain platform (SCP) solution from Exostar that would deliver the following benefits:

- Processes automated as much as possible.
- Existing infrastructure leveraged to minimize impact and cost.
- Increased collaboration between buyers and suppliers enabled.
- Standardization and integration across all existing MRP systems.

Results

Raytheon's Integrated Defense Systems (IDS) group was the first business unit to transition to SCP and connect its existing MRP systems to the SCP. It has been able to modify its existing MRP process to make it a leaner, more automated, standardized, and collaborative process that reduces manual processes, increases productivity, and increases integration with suppliers.

Overall, Raytheon anticipates that, after full implementation at all business units, it will be able to have savings of up to $3 million per year by:

- Increasing reliability – on-time delivery of goods from suppliers will increase by 10 percent or more.
- Streamlining the process – the new system should reduce manual re-entry of information, printing/faxing, and phone/email communications.
- Optimizing resources – move 12–15 employees per business unit from administrative to higher-value tasks.
- Reducing supply chain risk – better performance visibility and exception management.
- Improving consistency – implement the cMRP solution across all six Raytheon business units over time [www.exostar.com, 2013].

Finite Capacity Scheduling

Case 1 – *Mueller Stoves Reduces the Assembly Line Stops after Preactor Deployment*

Challenge

Mueller Stoves, founded in 2001, produces a variety of stoves, domestic ovens, and cook-top stoves. It had been using the concept of mini factories pulled by kanban from the assembly line.

Despite all the efforts of its lean manufacturing team, the kanban was not bringing the expected results, mainly owing to the fact that the assembly lines are extremely dynamic because of the high variability of items per day on each assembly line and the high volatility of quantities and reschedules caused by unforeseen events.

While each mini factory was producing its own scheduling, other information was not considered, such as the availability of material (supplied by other areas or outsourced). As a result, the assembly lines often did not produce as planned because the mini factories could not respond in time to changes. They tried to supply the components for the items scheduled on the assembly lines through daily inventory lists and urgent production requests for missing parts, but often had to stop the lines owing to lack of parts.

Additionally, the company had:

- Difficulties balancing loads across several resources.
- Difficulties properly evaluating production bottlenecks.
- No visibility of the consequences of unforeseen events.
- No possibility of coordinating a preventive maintenance plan without sacrificing productivity.
- Lack of capacity analysis to give adequate responses to demand.

Approach

As a result of these limitations, both the planning and production departments independently began to look for other solutions.

Both departments independently found Preactor and APS3 (Siemens's partner for Simatic IT Preactor products) and realized that a scheduling tool based on finite capacity, which took into account materials and resources, represented a possible solution to the challenges they faced.

The first step for the project was to generate finite scheduling only on the stamping area in order to level load the assembly lines, to prevent the internal parts supply shortages that were causing lines to stop.

Results

The results were impressive and highlighted that there was also an opportunity to schedule the painting area with the same principle adopted for stamping.

The most immediate results included:

- Improved visibility reducing production uncertainty through a scheduling horizon of five days and a firm schedule of one day.
- Increased reliability of the supplier to the JIT process due to its perception of the improving factory scheduling process.
- Reduction of stamping stocks from 3 days to 1.5 days of parts needed for future assemblies.
- Significant reduction of semi-finished stocks.
- Unplanned stoppages on the assembly lines went from 13 to 6 hours, a 22 percent reduction in WIP and a 98 percent improvement in overall inventory turns [www.preactor.com, 2015].

Procurement and Purchasing

Case 1 – Enabling Online Supplier Collaboration at Toshiba Semiconductor Company

Challenge

Toshiba Semiconductor Company wanted real-time information for its global operations to stay a global leader in the industry, and the lack of this information would limit the company's success in the future.

At the time, purchasing employees bought products locally, with no sharing of information among buyers, factories, or headquarters, as these activities were being conducted separately, primarily because no central database existed.

Approach

Toshiba selected JDA Software for spend optimization to help manage its supplier relationships, using a web interface with its customers and suppliers. This would enable Toshiba to operate on a real-time basis using accurate information, enabling it and its suppliers to collaborate on sourcing and procurement for supply management. In this way, it could integrate product development, sourcing, supply planning, and procurement across the entire supply chain.

Toshiba decided to implement JDA Negotiate and Strategic Sourcing for direct materials and information-gathering and decision-making processes.

This would enable it to send out RFQs to suppliers via the internet and help the company to create a supplier database shared by all of its purchasing staff to assist in the selection of the best suppliers in future negotiations and to make balanced scorecards for each supplier.

Results

As a result of its successful implementation, JDA solutions enabled Toshiba to gain competitive advantage by refining its supplier base and adding speed, efficiency, and reliability to purchasing.

It can now handle between 7,000 and 8,000 RFQs per site at six of its major factories in Japan.

Toshiba feels that it has achieved a competitive edge owing to the increased level of speed and intelligent decision-making from using JDA software.

It firmly believes that it will help the company reduce its number of preferred suppliers using a balanced scorecard from information contained in the new database, and that purchasing agents will become more strategic by being enabled to collaborate with product designers at the design stage, where 80 percent of a product's cost is determined [www .jda.com, 2016].

Case 2 – Clariant: Increasing Interenterprise Productivity and Extending Its SAP Software Investment Value

Challenge

Clariant, a global leader in specialty chemicals, markets innovative chemicals in a variety of business areas. It wanted to improve the accuracy of its catalogs for its global supply base and to develop more collaborative supplier relationships. Additionally, it wanted to improve invoice cycle times.

Approach

By deploying Ariba Procurement Content, PO Automation, and Invoice Automation solutions, it determined that it would be able to purchase all indirect goods and services through its existing SAP ERP software system.

Results

Clariant eventually deployed the Ariba Procurement Content solution to manage more than 300 catalogs, deployed the Ariba PO Automation solution in 21 countries, and rolled out the Ariba Invoice Automation solution in Germany and Switzerland.

This integrated smoothly with the existing SAP Supplier Relationship Management application for order initiation.

It enabled a consumer-like shopping experience, covering all countries with one user-friendly solution. To accomplish this, it utilized Ariba services, which incorporated catalogs and suppliers on the Ariba Network.

Clariant reached its goal of purchasing all its indirect goods and services through the integration of Ariba PO and Invoice Automation with its SAP ERP application, thereby increasing order accuracy, reducing non-catalog orders, and streamlining invoice processing in Germany and Switzerland. It allowed procurement personnel to focus on higher-value activities and improved collaboration internally and with suppliers [www.sap.com, 2016].

Case 3 – New Purchase-to-Pay System
Allows Smarter Processes at Atea

Challenge

Atea is a leading supplier of IT infrastructure in Europe which helps to enable its customers' IT purchasing, delivery, and service processes running smoothly by delivering the necessary hardware and solutions.

Other than its hardware purchases, which form the majority of items purchased and are handled by central purchasing, Atea lets employees do their own purchasing for indirect items.

Currently, department heads have to provide authorization twice: once to authorize a purchase and later to authorize the invoice after delivery has been made.

Approach

Atea looked for a combined technology solution that included purchasing, automated invoice processing, and travel and expense management. It had to support its decentralized (indirect-item) purchasing strategy and integrate with its existing ERP and payroll systems, all the while being user-friendly.

It needed the solution to help optimize its purchasing, invoicing, and expense handling processes as well as integrate its invoice processing and travel and expense management systems – a system that would enable department heads to deal with purchases just once.

Results

Atea licensed a purchasing system from Basware. Employees can now create a purchase requisition and get it approved electronically by their department head. When the invoice arrives, it has already been approved and can be sent for payment automatically, thereby reducing the work of two people by 50 percent.

Employees no longer have to search for invoice documents, ownership of invoices, or approvals, while at the same time they can ensure the right purchases are made.

The purchasing system now integrates with invoice and travel and expense processing and with the entire payables side, enabling many approvals to be granted automatically.

The responsibility for invoice posting has now been delegated to individual departments with decentralized invoice posting.

There is no need to send invoices from one department to another anymore, and departments have a better idea of what they are actually spending.

Atea also chose to shut down expensive manual advances and is switching as many staff as possible to personal liability credit cards [www .basware.com, 2016].

Appendix B: Chapter Discussion Questions

SECTION I: SUPPLY CHAIN STRATEGY

Chapter 1: Introduction to Demand and Supply Chain Planning in Today's Complex and Increasingly Uncertain Global Economy

1. What is meant by a "whitewater rapids" period, and how does it impact the supply chain?
2. What are some areas to focus on in terms of people, processes, and technology in today's volatile global supply chain?

Chapter 2: Understanding the Importance of Supply Chain to an Organization and Developing a Strategy for a Sustained Competitive Advantage

1. What is the difference between a mission statement and a vision statement?
2. What is a business model canvas, and how can it be applied to the supply chain?

Chapter 3: Supply Chain Performance

1. Compare and contrast efficient (i.e. low-cost) vs. responsive (i.e. flexible) supply chains.
2. How do the supply chain drivers of production, inventory, location, transportation, and information determine the blend of responsiveness and efficiency a supply chain is capable of achieving?

Chapter 4: Supply Chain Metrics and Measures

1. What are some financial metrics of supply chain performance?
2. There are four major categories that provide a useful way to classify supply chain performance metrics. Name them, and select one to discuss in more detail.
3. Discuss the metric classification scheme that has been developed by the Supply Chain Council and defined in the Supply Chain Operations and Reference (SCOR) model to measure the performance of Process D1: Deliver Stocked Product.
4. Discuss the supply chain's financial impact on an organization.

Chapter 5: Supply Chain Network Design

1. Discuss the trade-offs with locating inventory at a factory vs. locating it closer to the customer at a warehouse, distribution center, wholesaler, or retailer.
2. List four factors involved in locating manufacturing facilities, as discussed in the book.
3. What are the trade-offs among on-site expansion, new location, and relocation?
4. Which of the location decision tools is the most objective and can be used by the greatest number of decision-makers to arrive at the same site decision, and which would result in the least consistent choice when used by different decision-makers?

Chapter 6: A Lean, Agile, and Smart Supply Chain to Meet the Volatile Demand and Supply Conditions of the 21st Century

1. What are the supply chain implications of the lean system emphasis on small lot sizes?
2. What are the supply chain implications of the lean system emphasis on close supplier ties?
3. Briefly outline the steps to be followed in evaluating and improving a process using value stream mapping.

Chapter 7: Strategic Sourcing and Procurement

1. What is e-procurement?
2. Identify the reasons for "making" in the make-or-buy decision.

3. Identify the reasons for "buying" in the make-or-buy decision.

4. Identify some business processes that are outsourced.

5. How are outsourcing and vertical integration related? Can a firm do both successfully?

6. Identify the advantages and disadvantages of using the few suppliers approach.

Chapter 8: Integration, Coordination, and Collaboration in the Supply Chain

1. What is collaboration? Name the three levels, and discuss one of them in some detail.

2. What is the impact of lack of coordination on the performance of the supply chain?

3. How do improperly structured incentives lead to a lack of coordination in the supply chain?

4. How do cooperation and trust improve performance in a supply chain partnership?

5. Describe vendor-managed inventory (VMI) and an example of its use.

SECTION II: DEMAND-SIDE PLANNING

Chapter 9: Demand Planning

1. Why are forecasts for product families typically more accurate than forecasts for the individual items within a product family?

2. Which forecasting technique would you consider for technological forecasts?

3. What is the difference between mean absolute deviation (MAD) and mean squared error (MSE)?

4. What are reasonable criteria for selecting one time-series method over another?

5. What are the steps in a "generic" forecasting process as described in this book?

SECTION III – SUPPLY-SIDE PLANNING

Chapter 11: Supply Chain (Independent Demand) Inventory Management and Control

1. Explain the difference between independent and dependent demand and illustrate your explanation with an example.
2. What are the components of holding cost?
3. Although lower inventories and a just-in-time approach receive considerable attention in the business media, some organizations prefer high levels of inventory. Why would they want to hold a large inventory?
4. What is ABC analysis, and how does it work?

Chapters 12–14: Sales and Operations (Aggregate) Planning, Resource Planning – Dependent Demand Inventory and Purchasing, and Resource Planning – Short-Term Scheduling and Omni Channel Delivery

1. What is the impact of the sales and operations plan on the human resources and finance functions of a firm?
2. What is a product family?
3. Pick an example of a service organization and describe some demand options at its disposal for sales and operations planning.
4. Pick an example of a manufacturing organization and describe some supply options at its disposal.
5. Describe the sales and operations planning process.
6. What is the difference between a chase strategy and a level strategy in sales and operations planning?
7. What are the key inputs to an MRP system?
8. What is the explosion of the MPS, and what are the outputs?

Chapters 10 and 15: Information Technology in Demand Planning and Information Technology in Supply Planning

1. Define electronic data interchange (EDI).
2. What are supply chain execution tools?
3. What is enterprise resource planning (ERP) software?

4. Discuss how advances in mobile computing have led to the development of supply chain capabilities.
5. Define and discuss the history of RFID adoption and the associated issues with the technology.

SECTION IV – THE ROAD AHEAD

Chapter 17: Global Supply Chain Risk Management: Identification and Mitigation

1. List and describe typical disruptions to external supply chains.
2. List and describe typical disruptions to internal supply chains.

Chapter 18: Harmonized Demand and Supply Chain Planning – It Is the Journey, Not Just the Destination

1. Name and discuss some trends that are driving the need to be prepared for increased uncertainty and volatility with an efficient and agile supply chain.
2. Why are data analytics and simulation important technological supply chain trends to keep an eye on?
3. How can technology help manage the trend for sustainability in the supply chain?

References

"3 Ways How Technology Simplifies Demand Forecasting", *Intuendi*, Blog, July 13, 2020. Last accessed at www.intuendi.com November 2021.

"9 Steps to Establish the Lean Supply Chain: A System of Interconnected & Interdependent Partners", *Globaltranz*, May 6, 2015. Last accessed at www.globaltranz.com November 2021.

"AI For Business Forecasting", *Anodot*, 2022. Last accessed at www.anodot.com, 2022.

Andrews, Jerry. "CPFR: Considering the Options, Advantages and Pitfalls", *Plan4Demand Solutions*. Last accessed at www.sdcexec.com, 2014.

Bartholomew, Doug. "Can Lean and ERP Work Together?", *Industry Week Magazine*, April 12, 2012.

Blascovich, John, Ferrer, Alejandro, and Markham, Bill. "7 Ways to Procurement Excellence", *Supply Chain Management Review*, November 2011. www.scmr.com.

Bonner, Henry. "Efficient vs. Responsive Supply Chain or Can You Have Both?", *Riskpulse blog*, September 22, 2020. Last accessed at www.riskpulse.com October 2021.

Bozarth, Cecil, and Handfield, Robert. *Introduction to Operations and Supply Chain Management*. 2nd Edition, Pearson, 2008, pp. 516–518.

"Caribou Coffee Case Study, Logility Software", Last accessed at www.logility.com, 2015.

"Case Study: Manufacturing Production Planning, Corporate Technologies", Last accessed at www.cptech.com, 2015.

CCH® Tagetik, "Supply Chain Planning: A Look at What to Expect and Consider in 2022", *Wolters Kluwer*, January 20, 2022. Last accessed at www.woltrskluwer.com, 2022.

Chopra, Sunil, and Meindl, Peter. *Supply Chain Management – Strategy, Planning and Operation*. 6th Edition, Pearson, 2016, pp. 22–30.

Christopher, Martin, and Peck, Helen, Cranfield School of Management. "Building The Resilient Supply Chain", *International Journal of Logistics Management*, Vol. 15, No. 2, 2004, pp. 1–13.

"Clariant Cuts Costs with Ariba Solutions - Automating and Enhancing Procurement Processes", *SAP Software Case Study*. Last accessed at www.sap.com, 2016.

Clegg, Helen and Montgomery, Susan "Seven Steps for Sourcing Information Products", *Information Outlook*, Vol. 9, No. 12, December 2005. Last accessed at www.procurement-academy.com, 2017.

"Continental Mills, Logility Voyager Solutions Case Study", Last accessed at www.logility.com, 2015.

Cooke, James A. "Kimberly-Clark Connects its Supply Chain to the Store Shelf", *Quarter 1 2013 Issue of CSCMP's Supply Chain Quarterly*. Last accessed at www.supplychainquarterly.com, 2015.

Copeland, Michael V. "Death by a Billion Clicks", *Wired Magazine*, November 16, 2012. Last accessed at www.wired.com, 2019.

"Customers are Calling the Shots: It's Time for Retailers to Get Fit for the Digital Age", *White Paper, PwC and SAP*, January 2017. Last accessed at www.pwc.com, 2020.

Dittman, J. Paul. "Supply Chain Transformation", McGraw-Hill, copyright 2012.

Dominick, Charles. "Ten Types of Procurement Software", *College Planning & Management*, July 1, 2015. Last accessed at www.webcpm.com, 2017.

"Enabling Online Supplier Collaboration at Toshiba Semiconductor Company", *JDA Software Case Study*. Last accessed at www.jda.com, 2016.

Feizabadi, Javad, and Shrivastava, Apurv. "Does Artificial Intelligence Enabled Demand Forecasting Improve Supply Chain Efficiency?", *Supply Chain*, Vol. 247, November 20, 2018. Last accessed at www.supplychain247.com, 2021.

"Gables Engineering: Case Study, IFS Software", Last accessed at www.top10erp.org, 2016.

Gonzalez, Adrian. "Transportation Sourcing in an Omni-Channel World", *Talking Logistics*, April 29, 2015. Last accessed at www.talkinglogistics.com, 2019.

Hanks, Jeremy. "Evolving the Supply Chain in the Ecommerce Age", *Multi-Channel Merchant*, August 12, 2013. Last accessed at www.multichannelmerchant.com, 2018.

Harris, Daniel. "Compare Demand Planning & Forecasting Software", November 15, 2015. Last accessed at www.softwareadvice.com, 2015.

Hayes, Robert H., and Wheelwright, Steven C. "Link Manufacturing Process and Product Life Cycles" and "The Dynamics of Process-Product Life Cycles", *Harvard Business Review*, 1979. https://hbr.org/1979/03/the-dynamics-of-process-product-life-cycles

Heizer, Jay and Render, Barry *Operations Management*. 11th Edition, Pearson, copyright 2013, pp. 329–330.

Heizer, Jay and Render, Barry *Operations Management*. 11th Edition, Pearson, copyright 2013, p. 438.

Heizer, Jay and Render, Barry *Operations Management*. 11th Edition, Pearson, copyright 2013, pp. 106–107.

Hugos, Michael. "Five Supply Chain Drivers", *SCM Globe*, March 21, 2020. Last accessed at www.scmglobe.com October 2021.

IBM Solution Brief, IBM Supply Chain - Control Tower Orchestrate Your End-to-End Supply Chain with AI-Powered Visibility and Actionable Workflows, 2021. Last accessed at https://www.ibm.com/products/supply-chain-intelligence-suite/control-tower, 2021.

"Infinite Possibilities: Infineon Technologies Takes Planning to the Next Level With JDA S&OP", *Case Study*, 2014. Last accessed at www.jda.com, 2015.

Kahn, Kenneth B., and Mello, John. "Lean Forecasting begins with Lean Thinking - On the Demand Forecasting Process", *Journal of Business Forecasting*, Vol. 23, No. 4, Winter 2004–05, pp. 30–32.

Kaplan, Deborah Abrams. "The Real Cost of E-Commerce Logistics", *Supply Chain Drive*, June 6, 2017. Last accessed at www.supplychaindrive, 2019.

Kauffman, Ralph G., and Crimi, Thomas A. "A Best-Practice Approach for Development of Global Supply Chains", 90th Annual International Supply Management Conference, May 2005.

KPMG. "Forecasting with Confidence", *Advisory*, 2007. Last accessed at www.kpmg.com, 2014.

Kreipl, Stephan, and Pinedo, Michael. "Planning and Scheduling in Supply Chains: An Overview of Issues in Practice", *Production and Operations Management Society (POMS)*, Vol. 13, No. 1, Spring 2004, pp. 77–92.

Kourimsky, Hans, and van der Berk, Marc. "The Impact of Omni-Channel Commerce on Supply Chains: How to Make Sure You Effectively Deliver Products That Meet the Customer's Expectations", *White Paper, Itelligence*, 2014. Last accessed at www .itelligencegroup.com, 2019.

Kowalke, Mae. "5 Trends in MRP Technology", *Inside-ERP*, July 21, 2015. Last accessed at www.it.toolbox.com, 2015.

Lance, Logility. "Voyager Solutions Case Study", Last accessed at www.logility.com, 2015.

"Lean Procurement: The Future of Supply Chain Management in a Demand-Driven World", An Oracle White Paper Written in Collaboration with CSS International, Inc., June 2006. Last accessed at www.oracle.com, 2017.

"Lean Sourcing: Creating Sustainable Purchasing Savings", Executive whitepaper, 2005. Aptium Global, Inc. Last accessed at www.aptiumglobal.com, 2017.

Lee, H. L. "The Triple-A Supply Chain", *Harvard Business Review*, Vol. 82, No. 10, 2004, pp. 102–112.

McTaggart, Jennifer. "The Golden Years", *Progressive Grocer*, May 2012. Last accessed at www.progressivegrocer.com, 2013.

Montané, Javier González. "Supply Chain Management Canvas", *Strategok*, June 22, 2018. Last accessed at www.strategok.com October 2021.

"Mueller Stoves Reduces the Assembly Line Stops after Preactor Deployment", *Case Study*. Last accessed at www.preactor.com, 2016.

Myerson, Paul. "A Lean and Agile Supply Chain: Not an Option, But a Necessity", *Inbound Logistics Magazine*, October 16, 2014.

Myerson, Paul. "Demand Accuracy in Your Supply Chain", *Inbound Logistics Magazine*, July 22, 2021a.

Myerson, Paul. "IBP and Lean: A Match Made in Heaven", *Inbound Logistics Magazine*, July, 2019 issue.

Myerson, Paul. "It's Time to Bring the Outside-in to Your S&OP Process", *Inbound Logistics Magazine*, January, 2022 issue.

Myerson, Paul. *Lean Retail and Wholesale*. McGraw-Hill Professional, copyright 2014, pp. 128–132.

Myerson, Paul. *Lean Supply Chain & Logistics Management*. McGraw-Hill Professional, copyright 2012, p. 163.

Myerson, Paul. *Lean Supply Chain & Logistics Management*. McGraw-Hill Professional, copyright 2012, pp. 11–16.

Myerson, Paul. "Managing Change in Turbulent Times", *Inbound Logistics Magazine*, May 31, 2019.

Myerson, Paul. "Plan and Deliver", *Industry Week*, July 2, 2014.

Myerson, Paul. "Riding Out the Rapids", *Inbound Logistics Magazine*, January, 2019 issue.

Myerson, Paul. *Supply Chain and Logistics Management – Made Easy*. Pearson Education, 2015, pp. 13–15.

Myerson, Paul. "Supply-Side Accuracy and Timeliness in Volatile Times", October 2021b.

Myerson, Paul. "The Road Map Out of This Mess", *Inbound Logistics Magazine*, May, 2020 issue.

Myerson, Paul. "The Smart Supply Chain", *Inbound Logistics Magazine*, July, 2022.

Myerson, Paul. "The View From the Control Tower", *Inbound Logistics Magazine*. September, 2019 issue.

Myerson, Paul. "We're All in This Together: Teamwork in a Lean Workplace", *Inbound Logistics Magazine*, August 2013.

Myerson, Paul A. "Distribution Disruption: Ready or Not, Here It Comes", *Industry Week Magazine*, May 6, 2016a.

Myerson, Paul A. "E-Commerce is Driving the Industrial Real Estate Market", *Industry Week Magazine*, September 30, 2016b.

Myerson, Paul A. "Omnichannel Multiplies the Challenges for Distribution-Centric Supply Chains", *Industry Week Magazine*, June 1, 2018a.

Myerson, Paul A. "Store Delivery Keeps Retailers in the Game", *Inbound Logistics Magazine*, September 14, 2018b.

"New Purchase-To-Pay System Allows Smarter Processes at Atea", *Basware Software Case Study*. Last accessed at www.basware.com, 2016.

Nicholas, Clayton. "Building a Future-Ready Supply Chain", *Vibronyx.com*. Last accessed at www.vibronyx.com, 2022.

"Omni-Channel Retail, A Deloitte Point of View", *Deloitte*, 2015. Last accessed at www2.deloitte.com.

Perez, Hernán David. "Supply Chain Strategies: Which One Hits the Mark?", *CSCMP Supply Chain Quarterly*, Quarter 1, 2013 issue.

"Production Planning Case Study, ORM Technologies', Last accessed at www.orm-tech.com, 2015.

PwC and the MIT Forum for Supply Chain Innovation. "Making the Right Risk Decisions to Strengthen Operations Performance", 2013. last accessed at www.pwc.com, 2014.

"Raytheon Streamlines and Automates its Material Requirement Planning Processes with Exostar's Supply Chain Platform", *Exostar Raytheon Case Study*. Last accessed at www.exostar.com, 2016.

"Recipe for Success", *Case Study, JDA Software*. Last accessed at www.jda.com, 2015.

Rethink Data - Put More of Your Business Data to Work - From Edge to Cloud. With Research and Analysis by IDC, A Seagate Technology Report, 2020. Last accessed at https://www.seagate.com/files/www-content/our-story/rethink-data/files/Rethink_Data_Report_2020.pdf October 2021.

"Re-engineering the Supply Chain for the Omni-Channel of Tomorrow", EY in Collaboration with the CGF: Re-engineering the Supply Chain for the Omni-Channel of Tomorrow, September 2015. Last accessed at www.ey.com, 2019.

SAP White Paper: "Supply Chain Collaboration: The Key to Success in a Global Economy", 2007. Last accessed at www.sap.com, 2014.

SAS. "The Lean Approach to Business Forecasting - Eliminating Waste and Inefficiency from the Forecasting Process", *White Paper*, 2012. Last accessed at www.sas.com, 2015.

"Scapa Case Study", Consumers Interstate Corporation. Last accessed at www.lean-procurement.com, 2017.

SC Digest Editorial Staff. "The Five Challenges of Today's Global Supply Chains", August 12, 2010. Last accessed at www.scdigest.com, 2014.

Schiff, Jennifer Lonoff. "9 Tips for Selecting and Implementing an ERP System", *CIO Magazine*, July 30, 2014. Last accessed at www.cio.com, 2016.

Sheffield, Yossi, and Rice Jr., James B. "A Supply Chain View of the Resilient Enterprise", *MIT Sloan Management Review*, Vol. 47, No. 1, Fall 2005, pp. 41–48.

Småros, Johanna, and Angerer, Alfred et al., "Retailer Views on Forecasting Collaboration", Logistics Research Network Annual Conference, September 9–10, 2004, Dublin, Ireland.

"Sourcing as Strategy", Advisory Services Manufacturing, August 2014, *PricewaterhouseCoopers LLP*. Last accessed at www.pwc.com, 2017.

Srinivasan, Mandyam M. "The Goal of the Lean Supply Chain - Seven Steps to Building a Lean Supply Chain", *Industry Week Magazine*, September 10, 2007. Last accessed at www.industryweek.com November 2021.

Staff Contributors. "Achieve Lean in Procurement: Eliminate Waste But Don't Neglect to Add Value", June 13, 2016. blog.ivalua.com.

"Strategic Sourcing MRO Case Study by Source One", Case Studies and Examples, Source One Management Services LLC. Last accessed at www.sourceoneinc.com, 2017.

"Supply Chain 4.0 – The Next-Generation Digital Supply Chain", Article, McKinsey & Company. October 27, 2016. Last accessed at www.mckinsey.com, 2022.

Supply Chain Digest Editorial Staff, "Leading High Tech Company has to Improve S&OP Process, Supporting Tools Rapidly after Outsourcing Strategy Leads to Real Challenges", July 24, 2013. Last accessed at www.scdigest.com, 2015.

"Techlogix helps Nestlé Innovate in Milk Production Planning", *Case Study, Techlogix*. Last accessed at www.techlogix.com, 2015.

Thomson, James. "Lean Review of Procurement Arrangements: A Case Study", June 17, 2015. www.scott-moncrief.com.

Thompson, Scott. "Analysis: Walmart Accelerates Omnichannel Innovation", Essential Retail, February, 2018. Last accessed at www.essentialretail.com, 2019.

Verwijmeren, Martin. "Is Your Supply Chain Strategy Inside-Out or Outside-In?", *Supply Chain Minded*. Last accessed at www.supplychainminded.com October 2021.

Waldron, John. "How Home Depot Nails Omnichannel Supply Chain Fulfillment", 2019. Last accessed at www.etaileast.com, 2019.

"What is Going on in Last Mile Delivery, Omnichannel Retail and Transportation and Logistics?", Datex Corporation, 2019. Last accessed at www.datexcorp.com, 2021.

"What is Going on in Last Mile Delivery, Omnichannel Retail and Transportation and Logistics? 2019 Trends in Last Mile Delivery, Omnichannel Retail, Transportation and Logistics", *Datex Corp*, 2019. Last accessed at www.datexcorp.com, 2019.

Index

Printed in the United States
by Baker & Taylor Publisher Services